Marketing Research Tourism, Hospitality and Events Industries

This is a user-friendly textbook that covers qualitative, quantitative and social media methods, providing tourism, hospitality and events students and course leaders with an accessible guide for learning and teaching marketing research.

The book contains essential information on how to conduct research on visitor trends, experiences, preferences and lifestyles, shedding light on customer preferences, product changes, promotional efforts and pricing differences to ensure the destination is successful. It offers guidance on how to write, conduct and analyze the results of surveys, or use qualitative methods such as focus groups, interviews, projective techniques and observation. It also illustrates how social media can be used as a new means to determine visitor preferences by analyzing online data and conversations. Other content includes suggestions and examples on turning research data into actionable recommendations as well as advice on writing and presenting the final report.

Integrated with a wide range of case studies per chapter, this short and accessible textbook is essential reading for all students wishing to gain knowledge as to what visitors want from the travel, hospitality and/or event experience.

Bonita Kolb is Emeritus Professor at Lycoming College, Williamsport, USA, currently living in Nashville, Tennessee.

Marketing Research for the Tourism, Hospitality and Events Industries

Bonita Kolb

Routledge
Taylor & Francis Group

LONDON AND NEW YORK

First published 2018
by Routledge
2 Park Square, Milton Park, Abingdon, Oxon OX14 4RN

and by Routledge
711 Third Avenue, New York, NY 10017

Routledge is an imprint of the Taylor & Francis Group, an informa business

© 2018 Bonita Kolb

British Library Cataloguing-in-Publication Data
A catalogue record for this book is available from the British Library

Library of Congress Cataloging-in-Publication Data
A catalog record for this book has been requested

ISBN: 978-1-138-04214-8 (hbk)
ISBN: 978-1-138-04216-2 (pbk)
ISBN: 978-1-315-17390-0 (ebk)

Typeset in Iowan Old Style by
Servis Filmsetting Ltd, Stockport, Cheshire

Visit the eResource: www.routledge.com/9781138042162

Contents

Contents

Case studies

Chapter 1

Researching changing visitor preferences

Learning objectives

- Who are the service providers in the tourism, hospitality and events industries and how are they connected?
- What is the connection between developing a marketing plan and the process of conducting marketing research?
- Why should a process be followed when planning and conducting marketing research?
- What are the current challenges faced by the tourism, hospitality and event management industries because of social media technology?

Chapter summary

- While tourism, hospitality and events have always existed, the management of these industries as a profession is newer. The industries are connected as people want an experience that includes a destination, food, lodging and events. Because of the competition between the many destinations and events available to consumers marketing research is necessary to ensure that the benefits desired by visitors are understood and provided. A knowledge of the industry and its challenges is necessary for marketing success.
- All marketing is an honest relationship between a seller and a buyer where both obtain what they want. Writing a marketing plan starts with planning the development of a product, pricing it correctly, and having it available at the right location. The plan then describes the promotion methods that will be necessary to communicate the product benefits to a target market segment of consumers.
- Marketing research can be used to explore various aspects of the marketing mix detailed in the marketing plan. Needed improvements in the design of the hospitality product can be discovered. The correct pricing level, promotional message and aspects of the venue can all be explored. Finally, analyzing the demographic

1

and psychographic makeup of the visitor is critical to organizational success. The marketing research process consists of determining the research question, sources of information, finding research subjects, deciding upon the method and conducting the research. Finally, the data is analyzed and reported.

- The development of communications technology and social media sites has provided both opportunities and challenges to the tourism, hospitality and event management industries. The opportunity is that even small businesses and organizations have a means of reaching potential customers by directly connecting with potential visitors. The challenges include a visitor's desire to experience local authentic and personalized experiences. Also, the purchase process has changed to one in which the visitor is in control. Finally, the expectation of service quality has changed.

Categorization of the tourism, hospitality and event management industries

Tourism and hospitality is an activity with a long history. After all, people traveling to visit other places is not a recent phenomenon as the first tourism occurred in the ancient world. For example, people living in Rome traveled from the cities to villas and coastal resorts to enjoy sea air, good food and local wine. During medieval times in Europe religious pilgrimages to historic holy sites became popular. Travel also occurred in other parts of the world. In fact, during this same time period travel literature became popular in China. These types of tourism activities and travel literature are still seen today.

It was the Grand Tour of Europe that was the first example of travel that resembles the modern tourism industry because lodging, food, transportation and information were provided. During the eighteenth and nineteenth centuries it was expected that young men in England with the financial means to do so would further their

Figure 1.1 The Grand Tour of Europe was an early example of planned tours.

Photo Credit: canadastock

education through travel. Young men with the social connections and family wealth undertook long trips that included stops with an educational focus, such as studying classical culture in Italy.

If these young wealthy men were going to be able to travel, they needed places to sleep and eat while on their trip. Because the Grand Tours of Europe had standard destinations, a series of guest houses that provided lodging and food were established to cater to these travelers. In addition, local citizens were hired to provide guiding and other services. Transportation links were also created to make travel easier for people undertaking the Grand Tour. Finally, guide books detailing where to stay and what to do were published.

While the Grand Tour was only available to the wealthy, tourism started to develop more widely in Europe during the mid-nineteenth century. Tourism increased because the growth of the middle class meant more people could afford to travel. During this time period, Thomas Cook started his package tour business in England. The pre-planned and packaged Cook tours took tourists to historical sites and also holiday destinations. Because the trip was packaged with transportation, food and lodging included, no prior knowledge of the places visited was necessary.

Traveling to events is also part of the history of tourism. Attending festivals and markets were some of the reasons travelers had for undertaking a trip. While local residents could attend an experience in their home community, to be successful most events wanted to draw attendees and their money from a wider geographic area.

In the twentieth century with the introduction of cheap flights after airline deregulation, more people started to travel on their own without packaged tours. With the use of the internet, they were now able to obtain information on how to travel to the most distant and previously difficult to visit destinations, without the assistance of travel professionals.

Tourism is now a multi-billion-dollar industry worldwide. The industry consists of transportation, food and beverage, lodging, events and travel services. The hospitality industry comprises separate service producers, although in the case of a resort all the components might be provided by the same organization.

Industry components

- Transportation: to and within the destination
- Accommodation: all forms of lodging
- Food and beverage: at all price levels
- Events: either the core attraction or supplementary
- Travel services: information and assistance

Types of tourist travel

Although tourism, hospitality and events include a variety of experiences that can motivate travel, they can be grouped into four categories. The first would be attractions, which can be separated into natural, built and historical. Natural attractions might be large in scale such as the Grand Canyon in the United States or smaller such as a local river front. Built attractions were created for local residents, but now attract visitors or they may have been built specifically for tourists. Examples of such attractions would include amusement parks and botanical gardens. Historical

Case Study 1.1: Solo traveler vs. single travelers: are you a Yuccie?

The travel industry formerly thought of single travelers as sad, lonely, and looking for love. They traveled alone because they had no one with whom to travel – a situation they hoped to fix while on the trip! This may have been true in the past but it is not an accurate description of today's solo traveler.

In 2015 a research report on the holiday industry discovered that one out of three trips taken by British travelers was solo. Why? First, 25 per cent of British adults are unmarried, divorced or widowed. Second, this group has money to spend and, rather than looking for love, are seeking life-changing experiences. While they want to socialize, this is not the main reason for the trip.

Who are these travelers? Many are Yuccies, urban creatives in their twenties and thirties. If they are single with no other commitments, they indulge themselves with premium products, and that includes travel. They want to enjoy travel that combines cultural adventures with the consumption of luxury. However, it is not just the young, as many older people are traveling solo for adventure and cultural opportunities. In the UK, over 50 per cent of travel expenditures are made by people over 50.

The tourism industry is responding. Cruise lines used to shun single travelers as a waste of cabin space. Now the major cruise lines, such as Norwegian and polar specialist Quark Expeditions, are introducing single occupancy cabins along with shared spaces for solo travelers to socialize, if they desire to do so. In addition, hotels are developing specialty 'lifestyle' brands targeted at solo leisure travelers.

The solo traveler is independent but wants connection to the places they visit and the tourism industry is responding (Kasriel-Alexander 2016)!

Question: What research would you conduct to group solo travelers into different segments?

attractions are present in almost every community though some, such as Stonehenge, will be more well known than the site of a local battle.

Another category in the industry covers performances. Performances are usually associated with arts and culture, such as dance, concerts or theatre. Most often the organization that is responsible for the performance was created to serve the community but also wants to attract visitors.

Celebrations include festivals, events and sports. Festivals happen on a repeating schedule such as a yearly Apple Blossom Festival or a Mardi Gras carnival. Also included would be parades, such as Macy's Thanksgiving Day Parade in New York City. Events differ as they are usually categorized as single occurrences such as the hundredth anniversary of the founding of a town. Sporting events that attract an audience from out of town also fall into the tourism category.

An additional category of motivation for tourism are business conferences and meetings. These also fall into the category of tourism as they bring in visitors.

These may be particularly sought after by a city because the visitors may have their expenses covered by their employer, allowing them to spend more money.

Categorization of tourism

- Attractions: natural, built, historical
- Performances: dance, theatre, music
- Celebrations: festivals, events, sports
- Business: meetings, conferences

What connects all of these categories is the need for information, food, lodging and activities to enjoy. Everyone coming in for an attraction, performance, celebration or business will have the same basic needs. Because of this they can all be served by visitor centers, tourism promotion agencies and websites aimed at travelers.

An aspect of tourism that is changing is that visitors who arrive for a specific tourism event now want all aspects of the experience to reflect their interest. They want an experience that packages together all aspects of tourism. For example, someone coming to a town for a major sporting event may also expect to have other experiences built around the sport. They may want to eat at sports bars and stay at the same hotel as other fans. If possible the community can even build a celebration around the sporting event such as a fan fair where people can meet their favorite players. A community will start such an event as a means to attract even more visitors who will spend money. People coming for a music celebration may also want to take in the historical sites related to a local musician. Business visitors now also

Figure 1.2 Visitors today want to experience local culture.

Photo Credit: Karel Gallas

want to experience local culture and can be encouraged to attend performances on offer by giving group discounts to the meeting or conference organizers.

Need for visitor research

The tourism, hospitality and event management industries are interrelated because the same consumer will most likely need all three industries. All tourists need food and lodging. While at the location they are visiting, these same individuals need events and activities to occupy their time. Or the process might be the opposite. Someone traveling to any event will also need tourism and hospitality services so they can enjoy the visit experience.

The tourism industry is unique as it is a combination of government funded organizations, nonprofits and private businesses. Tourism promotion agencies such as destination marketing organizations and visitor bureaus that provide information are often funded by the government. Some tourism attractions may be governed by boards of nonprofits such as museums and historical sites. Finally, there will be private businesses such as restaurants, hotels and attractions. The size of any of these organizations can range from large, such as Disneyworld, to a local farmers' market run by volunteers. What all these groups share is a need to conduct research of their current and potential visitors to determine how to best meet their needs.

The hospitality industry is a subset of tourism industry as it consists of companies that focus on providing lodging, food and beverages. Almost always these companies are private businesses. The lodging industry is very fragmented between global companies that have chains of hotels and a person who rents out a spare bedroom to visitors as part of the sharing economy. Most hotels are differentiated by the type of amenities they provide and the level of service, resulting in wide range of prices.

The event management industry is a newer field of academic study. It is a fragmented industry as there are so many different types of events that can be produced. Cities can become branded by the type of events that are held. For example, one city may be known as the location for romantic weddings while another is known for world class sporting events. The event management industries in the cities will have developed to handle each type. There are few national or global branded event management companies. Most are smaller private companies that focus on a type of event, geographic area or both.

The types of events that are produced include music, theatre, conferences, festivals, carnivals and parades. All of these events need to attract visitors to be successful. In doing so they help make the community more exciting for local residents while also helping to brand the community in the minds of potential tourists.

Providing assistance with transportation, lodging and experiences for travelers is still at the heart of the tourism, hospitality and event management industries. They are now striving to provide unique experiences in a consumer environment that is rapidly changing. As a result, while the products they offer will differ, they share a similar need to conduct consumer research to understand changing visitor expectation.

Growth of the tourism city

Small local events have always been held in communities. However, with industrialization and the growing wealth of cities there was a corresponding growth in built cultural institutions. While the local citizens provided an audience for these opera houses, theatres and museums, they also soon became a reason to visit the city. Governments eager to demonstrate the prosperity of their city also started to host festivals that showcased both local culture and products, such as World Fairs and Industry Expos. Cultural institutions also started their own events, such as the Promenade Concert series in London first held in 1895. During the second half of the twentieth century there was a movement to create festivals specifically to attract tourists (Richards and Palmer 2010). It was believed that such tourism would strengthen global understanding and connection.

With the decrease in manufacturing in many cities in the later decades of the twentieth century the reason for developing tourism changed. Many cities, looking for new sources of economic development, focused on entrepreneurship and creativity. Tourism was a natural partner with this movement because of the changing desires of visitors. Visitors were now less interested in large-scale staged events but instead wanted to discover the unique culture of a community. This new focus encompassed all components of tourism as visitors wanted authentic experiences, local food and unique lodging.

Staging events has several distinct advantages for cities. Events can create the atmosphere or ambience that visitors now seek. The only way to experience an event is to be physically present, which means people must visit, which helps the economy. A further benefit to cities that host events is that they are harder for competing cities to replicate. While it is easier to copy a sports stadium, living history museum or hiking trail, an event based on the specific character of a city is unique to that city. In addition, an event created by a city or community, while involving expenses, is much less costly than building an attraction. Finally, because so many cities are now intercultural, events have become an effective way of sharing culture with visitors while building community at home.

Connection between marketing strategy and marketing research

Marketing has been defined by the American Marketing Association on its website www.marketingpower.com as:

> the activity, set of institutions, and processes for creating, communicating, delivering, and exchanging offerings that have value for customers, clients, partners, and society at large.

The definition describes marketing as an equal exchange that offers value for both the provider of a good or service, and the individual who pays for the benefits the product will provide. Marketing is sometimes misunderstood as only the promotion of a product. In this view, all that is necessary is to create the most compelling or clever marketing message and the tourist will visit, the guest will check in, or the event ticket will be sold. This approach does not take into consideration that today marketing messages are only one way that consumers discover information about products. In fact, professional marketing messages are much less believed and relied upon than former customer reviews.

While tourism promotion is still necessary, marketing must start with ensuring that the product has the benefits and level of quality that will satisfy the requirements of the specific group of visitors most likely to be interested. While creating the product is part of the definition of marketing, companies with existing products and services will start the marketing process by analyzing what their product has to offer visitors. Part of what the product offers are the core benefit or the reason the product exists. This might be a tour of an historic site, a bed for the night, or a ticket to a concert. The challenge facing tourism organizations is that many other destinations offer similar core benefits. Therefore, the organization must analyze their product for benefits beyond the core, such as educational opportunities, a unique ambience or a special opportunity to engage with an entertainer.

In addition, the definition of marketing includes the pricing of the product. While it is easy to understand that the organization must cover its costs from the revenue received from product sales, determining the correct price is difficult. A price that is too high will result in less sales while a price too low means a missed opportunity for revenue. In making the purchase decision visitors will consider the value of the product, which is a comparison of the financial cost versus the benefits received.

The consumer will also consider the convenience of obtaining the product. While most tourism, hospitality and event revenue is from providing services not physical products, distribution is still an issue. The concept of distribution in tourism covers how easy it is to obtain the product, which includes not only transportation to the venue but also the ease of payment.

Marketing strategy

Writing a marketing plan forces the tourism organization to answer difficult questions about their current and potential customers. While the organization may have a vague idea of their visitors, such as people who like to visit sites of natural beauty, the marketing plan will force them to develop a clear description including demographic facts, psychographic characteristics and geographic location. Finally, writing the marketing plan will force the organization to answer questions about their competitors. Visitors will certainly compare products, so the organization must also do so. All of these questions will require the organization to conduct research to learn the answers.

Once the tourism organization has decided on a course of action by conducting research, a well written, detailed marketing plan keeps everyone moving together towards the same goal. People in the organization will understand what actions must be taken and in what order. In addition, people will understand which tasks they have been assigned to complete. A marketing strategy that starts with producing the tourism product and ends with a visitor satisfied with the travel experience includes many steps. It may be that only those responsible for writing and implementing the marketing plan are able to understand the entire process, but the plan will keep everyone else in the organization on task.

Marketing research

Marketing is much more than just the promotion of a product. The concept of marketing can be described as a circle with the customer in the middle surrounded by the four 'P's of promotion, price, product and place. All four of these components of marketing must provide the customer with a wanted or needed product at an

Case Study 1.2: Bad weather affecting your flight? No problem!

In the past if bad weather was forecast, all travelers could do was show up at the airport hoping that their flight could take off. The airline also hoped the flight could take off as planes on the ground make no money. If, at the last minute, the flight had to be canceled, passengers were upset and lined up at the help desk trying to rebook.

No more! Airlines have learned that to keep customers happy, they need to give them more control over their travel plans. Now if bad weather is predicted, a weather waiver is issued for the airport. Any passenger booked on an affected flight can go on to their smartphone and change their plans. They can cancel their trip and get a 'no questions asked' refund, rebook on another day, or rebook on the same day but to a different airport, all with no fees.

Why did airlines change their approach to flight cancellations? Anyone who follows the Twitter streams of angry comments when flights are canceled at the last minute will know that the new policy generates goodwill. Does it make sense financially? The airlines believe that they save staff time in not handling complaints and rebooking flights at the airport (Weed 2017)!

Question: What information could you gather through research to support the claim that the change in policy to let people rebook for no fees was successful?

acceptable price, in an appropriate place, and with effective promotion. However, to accomplish this goal the organization must first listen to the customer's wants and needs. The only means of doing so is by conducting marketing research.

The official definition of marketing research, according to the American Marketing Association, can be found on the website www.marketingpower.com:

> Marketing research is the function which links the consumer, customer, and public to the marketer through information – information used to identify and define marketing opportunities and problems; generate, refine and evaluate marketing actions; monitor marketing performance; and improve our understanding of marketing as a process.

Before marketing research can be conducted by a tourism organization it must determine what information it needs from their current and potential visitors. It must design a method for gathering this information, after which it will be analyzed. Finally, the information must be communicated so that it can be used to guide marketing strategy.

Although the AMA definition is a useful summary of all that marketing research can accomplish, a simpler definition can be constructed. According to the dictionary, the word 'research' means to search or investigate exhaustively or in detail. The thesaurus gives as a synonym for 'research' the word 'inquiry', which means the act of seeking truth, information or knowledge. So market research can be defined as a detailed search for the truth.

Marketing research will need to be conducted so that the organization is aware of the many changes in consumer wants and needs. The process will start with qualitative research methods such as focus groups and interviews to explore the nature of the issue. Once this is done, a quantitative study, such as a survey, will be conducted to confirm the answer to the issue. All of these methods will either be entirely on social media or be distributed on social media sites.

Marketing research on tourism can be conducted by government agencies, academics and tourism service providers. Government agencies will conduct research on the number of visitors, the amount of money spent by visitors, and the impact of tourism on the community. They conduct this research in order to determine what policies, regulations or laws are needed to promote economic growth while protecting the community from the negative effects of tourism. Academics conduct research to explore new areas of enquiry such as the effect of tourism on the environment. Both types of studies may be of interest to providers of tourism information and services, but their research needs are more specific. They need to answer the question as to who is visiting, why they are visiting and what they want from the visit experience. A tourism promotion organization may take on such research for the community as a whole, but each service provider will need to conduct their own research on their product offerings. Each provider will have a unique market segment they serve with their unique services. The findings from this research will then be used in their strategic planning.

Uses of marketing research

Marketing is often described as consisting of the four 'P's' of price, product, place and promotion. Some definitions add the 'P's' of people and presentation. Tourism, hospitality and event organizations must provide a product, whether a good, service or experience, that is needed or desired by visitors. They must also price this product correctly and provide it at a location convenient for the visitor. The information on the product, its price and location must then be promoted using effective words and images. The most relevant issue for people is delivering the quality of service visitors desire. Finally, the presentation involves offering the ambience desired by the targeted visitors. This information will be needed to create the visitor experience.

Researching the tourism experience

The purpose of marketing research is to provide the information the organization needs to determine the correct product, price, place, promotion, people and presentation that will motivate the potential visitor. In addition, a company or organization can research the visitors' opinions and ideas and also their competitor's actions.

The organization needs to research its tourism product to determine what benefits it can provide. This research must go beyond the fact that a hotel provides a place to spend the night. Instead it should focus on what other needs it meets, such as safety, excitement, relaxation or socialization. The hotel should not assume it knows the answer but instead conduct research of current guests to obtain this information.

Price is one of the most complex issues facing an organization. It needs to charge enough to cover expenses and make a profit. At the same it is trying to keep its prices low as it knows potential visitors are comparing prices online. The purpose of pricing research is not just to determine the correct price but also to discover if there are added services and experiences for which visitors are willing to pay. For example, visitors may be willing to pay more for early access to tickets, specialty food in their room or a personal tour of a site. The only way to determine the correct pricing is through research. Furthermore, research may find that different groups of visitors have different abilities and willingness to pay, which means that the organization can develop pricing that meets each visitor segment's needs.

Place or distribution refers to the physical location where the good or service is made, such as the location of the attraction, hotel or venue. Visitors understand that the location is related to price as more upscale locations, such as near an ocean with a view, will cost more. Location can also deal with convenience as business people may be concerned about saving time and be willing to pay more for a stay close to the airport. Only research will determine if the location is acceptable.

Promotion may be the marketing component that is most frequently researched. A good deal of money and time is spent on designing promotional material in the hopes that it will effectively communicate a compelling marketing message. Using marketing research before designing the campaign means that there can be less reliance on hope and more reliance on fact regarding what types of words and images motivate a visit.

The organization needs to determine what type of staffing is preferred by visitors. Some visitor segments will want a high level of personal attention from staff while others are willing to forego this level of staffing in exchange for a lower price. Personal customer service can be costly to provide so research will need to be conducted to determine the correct level.

The presentation of the attraction, hotel and venue is critical in tourism. After all, it is the experience that is being purchased. Because the ambience is an essential part of the experience, research needs to be conducted on what style is preferred. In addition, the association of the destination or tourism brand in the mind of the visitor needs to be researched.

If the organization is going to offer a product with the benefits visitors want at the right price, in the right location, the organization must know as much as possible about its current and potential visitors. This would include demographic data such as gender, age, income and education level. It would also include psychographic information such as their values, attitudes and lifestyles.

Another use of marketing research can be to examine the strategies of competitors. Competing tourism organizations can be a useful source of ideas regarding product, price, place and promotion. Successful ideas used by competitors can possibly be adapted by the researching organization for their own use.

Uses of marketing research

- Product: discovering benefits provided to visitors
  - Why do people visit? How can the visit experience be improved?
- Price: choosing price level and additional fees
  - How much should be charged for tour, room, meal, or ticket? For what additional services are visitors willing to pay?
- Place: assessing effect of location on visitors

Case Study 1.3: How local can you go?

With the success of Airbnb every hotelier has been considering how to incorporate the local experience into their hotel. However, the issue of consistency of experience should not be forgotten. After all, it is the reason that hotel chains were started.

The first Holiday Inn Hotel in the United States was opened in 1952. Within 12 years there were 500 more opened. Why the success? People had the money to travel and owned an automobile (airfares were still far too expensive for the average family). Most existing motels were mom and pop enterprises and there were limited means to ascertain quality standards such as comfort, safety and quality. Unwelcome surprises were not uncommon.

The hotel chain was preferred because it could provide a consistent quality experience by maintaining uniform standards for all participating hotels. For the traveler, no surprises were good! Today quality is assumed as it can be quickly determined by looking at reviews. Now the traveler is looking for quality plus a local experience. This trend is affecting hotels at all levels.

When even the Ritz Carlton has local food trucks you know that going local, which may have started at the farmers' market, is now mainstream. But it is not just local food but local retail. The Roger Smith New York Hotel has contracted for retail pop up shops. People still want a souvenir, but local is best (Minett 2017)!

Question: How can research be helpful in making decisions on how to incorporate the local experience?

- ○ Where is the most convenient location to provide the tourism product? How can the location be improved?
- Promotion: determining effectiveness of promotion
  - ○ Does social media promotion motivate action? What media will reach potential visitors?
- People: assessing staffing and customer service
  - ○ What staffing level is appropriate for a family style hotel? What services are desired at a luxury resort?
- Presentation: analyzing ambience and branding
  - ○ What style of presentation is preferred at an event venue? Does the restaurant brand have a positive association to visitors?
- Consumer: understanding the visitor
  - ○ How would frequent visitors be described? What non-visitors can be reached?
- Competitor: understanding competitors
  - ○ Why do visitors visit other destinations? What competitor attractions could be added?

The marketing research process

To conduct effective marketing research, an organization needs to understand the entire research process. Understanding the process will help the tourism organization

Figure 1.3
Technology has
changed how tourism
is both researched
and purchased.

Photo Credit: rawpixel.
com

plan its research so that its efforts will be successful in providing the needed information. Without planning, either the organization will not obtain enough information to justify the research cost and effort or it will obtain information, but not what is needed.

The research process can be summarized as the need to determine, decide, choose, design, conduct, analyze and report. The first step involves the organization in determining what information is needed, which will require determining the research question. For example, a tourism organization may need to know what would attract visitors during the off season. While this might seem an adequate question, it is too broad. The question needs to be narrowed to a specific type of visitor that will be the subject of the research. It might also need to be narrowed by activity. For example, an event management company may want to know what type of venue couples prefer for their wedding during the winter months.

Next, the organization must decide where this information can be obtained. If the research question is general to the population, such as how many people booked destination weddings last year, the data is probably already available. For example, a wedding trade association has the means to conduct this type of research and will have this data available. If the research question is where local people prefer to get married, then the organization will need to conduct its own primary research. The organization must then choose the appropriate research approach and design the research method. Only then is it ready to conduct research. Finally, it must analyze and report the findings.

Marketing research process

1   Determine the research question: What knowledge is needed that is not known now?

2   Decide on source of information: Where will the answer be found?
3   Choose the research approach: Is the research looking for facts or ideas?
4   Design the research method: What kind of tool should be used?
5   Conduct the research: When, where and who will conduct the research?
6   Analyze findings: Do we know what the answers tell us?
7   Report findings: What actions should we now take?

Social media and changes in tourism behavior

Tourism has been affected by the development of technology that allows rapid two-way communication between people across distance. Access to social media has increased the desire for authentic personalized experiences as people want to interact with the local community when they travel. Technology has also changed the trip purchase process and the expectation of quality. It is now much easier for potential visitors to research and book their own trip. Technology also makes it easy for visitors to complain when a tourism product is not meeting their expectations. In fact, consumers will not only let the company know; they will also let everyone else know by posting their opinions online.

The product preference information posted online is a form of marketing research data that already exists for use by researchers. Social media allows market researchers to understand visitor preferences by reading reviews, following bloggers and watching trends. Familiarity with the ever-evolving apps that people use to access and share product information is necessary so that marketers can keep abreast of visitor preferences.

There is so much data available that there is now data collection software that will search the social media landscape to find comments, both positive and negative, about an organization or destination. As a result, the ability to use this software to analyze data is often now a required skill for market researchers.

Desire for authentic and personalized experiences

Another issue that relates to the current change in tourism consumer behavior is the type of experience desired. Earlier studies of tourism were built on the idea that tourists wanted to have an experience different from daily life. While they knew that there was an 'everyday' life happening behind the scenes while they visited, they were not interested in that part of the experience. Now what travelers want is to be part of an authentic local experience that fits their individual interests.

Authenticity can have a variety of meanings depending on the context in which the word is used (Knudsen and Waade 2010). Applying the term to destinations means that they are both credible and reliable in how the reality is represented. Disneyland is authentically Disney in that it provides the experience that the tourist expects when visiting. Authenticity can also mean that something exists and is not imaginary. While people can view videos about a country and culture online, this is not considered as authentic an experience as would be visiting personally. Lastly, authenticity can mean that a place is the original and not a copy. The intensity of an experience is increased and an emotional relationship is created when encountering an original place or culture. The most authentic tourism experiences can be said to be a credible encounter with the original place that generates a feeling of relationship. The search for authenticity by tourists can be defined as a desire to experience life as it is really lived somewhere else.

Even if in the past travelers wanted an authentic travel experience, they lacked both the knowledge of the destination and the ability to access tourism providers directly. As a result, they needed to rely on travel intermediaries to book their trip. To please the most travelers, these intermediaries tended to standardize the travel experience by providing similar experiences. Now people are no longer satisfied with this standardized approach to tourism. Because they are globally aware through reading about and viewing destinations online they want to do more than simply see a place. Instead they want to experience the local culture in a way that technology can't provide. Tourism providers will need to conduct research to determine what type of authentic experience is desired so that it can be provided and promoted to visitors.

Today travelers are savvy consumers who have a resistance to packaged products and generalized marketing messages. The packaging and marketing done by tourism intermediaries is often seen as making travel just another commodified product rather than a personalized experience. Travellers will have very specific desires as to what they wish to experience, including sites, culture, activities and people. While they are looking for cultural difference, they want experiences that mirror their already existing interests and lifestyles (Bosangit 2014). As a result, tourism organizations will need to research what they prefer. If they are interested in music, photography or sports at home, travellers will want to experience the local cultural expression of the same.

Changes in visitor expectations

The easy access to products because of technology has changed consumers' expectations of how products should be marketed. They want the product to be represented accurately in marketing as the consumer's self-image depends on this factor. Because the product must enhance their sense of identity, purchasing a product that is not as it was promoted honestly is not only a purchasing mistake; it affects the consumers' sense of who they are.

It is the issues of quality and authenticity that most affect the consumer purchase behavior when buying tourism products. Quality is critical when purchasing tourism products as it is difficult to ascertain before purchase. In addition, authenticity is the deciding factor when purchasing experiences such as travel. The problem for the consumer is how to obtain the desired high quality authentic travel experience.

To get accurate information, potential travelers rely on the advice of those who have already visited. In fact, sharing information on travel has become part of the travel experience. This behavior starts even before the trip as can be seen by the fact that 50 per cent of travelers download phone apps for the location they will be visiting when researching a potential travel destination. Because they know so much about a destination before visiting, visitors are no longer satisfied with the standard tourist experience; instead they want a local experience that is personalized to their interests. The challenge for tourism organizations is learning more about visitor desires so that this local experience can be provided.

Case Study 1.4: Are Millennials always on their smartphones? Yes

A global survey was conducted of 9,000 Millennials on their use of technology. Looking for someone of that age that does not use technology daily? You will need to look long and hard. Less than 1 per cent do not connect via a smartphone, computer or tablet daily. Who is on their phones the most? Germans have a daily use percentage of 93 per cent. This is followed with the British at 92 per cent, Brazilians at 91 and Americans at 89 per cent. What was surprising was that of all the technology use surveyed, including smartphones, tablets, computers and smartwatches, Japanese Millennials had the smallest percentage of daily use for each.

What are Millennials using this connectivity to do when staying at hotels? Forty-six per cent book online while less, 20 per cent, check in online. Only 12 per cent order room service online. The low percentage does not mean that they are not interested in doing so. In fact, online room service menus were the highest ranked request when the survey asked how else hotels could use technology.

What about restaurants, coffee shops and bars? While 39 per cent of Millennials are already ordering their food online for takeout, 46 per cent are interested in ordering their food online while in the restaurant. When it comes to tracking their upcoming free cup of coffee, over half of respondents want to manage their restaurant loyalty programs using technology.

Millennials want both online convenience and customization of the travel experience. They want to go on the hotel website and not only check in, but also to specify all of their preferences (type of pillow preferred), provide information (weather forecast), and suggest services based on their profile (spa, workout or both) (Renner 2017).

Question: How would you personalize the travel experience using technology for your organization?

Consumer purchase model changes

Consumer behavior is the process of both why and how the decision to purchase a specific product is made. As the motivations for travel can vary widely from one traveler to another, the marketing of tourism has always been challenging. Now a new challenge has arisen as consumers rely less on tourism intermediaries as a source of information.

There have been a number of models that have attempted to explain how consumers make the decision to purchase a product. The most accepted model of the process involves need recognition, search for information, evaluating alternatives, purchase and post-purchase evaluation. This model led marketing professionals to focus on the role of promotional information in motivating a purchase decision.

In fact, the use of social media has changed every step of how consumers purchase products, including tourism. During the first step of need recognition, the desire for travel might not be based on information from a travel intermediary, which then prompts a search for information. Instead consumers might be online updating their Facebook page or perusing information on a video or photo sharing site when they might notice that someone has posted information on their travel experiences. This might start consumers developing a need to travel to a specific destination that was not prompted by any promotional material produced by an intermediary. The evaluation of alternatives stage has also changed. Rather than requesting information from tourism intermediaries, the travel consumer is much more likely to then search consumer review sites such as TripAdvisor to compare the benefits of different destinations (Rudnansky 2015). As a result, consumers no longer rely on professional travel intermediaries to provide access to information. Instead the average traveler now uses 22 websites before booking travel.

Once the decision has been made and the trip purchased it was thought that the search for information and evaluation of alternatives was completed. However, social media has also changed this step in the tourism consumer behavior process as travelers continue to search for information and evaluate alternatives during the trip. The traveler now becomes a co-creator of tourism content by continually customizing their travel experience.

Another change resulting from social media is that the post-purchase evaluation now starts during the trip. While in the past a common motivation ascribed to travel was a desire to get away from everyday life, now the tourist stays in contact with home while away. Almost as many of the conversations with people at home about a trip take place during the trip via social media as when the trip has been concluded. Even the most adventurous of backpackers takes at least a smartphone with them. They do so as part of the travel experience is now sharing online. While social media is used to enrich the trip by sharing information with those back home, it is also used to communicate with local residents to find desired experiences. After the trip social media is used to critique the trip by writing reviews and sharing the trip by posting photos. While it may have been the technologically sophisticated trend setters who first used online sites to directly access tourism products and social media to share experiences, this change in consumer behavior has spread rapidly.

References

Bosangit, C., 2014. Online Blogs as a Marketing Tool. *The Routledge Handbook of Tourism Marketing*. London: Routledge, pp. 268–280.

Kasriel-Alexander, D. 2016. Top 10 Global Consumer Trends for 2016 [online]. *Euromonitor International*. Available from http://go.euromonitor.com/rs/805-KOK-719/images/WP_Top-10-GCT-2016_1.3-0116.pdf. [Accessed 9 January 2017].

Knudsen, B. and A. Waade. 2010. Performative Authenticity in Tourism and Spatial Experience: Rethinking the Relations Between Travel, Place and Emotion. *Re-investing Authenticity: Tourism, Place and Emotions*. Bristol, UK: Channel View Publications, pp. 1–19.

Minett, D. 2017. Why Are Hotels Embracing Local Culture? *Hotel, Travel & Hospitality News*. 4Hoteliers, 16 January. Available from www.4hoteliers.com/features/article/10209?awsb_c=4hdm&awsb_k=dnws. [Accessed 16 January 2017].

Renner, S. 2017. Global Study: Millennials Mobile Use Reshaping Hospitality Industry [online]. *Oracle Hospitality Blog*. Oracle. Available from blogs.oracle.com/hospitality/

global-study:-millennials-mobile-use-reshaping-hospitality-industry. [Accessed 3 January 2017].

Richards, G. and R. Palmer. 2010. *Eventful Cities: Cultural Management and Urban Revitalization*. Oxford, UK: Butterworth-Heinemann.

Rudnansky, R. 2015. Why Are More Hotels Heavily Promoting Direct Booking Today? [online]. *TravelPulse*. 2 September. Available from www.travelpulse.com/news/hotels-and-resorts/why-are-more-hotels-heavily-promoting-direct-booking-today.html. [Accessed 18 September 2017].

Weed, J. 2017. Airlines, Now More Proactive on Weather, Allow Fliers to Shift Their Own Travel Plans [online]. *CNBC Travel*. CNBC, 03 January. Available from www.cnbc.com/2017/01/03/airlines-now-more-proactive-on-weather-allow-fliers-to-shift-own-travel-plans.html. [Accessed 13 January 2017].

Chapter 2

Understanding cultural and ethical research issues

Learning objectives

- What effect do cultural differences have on the choice of research method?
- How can the Hofstede model of cultural dimensions be used to ensure the research method will be successful?
- What are the ethical guidelines that researchers should follow when conducting research?
- Why does using social media to conduct research present new ethical issues for researchers?

Chapter summary

- Research may need to be modified when conducted with visitors from areas that have different cultures. Culture is the way life is lived including the choices made when engaging in daily activities such as what to wear and what to eat. It also includes beliefs and values, such as the role of family relationships. Ethnocentrism, prejudice and stereotyping can cause a researcher to not see the other person as a unique individual.
- Geert Hofstede developed a well-known model that groups cultural values and behavior by dimensions that determine how people will act in social situations. Hofstede proposed four dimensions: power distance, uncertainty avoidance, individualism versus collectivism, and masculinity versus femininity, that could be used to categorize cultures.
- A researcher can use dimensions to adjust research methodologies based on how people in a cultural group will react. When designing research methodology the culture of the research subjects will affect the type of method chosen. Some tasks may require independent action and types of communication with which members of cultural groups may be uncomfortable. In addition, they will affect the skills needed by the moderator chosen for focus groups.

- Marketing research involves asking individuals to share their opinions and ideas and to reveal information on their behavior. Because this information can be very personal, research subjects should be treated with respect. A consideration of ethical issues before research begins can avoid unintentional problems. Social media presents additional ethical challenges as while comments posted are meant for the public, the posters have not agreed to be part of a research study.

Conducting research across cultures

Culture can be defined as underlying values held by a group of people about how life should be lived. Culture is transmitted from generation to generation, often unconsciously. It includes both the languages spoken and values that are held.

Most researchers are aware that because of language differences they may need to translate survey questions. In addition, participation invitation letters and emails, along with research instructions, may need translation. What is more difficult to understand is how cultural values may differ between groups of people. These values must be understood as they provide guidance on the many decisions people make each day on how they live their lives. These decisions range from the routine, such as what type of food should be eaten for breakfast, to the significant, such as what is the proper relationship between a parent and a child. While these values cannot be seen, the behaviors that result from them can be observed. Behavior patterns are not random and patterns can be observed because 'most' people in a group act in a similar way. Of course, while not every person in a culture follows the same behavior patterns, the individual will feel the pressure to conform to the cultural norm.

For example, an important part of culture is religious beliefs. If a culture holds strong religious values, it is expected that certain behaviors can then be observed, such as an unwillingness to participate in certain activities on the Sabbath. People who hold religious values may also restrict their diet to certain foods and may have rules regarding the type of clothes they wear. It can also be observed that the cultural group's socialization may revolve around religious holidays and festivals. People inside the cultural group will accept this way of life as normal behavior. This is true whether the group is the majority or a minority cultural group.

These cultural differences can be observed when people visit from other countries. However, visitors from within the same country or even community may have different cultural backgrounds. Misunderstandings can result because while the minority cultural group will certainly be aware of the culture of the majority group, the opposite may not be true. The cultural values of the group that is a majority in a country or community are communicated through the media, education system and other social institutions. This majority cultural awareness is the inevitable result of having most of the people exposed to the majority culture. On the other hand, members of the majority culture may be less aware of the values and assumptions of minority groups as they may not encounter them on a daily basis.

One of the primary reasons for tourism is to experience other cultures. Therefore, when hospitality, tourism and event management organizations need to study current and potential consumers, they will most likely be conducting cross-cultural research. Understanding the differences in cultural value will affect how marketing research is conducted. It would be a rare tourism research project that did not need to consider how the methods used might need to be adapted to different languages and cultural values.

Types of cultural differences

There can be different types of cultural differences between the marketing research-ers and the cultural group that is the focus of the research. These differences can result from having different languages, cultural values or both (Markgraf 2013). If the potential participants share a similar culture but speak a different language, the research will be easier to conduct. In this case, all the researchers need to do is translate the survey form and other research materials. If there is a shared language, but different cultural values, the research process can be more challenging. A local ethnic community may speak the same language as the majority culture but have very different values. If the researchers are from the majority culture they may need help in understanding the cultural differences. To do so, they may learn the cultural values from a local cultural association or educational institution.

Of course, research becomes increasingly difficult if the groups do not share the same language and have different cultural values. This would most likely be the case with international tourists. While there may be regional similarities, such as with European and Latin American countries, there are also critical cultural value differ-ences between even neighboring countries that must be considered (Pashupati and Couright 2013). When designing a research study both the need for translation and the need to modify the research methodology need to be addressed.

Language differences

One of the more practical issues when researching across cultural boundaries is lan-guage. Effective research is dependent on clear communication of meaning between the researcher and the subject. This is difficult enough when they both share a first language. It becomes even more challenging when they don't. The best solution to

Figure 2.1 Translation isn't the only issue when researching other cultures.

Photo Credit: Maxx-Studio

Case Study 2.1: How do focus groups differ in China?

China's middle class continues to grow. As a result, many companies are interested in selling products to the Chinese. To do so, they need to conduct research to better understand the Chinese consumer. If the company is planning to use focus groups as a research method, they need to consider how Chinese cultural traits may affect how they will be conducted. First, not all cultural groups consider punctuality important. Your focus group in China may not start on time. A more casual lifestyle may result in not all focus group members attending even if they stated that they would, so you need to invite more people than needed.

When the group starts, the warm-up period may need to be longer. Ethnic and social differences within the group of Chinese research subjects may result in it taking longer for the group to bond. Chinese people are conditioned from youth to keep their opinions to themselves. Getting answers from Chinese research subjects may take longer. In addition, they may believe that there is only one right answer to a question and keep quiet, due to a fear of being wrong. A last consideration is that in China having a group with a mixed age range may not work. Young people may be hesitant to voice an opinion at variance to the one given by an older group member (Joseph 2016).

Question: What other cultures might require changing how a focus group is designed and conducted?

this issue is to use researchers to conduct the study who share a common culture and language with the research subjects.

When conducting qualitative research much of the information is communicated orally. It is critical for the researcher to understand not just what is being said, but how it is being said. For this reason, having a researcher who can communicate in the subject's language is imperative to build trust and ensure accurate communication. Only using someone to interpret during the interview or focus group will result in losing too much of the meaning.

Language issues are of less concern when conducting surveys. Of course, it will be necessary to have a survey form translated into the first language of the research subjects. In fact, if there is a language issue, all written communication must be translated including not only the survey form but also any directions that are provided.

Cultural differences

Most people do not think how culture affects the decisions they make. In fact, cultural values are learned at such a young age that they may be believed to be universal. How the elderly should be treated, which relatives are considered close family, and what is the correct balance between work and leisure, are all cultural values that are learned. Having learned the group's cultural values does not mean that everyone in the culture will act accordingly. However, when people act differently from their cultural values, they may feel uncomfortable. If the difference between community and individual value is too wide, an individual may choose to live elsewhere.

Figure 2.2 Chinese families celebrate New Year's together.

Photo Credit: wong sze yuen

Unfortunately, there are some individuals who believe that the values of the group that guide behavior are correct and that any other values are not just different but wrong. This is referred to as self-reference and leads to an outlook called ethnocentrism where all behavior by others is judged against how the individual would act in a similar situation. Ethnocentrism is usually not a problem if everyone belongs to the same group. However, when cultural groups interact, problems will result as negative judgements will be made about the actions of the other cultural group.

Such an attitude will certainly result in problems if communicated to members of other cultural groups. In tourism marketing research, it will lead to making assumptions about people's motivation for travel that are inaccurate. As a result, the tourism organization will not provide the travel experience desired by visitors from other cultures.

Avoiding stereotyping

Stereotyping is a form of mental shorthand that people use to help make sense of the world. It is human nature to group and categorize both objects and people. After all, life would be too difficult if we had to approach each new object and person as a completely unknown experience.

When stereotyping someone who has learned a few facts about a single member of a group applies them to all people in the cultural group. For example, a researcher with a friend from another culture will assume that the friend's qualities, either good or bad, are true of everyone in the cultural group. Stereotyping can be either positive, such as if the friend loves to travel, therefore all people from his or her culture also like to travel. Or it can be negative: if someone from another country is unadventurous, therefore no one from the culture would want to take trips to unusual locations. Both positive and negative stereotypes can be dangerous if they lead the researcher to make inaccurate assumptions about the group.

The issue is for researchers to be aware of the stereotypical views they hold so they do not affect the research process. If they do not understand their own stereotypical views, they may miss information because it does not fit in with their preconceived ideas. For example, a researcher conducting a focus group with members from a local cultural community may believe that all members are hardworking and therefore have little preference for leisure. As a result, comments from focus group members about their desire for more leisure activities while on holidays may be unconsciously ignored by the researcher.

Dealing with prejudice

Prejudice differs from stereotyping as it is always negative and can have no basis in fact. Prejudice can be based on any human characteristic such as age, weight, sexual orientation or ethnicity. Another significant difference between stereotyping and prejudice is that prejudice does not have to be based on an actual experience with someone. Instead it is a negative belief about a group that has been learned from others with no basis in reality. While no one wants to think that they themselves are prejudiced, it is actually very easy to have a prejudiced view of a group without even being aware.

Prejudice can be active or passive. Sometimes prejudice is so strongly held it becomes a part of an individual's belief system. People with strongly held prejudices may choose to associate only with others who also hold these beliefs. Prejudice can also be passive where the individual does not act on their beliefs.

Prejudice is learned early in life, which is why it is sometimes unnoticed and difficult to overcome. Of course, the researcher would not act on their prejudice, but even passive prejudice can be harmful to the research process. If researchers realize they have a problem with prejudice, it is best to avoid being involved in research with members of the group. It will be impossible for the researcher to hide their

Figure 2.3 Cultural differences must be considered when designing research studies.

Photo Credit: John Leung

negative feelings as members of groups which have experienced prejudice are very sensitive to negative attitudes.

Hofstede's cultural dimensions

Many of the decisions people make every day, including how they greet people, what they eat, the types of clothes they wear, and if they should travel in the summer, are made without much thought. After all, if everyone had to carefully consider each decision, they would never make it through the day. Instead they get up and have what they consider a 'normal' breakfast, whether it is cornflakes or fish soup and take a 'normal' vacation, whether it is for a weekend or six weeks. Because their choices are based on values and behavior that have been learned at a young age, they do not consider the reason why they are making a choice.

Even if the tourism researcher accepts the fact that they should consider the differences in other cultures, doing so can be difficult because there are so many aspects of behavior that are determined by unconscious cultural values. A model is needed to help think about these differences and similarities across cultures as these cultural values will determine the attitude toward travel, the type of experiences that are desired and customer service expectations.

A well-known model that groups cultural values and behavior by dimensions was developed by Geert Hofstede. He proposed that everyone carries around mental maps in their minds of how they should act in social situations. Most people will make decisions about action in accordance with their mental map. Of course, they may act differently, but if they do their actions will be in conflict with their values and they may feel uncomfortable or guilty as a result (Hofstede 2001).

Four of the dimensions Hofstede initially proposed – power distance, uncertainty avoidance, individualism versus collectivism, and masculinity versus femininity – can be used to categorize cultures. A culture's grouping on these dimensions can then be used to predict their actions or responses to situations. The researcher can use the dimensions to predict how people in a cultural group will react to different research methodologies. After all, the willing participation of the research participants is necessary if the research is going to be successful. Lists of how countries compare with each other based on these dimensions can be found online. If the research subjects are from other countries, these should be consulted before designing the methodology.

Power distance

The dimension of power distance measures how people react to authority and how accepting they are of role differences. In all cultures there are differences in equality. Even within families, some family members will have more power to make decisions than others. This power difference might be based on gender or on birth rank. At work, there are also power differences. There is someone who has the authority to tell someone else what work they must perform. There are also political power differences between those in power and those who do not have any or limited input into political decision making. These examples demonstrate the role of authority.

The important issue is not whether these power differences are right or wrong. After all, they exist to some extent in all cultures. The important issue is whether

Case Study 2.2: From zero dollar to FIT

Tourists from China to Thailand formerly all preferred to travel with tour groups. Since the Chinese tourists had little experience with international travel and little knowledge of Thailand this made sense. Unfortunately, unscrupulous tourism promoters developed what came to be called zero dollar tours. These were tours where every stop was not just planned but controlled. The tour group participants could only stay, shop and eat in Chinese owned establishments that had links with the tourism companies. Often, tour members were not allowed to travel outside of the established itinerary. Local tourism service providers were unhappy as they received no benefit from tourism. As a result of complaints, the Thai government shut down some of what were called zero dollar tour operators.

Chinese tourists were also becoming unhappy with the group tour experience. Now Thailand is experiencing the arrival of FIT travelers, who are free independent travelers from China. Often young, they know how to research destinations online and have the knowledge to travel independently. They use Google translate on their phones and are comfortable traveling only with their friends. While the number of Chinese visiting Thailand has decreased, the spending per tourist has increased (Macan-Markar 2017)!

Question: How could you research these FIT Chinese visitors to determine what experiences they desire?

they are accepted as appropriate and natural. In fact they may even be accepted as necessary to the effective management of a home, a business or a country.

Members of a high power distance culture will believe that decisions made by those in positions of authority should be accepted. After all, making these decisions is the responsibility of those in power because they have the knowledge to make the best decisions for all. Members of a low power distance culture will believe that everyone has the ability and knowledge to make decisions. Therefore, those in positions of authority should listen to the opinions of even the lowest ranking members. This dynamic would affect behavior such as who in the family makes the decision on where to travel on vacation. This dimension would also affect how the authority of the marketing researcher will be viewed. For example, in low power distance countries, children will be part of the decision-making process for where to go on vacation, while in high power distance countries, this may be the decision of an adult male.

Uncertainty avoidance

While risk is a part of life as the future is always an unknown, it would be psychologically impossible to live life with a constant awareness that the future is both unknowable and uncontrollable. As a result, a society will create laws and social norms that control current behavior. They will also use religious or civic rituals to assure people about the future.

Cultures vary on how accepting people are of the idea of an unknown future full of risk. Cultures with high uncertainty avoidance will avoid new behaviors because the results are unpredictable. They accept rules that govern behavior because they lessen anxiety. People in these cultures understand that if everyone follows the rules there will be few surprises, which are not welcomed. This aspect of culture affects travel behavior. People who wish to avoid uncertainty may prefer tours where the itinerary is planned by professionals. The opposite may be true of individuals who accept risk as part of the excitement and want to rent a car or buy a train pass and travel on their own without plans.

People in high uncertainty avoidance cultures will find challenges that force them to take unfamiliar actions troubling. As a result, research techniques that ask for the participant to be creative will not be viewed favorably.

On the other hand, cultures with low uncertainty avoidance will accept risk as a part of life. They will be interested in new experiences because the outcome might be successful. Because they anticipate a positive result from change rather than problems, they welcome new challenges and do not fear failure. They are open to new experiences, including research techniques. As a result, this dimension also affects the type of research method that should be used to successfully obtain the needed information.

Individualism versus collectivism

Humans are social beings who need to associate with other people. These social relationships between people involve responsibility for each other's welfare, which is how people survive. The importance given to social relationships differs between cultures. This differing level of importance of relationships results in different social behaviors.

If a culture focuses on collectivism, people learn to put the group's needs before their own. What is good for most people is more important than what is good for one individual. This fact affects decisions on where people live, the career they choose, and even who is considered family. In a collectivist culture, people are more likely to live at home and work at the same jobs as their parents. Even who is considered family will differ. In a collectivist culture family relationships will be much more broadly defined, with even non-related people considered relatives. In fact, the whole cultural group may be considered family and what is good for most people in the family is more important than what is good for one individual member. As a result, people tend to think and act in similar ways.

While people in individualist cultures also have family relationships, more emphasis is placed on the needs of the individual. In an individualist culture, people make decisions on their own personal goals rather than what is good for the group. For example, an adult in an individualistic culture will take a job that will further his or her own career goals even if it means a move away from family and friends. While people will sympathize about the move, people in an individualistic culture will understand why the decision was made. In a collectivist culture such a move may seem heartless and an abandonment of family responsibility.

Growing up in an individualistic culture affects how people think about the world around them and the possible choices they can make. People are expected to have their own ideas, thoughts and plans and to pursue them. It is believed that the more people pursue the plans that are best for them the better society will be as a whole.

This dimension affects how people wish to travel. Collectivist cultures will find traveling in groups not only acceptable but also more enjoyable. Travelers from individualist cultures do not want to have to follow someone else's plans. Acceptance of research methods that involve group dynamics will be differ based on this dimension.

Masculinity versus femininity

The terms masculinity and femininity when referring to cultures, use the traditional meanings of the words. Of course there are biological differences between the genders but how these differences are accepted and reinforced varies between cultures. For example, while differences in child bearing are biological, the importance of being nurturing is cultural. Most cultures will differ on what is acceptable behavior for males and females.

A masculine culture believes that aggression is natural. Therefore the members of the culture will be more accepting of aggressive behavior. Men in these cultures are believed to be biologically fitted for leadership. As a result certain occupations are considered masculine and reserved for men. In addition, the culture will be accepting of nurturing behavior, as long the behavior is exhibited by females. A culture is considered masculine when these role differences between men and women are reinforced.

A feminine culture does not define role differences as strictly. Men are allowed to be nurturing without being considered feminine. In such a culture women are more accepted into all types of occupations, as those that require strength, whether physical or emotional, are not seen as being fit only for men. However, a feminine culture as a whole encourages nurturing behavior in all its members and aggression in none.

Travelers from a more masculine culture will enjoy adventures that allow them to show their skills, while travelers from feminine cultures may gravitate to experiences that allow interaction with local community members. This will affect marketing research techniques such as how focus groups are moderated.

Adjusting research methods based on cultural differences

When designing research methodology, the four dimensions should be considered as they will affect the type of method chosen. In addition, they will affect the skills needed by the moderator chosen for focus groups.

Power distance

The cultural dimension of power distance has a direct application to marketing research. For example, the United States is a country that ranks low on power distance. A marketing researcher in the US expects that average consumers will have insights that they believe will be valuable to those making decisions in the company and will provide them if asked. In fact, a visitor to a city who is asked to participate in research may even assume they will have better ideas about tourism than those working professionally in the industry. They will expect that the professionals will want to know and also value their opinions.

Based on this assumption, the researcher will plan on focus groups or interviews to gather opinions. During the focus group, participants will speak freely and not defer to the opinions of others. They may even argue with the moderator of the group as to the process. They will become uncomfortable if the moderator dominates the discussion and ignores their input.

In this situation, the moderator must first earn the respect and trust of the group members. They cannot assume that people will be willing to stay on topic just because it is part of the research plan. Moderating such a group can be challenging as people will feel entitled to share their opinions even if they are uncomplimentary or differ from those of other group members.

In a high power distance country, such as Malaysia, the average consumer might find the notion that management should need their ideas rather absurd. Most participants in a focus group will see the moderator as someone in a position of power whose views are not to be challenged. As a result, they will be hesitant to voice complaints or make suggestions for changes. Research subjects will believe that management includes the best people to make decisions. If those in power have both the authority and the responsibility to make decisions, research subjects would wonder why they are being asked for their views.

Personal interviews rather than focus groups would work better in high power distance countries. The interviewer should plan enough time during the process to gain the trust of the participant until they are ready to share their ideas. It might be necessary to conduct research using surveys. As these are anonymous, participants are more likely to challenge authority by providing negative comments.

Power distance

- Participants from high power distance countries defer to researcher as a person with a position of authority.
- Low power distance country participants may be argumentative and not willing to follow research instructions.
- Use techniques that will allow participant to provide information anonymously.
- Focus group moderator must treat participants as valued equals.

Uncertainty avoidance

People from countries with high uncertainty avoidance cultures will find novelty as a threat rather than exciting. Because they fear failure more than they anticipate success, they will not be comfortable in a situation without directions. Therefore, projective techniques without any definition of what is to be expected would not be welcomed. People from low uncertainty avoidance cultures, such as Sweden, will find new challenges and unfamiliar situations exciting. Rather than worry about failure, they will focus on the possibility of success.

Research techniques that require the participant to take risks based on little information would make individuals in high uncertainty avoidance cultures, such as Portugal, uneasy. Creative projective techniques, such as asking participants to draw a visual ad for a product based on their opinions, provide little guidance as to what is expected so would not work well in a high uncertainty avoidance culture. Even open-ended questions in a survey form may go unanswered as there is too much risk of giving an answer that might be perceived as wrong. This reluctance can be partly

Case Study 2.3: Make mine halal!

Any group that follows a religious belief that prescribes certain behaviors for daily living may have unique needs when traveling. This is true of conservative Muslims who follow halal practices, a set of rules of what is permissible and what is not. While not every Muslim will feel the need to do so, some want hotels that reflect their beliefs. As a result, a growing number of hotels promote halal tourism.

These hotels do not serve alcohol, serve halal food, and have separate recreational facilities for men and women. Other ideas for making conservative Muslims feel at home are providing prayer rugs in the rooms and having staff dress conservatively. Why do so? It is estimated that by 2020 11 per cent of travelers will be conservative Muslims. This is a market segment worth over $200 billion. Turkey already has 40 hotels that cater to this segment. In 2016 the annual conference dedicated to halal tourism attracted attendees from 30 countries including Western countries as the need for such hotels is not just confined to Muslin countries but anywhere a conservative Muslin may wish to go (Youssef 2016).

Question: How would religious beliefs affect the design of a research study to learn more about Muslim travelers?

overcome by providing detailed instructions on how to proceed with a technique. In addition, a complete explanation of the research process and the reason it is being undertaken may make participants from high uncertainty avoidance cultures more comfortable.

People from low uncertainty avoidance cultures will find such detailed explanations both boring and unnecessary. They believe that they have the ability to figure out how to complete the process on their own. They are not unduly concerned about making mistakes or failure as they believe that nothing bad will happen as a result.

Uncertainty avoidance

- Participants from high uncertainty avoidance countries find techniques that provide little direction threatening.
- Low avoidance participants welcome techniques that allow creativity.
- When using such techniques more information on expectations needs to be provided.

Individualism versus collectivism

The marketing concept states that products and services should be developed to meet the needs and wants of the consumer. The purpose of marketing research is to uncover these needs and wants. While it is true that individuals differ because of their genetic makeup, their family experiences and their external environment, in collectivist cultures it will be much harder to prompt them to express their individual needs and wants. Particularly in focus group situations, research subjects from collectivist cultures, such as China, will be more likely to agree with other group members rather than explore differences that might cause disagreements. Also, when answering survey questions, people from collectivist cultures are likely to respond to questions based on the views of their families and friends rather than on their own opinions. It will take time and patience to establish a relationship and develop the trust before the research participant from a collectivist culture will be ready to express their views. Until then, they are more likely to express as their own opinions the views of others.

People from individualistic cultures will feel free to give their own opinions. In individualistic countries, such as Australia, people feel free to express their opinion even if it differs from most others. Their answers to questions on product benefits will be based on their personal experience. They will view a tourism product negatively if it does not meet their needs. They will not find relevant the fact that the product meets the needs of many others.

Individualism vs. collectivism

- Participants from collectivist cultures in focus groups tend to agree with other participants.
- Survey questions may be answered based on the opinions of the group rather than individual.
- In-depth individual interviews may be needed so that sufficient time is available to convince the participant that his or her views are valid and needed.

Masculine versus feminine

Masculine versus feminine behavior has a direct implication for consumer research as it affects who is the family member who makes the purchase decision. In a high masculine country, such as Hungary, men make the major shopping decisions involving expensive products while women will shop for food and everyday items. In Denmark, a country with a more feminine culture, men and women would play equal roles in decision making. Because of this difference, in masculine countries men should be asked to participate in research that asks opinions on expensive products such as long cruises. In feminine countries men and women would both be involved in making travel decisions. As a result, both genders will have impact on the decision when planning travel and should be included in research. Likewise, in a high feminine country, men may equally take on the task of food shopping. Research on dining preferences when travelling will want to also gather the opinions of men.

In masculine countries, the male participants may have difficulty with viewing a female researcher as having the necessary skill and authority to conduct the research. In this case the female researcher may need to take the time to define her credentials and also her role in the organization. These male participants will assume a male researcher is qualified without asking for any verification.

Another consideration is that having males and females together in a focus group might result in the women not speaking or differing as to the opinions of men. It may increase the effectiveness of the groups if men and women are separated.

Femininity vs. masculinity

- Who makes the purchase decision varies based on the cost of a product and its perception as something that is used by only men or women.
- Research sample will need to be adjusted to adapt for gender differences in product purchasing.

Marketing research ethics

Marketing research involves asking individuals to share with the researcher their opinions and ideas. In addition, they are asked to reveal information on their behavior. Because of its potentially intrusive nature, researchers should ensure that they treat every research subject with respect. While it would be the rare researcher that started to research with the intent to commit harm, a consideration of ethical issues before research begins can avoid unintentional problems.

Ethical code of conduct

Simply defined, ethics is a set of guidelines that distinguishes what is right from what is wrong. While ethics are general principles, a code of conduct is a set of guidelines that spells out what actions are right and wrong when engaged in a specific set of activities. Because of the importance of ensuring that the rights of research subjects are respected, organizations within the marketing research profession have established their own codes of conduct. The codes can be summarized as the need for researchers to seek truth, deal honestly, and to ensure no harm occurs to participants. A fourth principle is becoming accepted, which is the right of research subjects to see survey data.

Guidelines for conducting ethical research

- Conduct research without compromising the search for truth
- Deal honestly with research subjects
- Make sure no harm results
- Communicate research findings to participants

The first standard is that the purpose of the research itself must be ethical. It is the researcher's responsibility to ensure that the research is conducted objectively without a predetermined outcome. Researchers understand that by controlling who is asked and by changing the phrasing of a question, the outcome of a study can be manipulated. The pressure to predetermine the results may be caused by the need to have a specific outcome so that a grant or funding may be obtained or renewed. For example, survey participants may be asked questions that lead to a positive response on their use of the visitor center. By participating in such deceptive research, not only will the organization have failed ethically, all future research results will be suspect. It is both the principles and behavior of the organization's management that shape the behavior of the researchers with whom they work.

When conducting research, those working for the organization should always identify themselves accurately. If possible they should have, and be willing to show,

Case Study 2.4: Happy New Year! Not the same in every culture

While many people may think of 1 January as the day to say Happy New Year, this is not true in every culture. The Chinese use a lunar calendar to mark the date so the day to celebrate will vary.

How people will celebrate will also vary. The Chinese distribute red envelopes with cash (*hongbao*) at New Year and on other days of celebration. Why red? The story goes way back, but essentially has to do with warding off evil spirits. Also, the color red is associated with energy, happiness and good luck. While learning the reason for a custom is always interesting, it is vital to know the etiquette that is associated with a holiday.

The rules for giving hongbao include only using clean crisp bills and making sure the amount is appropriate for the relationship. Also, remember the symbolism of numbers is important in Chinese culture. Odd amounts are bad, even are good and an amount that starts or ends with the number eight is even better! When receiving hongbao always use two hands, don't open in front of the giver and say thanks. Technology now makes the process easier as a virtual hongbao can be sent over WeChat!

Why should someone working in tourism be aware of this custom? First, holidays important to employees should be acknowledged. Second, events that fall on cultural holidays should be themed. Most importantly, any hotel guests should feel that the hotel understands the significance of the day. Just as an American might feel welcomed in China when on Thanksgiving they see the decorations with turkeys, guests from China would feel welcome in the US when they see red decorations on Chinese New Year (Lee 2017).

Question: How can we learn more about the holidays of our international visitors?

identification. The emails that contain links to online survey forms should provide information on the organization conducting the research along with contact details. Researchers should also be honest with participants as to the purpose of the research. If this is not possible because of the research design, the information needs to be presented at the conclusion of the research.

An additional ethical issue is the responsibility to protect participants from harm. This should be of special concern to destination marketing organizations as they may be researching sensitive issues, such as attitudes toward personal safety in a tourist area. While marketing research uses techniques that are adapted from psychology, marketing researchers are not trained as psychologists. Researchers must be careful with how questions are worded so as to minimize any emotional distress. They must also be ready to handle any distress that does inadvertently result. For example, permissible questions in a focus groups might be 'Did you feel safe in all areas of our city?' or 'What could be done to improve the safety of our parks?' A question that is not part of marketing research would be 'How did you feel when you walked in the park after dark?' This question will not help the organization improve and may trigger unpleasant memories.

Finally, the participants should have access to the research findings if they are voluntarily participating. If a participant is paid, they are already being compensated for their time and cooperation. In contrast, a volunteer is owed transparency. Even if it is not possible to provide participants with the entire final report because of privacy issues, they should be allowed access to at least a summary of the analysis of the responses to the questions in which they participated. The organization may find that not everyone is interested, but still the offer should be made.

Ethical issues when conducting cross-cultural research

Researching across cultural differences has additional ethical issues because of the difference in cultural values. Unless the researcher understands that the expectations of ethical behavior can vary between countries, misunderstandings can lead to a breakdown in trust that may be difficult for the organization to repair (Lipman, 2016). This does not mean that researchers should lower their standards but that they need to be aware that research subjects may not always deal honestly with researchers.

Effective research depends on the willingness of research subjects to participate. This willingness is based on an understanding of the purpose of research and trust in the researcher. Issues that can affect this understanding and trust include the respect the organization and researcher have for the culture of the research subjects. In addition, it depends on the cultural value placed on the privacy of those involved in the study. Of course, having a shared language helps being able to communicate both respect and an understanding of cultural values but does not eliminate the issue.

Guidelines for conducting research across cultural boundaries

- Respect the culture of research subjects to build trust
- Understand the cultural values involving privacy
- Communicate in the language of the subject

Before designing and conducting a research study that involves subjects from a different culture, the organization and particularly those involved in the research should have a sincere respect for the culture. If this is not the case, the research subjects will not trust the researchers and may refuse to be involved in the research.

For many cultures trust depends on personal relationships. The idea that the researcher and the research subject are only acting in 'roles' and should not be considered a unique human being might not be understood or, if understood, may not be accepted. In this case for research to be effective, the researcher must first develop and maintain a relationship with the subjects. Asking someone to 'tell me what you did not enjoy about your visit' might be difficult to answer, as the participant may not wish to give offense to a stranger.

Part of respecting the culture of the participants is an appreciation of how cultures differ in their attitudes toward people in authority. In some cultures, the researcher might be seen as having some level of control over the subject's life. For this reason the researcher must clearly explain the purpose and limitation of the researcher's role. If the researcher is seen as someone having authority, simple demographic questions concerning family status, address or nationality may not be answered honestly. Such questions may be seen as too personal with the possibility that the information may be used against the research subject in some way. Rather than state this directly, it may be considered more polite to give a vague or misleading answer.

Marketing research techniques were originally derived from the area of psychology and are based on the sharing of personal information from the research subject to the researcher. It is important for the organization to understand that cultures differ in how they view sharing personal information. Some cultures are not hesitant regarding the sharing of information. In fact in some countries, people compete to get on reality and talk television shows to share their most personal secrets with the world. However, there are very good reasons why other cultures do not wish to communicate this information. If modesty or privacy are considered important cultural values, subjects will be reluctant to provide any information that they feel should not be discussed in public.

This aspect of the subject's culture should be considered when deciding upon a research method. While the researcher might feel that providing an anonymous survey form about travel preferences provides privacy, the subject might not trust that this is so and wish to speak personally with the researcher as personal interaction in a focus group or interview can build trust. Another cultural group might see an interview or focus group as a totally unacceptable invasion of privacy and prefer a survey form to provide information.

If the research method cannot be changed, a more complicated research design is necessary. The researcher might need to first hold a group meeting to explain the reasons for the research and how privacy will be respected. After trust is established then an anonymous survey might be administered.

Social media and ethics

When using social media as a source of data in research on travelers' opinions on destinations, lodging and events, some additional issues arise. The first issue is one of privacy. Some sites are public and anyone can look at the information that is posted. Most review sites are of this type. Other social media sites require a person to register. The criterion may be an address as the site is only available to a geographic area, such as a neighborhood. Some sites that require registration are for people with some special interests such as trivia nights at bars.

Even government agencies that deal in security concerns are receiving resistance in their efforts to gather data via social media (Johnson 2017). Marketing researchers should not sign into sites and pose as members of a community if their only purpose in doing so is to gather information for research.

The second issue is one of consent. A person may post reviews or information online for the use of other travelers. This can be done from the altruistic motive of wanting to save other people from an unfortunate experience or to provide a recommendation that will lead to a positive experience. This does not mean that the information is available to be used as part of a research study.

Lastly, an issue is that research should be a separate process from destination, hotel or event marketing. It is acceptable that a researcher goes on to social media identified as a researcher to ask research questions online. The problem arises when they then proceed to provide product information. This crosses the line into selling and the research subject will wonder if the only purpose of the study was to market.

References

Hofstede, Geert. 2001. *Culture's Consequences: Comparing Values, Behaviors, Institutions and Organizations across Cultures*. London: SAGE.

Johnson, T., 2017. Privacy Critics Assail U.S. Plan to Collect Travelers' Social Media [online]. *The Seattle Times*. The Seattle Times Company, 9 February. Available from www.seattletimes.com/nation-world/privacy-critics-assail-us-plan-to-collect-travelers-social-media/>. [Accessed 12 April 2017].

Joseph, D., 2016. How Do Focus Groups in China Differ? – Hub of China [online]. Available from www.hubofchina.com/2016/02/21/what-do-we-need-to-bear-in-mind-when-conducting-focus-groups-in-china/. [Accessed 13 December 2016].

Lee, C., 2017. Happy Chinese New Year, Folks! It's That Time of Year Again, When Red Envelopes — Also Known as 红包 (hongbao), 'red Packets' or Even 'lucky Money' — Holding a Monetary Value Are given to and Received from Friends and Families [online] *Hotel, Travel & Hospitality News*. Available from www.4hoteliers.com/news/story/16753?awsb_c=4hdm&awsb_k=dnws. 4Hoteliers, 23 January 2017. [Accessed 23 January 2017].

Lipman, V., 2016. New Global Survey Reveals The Most Ethical (And Unethical) Countries To Do Business In [online]. *Forbes Magazine*, 25 June. Available from www.forbes.com/sites/victorlipman/2016/06/09/the-most-ethical-and-unethical-countries-to-do-business-in/#14190d072303. [Accessed 12 April 2017].

Macan-Markar, M., 2017. Thailand Cracks Down on 'Zero-dollar' Tour Groups [online] *Financial Times*. The Financial Times Ltd., 8 January. Available from www.ft.com/content/698a002a-d3fd-11e6-b06b-680c49b4b4c0. [Accessed 16 January 2017].

Markgraf, B., 2013. Cultural Adaptation in the Global Marketplace [online]. Chron.com. 05 June. Available from smallbusiness.chron.com/cultural-adaptation-global-marketplace-68239.html. [Accessed 13 April 2017].

Pashupati, K. and M. Couright, 2013. Lost in Translation? [online]. *Research Live*. 12 November. Available from www.research-live.com/article/features/lost-in-translation/id/4010792. [Accessed 12 April 2017].

Youssef, N., 2016. Halal Tourism: A Growing Trend for Muslim Travellers [online] *Daily News Egypt*. Available from www.dailynewsegypt.com/2016/06/09/halal-tourism-growing-trend-muslim-travellers/. [Accessed 16 January 2017].

Starting the research process

Chapter summary

- The first step in research involves writing the research question about an issue or problem on which the organization might need additional information. Rather than make an assumption as to what needs to be known, critical thinking skill must be used. First the organization must identify the pre-existing assumptions regarding the cause of the problem or the potential opportunity. Then internal research data must be used to challenge whether these same assumptions are based on facts. The final step is to explore new ideas about the actual source of the problem and its possible solution.
- Once the research question has been determined the next issue the organization will face involves deciding whether to use secondary or primary data. Information that is already available as the result of some other organization conducting research is called secondary data. Since using already available data saves time and money, organizations should always first look for secondary data. The burden is on researchers to ensure that the secondary data they are using is credible.
- Researchers will choose whether to use a quantitative or qualitative research approach depending on the type of information that is needed. Quantitative research is useful for answering questions of fact involving where, who, how often and what. Qualitative research is used to explore opinions and ideas. Descriptive

research gathers facts about a known problem while exploratory research is used when little is known.

- Quantitative research is conducted using surveys that can be administered personally or self-administered online. The other commonly used tools in marketing research are qualitative focus groups, interviews, projective techniques and observation. This is because most marketing research asks the question of 'why'.

Determining the research question

The research process starts when the tourism, hospitality or event management organization determines what information is needed. This first step involves formulating the research question. While this sounds rather scientific it simply means the organization must ask itself, 'What do we need to know that we don't know now?' There are any number of issues or problems on which the organization might need additional information.

Critical thinking and narrowing assumptions

The most common difficulty faced by organizations when starting the research process is making a faulty assumption about the cause of a problem. This results in writing a research question that will focus on finding the wrong information. Assumptions can be thought of as facts that are believed to be correct without proof. Faulty assumptions are often based only on personal experience, rather than on objective facts. This rush to judgment over why a problem exists is simpler and quicker than searching for the true cause, as it takes little critical analysis. Yet, just because the cause of a problem seems self-evident, does not make it true. For example, an assumption about why visitation to an attraction is down can result in actions that are counterproductive. The organization might assume that its current offerings are of no interest and, as a result, then introduce a new tour or show. This can lead to expensive failures, as the reason for decreased visitation might not be lack of interest but a lack of promotion. Therefore, instead of making assumptions, researchers need to take the time to think critically about what is the true nature of the problem or opportunity.

If an inaccurate assumption about the cause of the problem or the potential success of an idea is made, the wrong research question will be asked. The company will then design and conduct research which will lead to information that is not useful, such as asking what new products should be offered, when the problem is a lack of promotion. As a result of the wrong assumption a great deal of research time, money and effort will be wasted. One way for market researchers to avoid this situation is to use critical thinking, which is a process of questioning and evaluating assumptions. Critical thinking is a difficult skill that requires effort and a creative imagination, but using it will improve research results.

Critical thinking process

Critical thinking can be thought of as a three-step process. The first step is identifying the pre-existing assumptions held by organization employees regarding the cause of the problem or the potential opportunity. The second step is to use internal research data to challenge whether these same assumptions are accurate and based on facts. The third step is to explore new ideas of the actual source of the problem and its possible solution.

If tourism officials are asked why tourist numbers have decreased, they are likely to state the reasons that are common knowledge. If the news has recently been full of stories about economic difficulties, they are most likely to state this reason. Careful questioning of the officials might find that they do not have accurate information about this affecting local tourism. If this questioning is not undertaken, focus groups might be conducted about what type of inexpensive tour packages to offer, even though this might not be necessary.

The second step in critical thinking is to challenge the assumption that is held by the organization. This can be done by examining internal data that already exists. For instance, an analysis of hotel room data might reveal that the most expensive rooms are still being booked. If it is found that upscale restaurants are also doing well, then despite the fact that the news is full of stories about people cutting expenses, this does not seem to be the reason for a visitor decline.

Now that the initial assumptions have been dealt with and any wrong assumptions have been discarded, it is time for the final step in the critical thinking process. This is to explore new ideas regarding the problem or potential opportunity. This step in the process demonstrates why the market researcher's knowledge of the product and target market is essential. Using this product and consumer knowledge shortens the process of generating and developing new ideas. This is because the researcher has already challenged many of the assumptions and has a base of knowledge about the product and consumers on which to form new ideas. A market researcher who is familiar with the tourism industry will understand that the motivation for travel might be even stronger when economic times are difficult. If the market researcher does not have this information, additional external secondary research will be needed.

Challenging assumptions and developing new ideas about the cause of the problem is difficult as there are often common patterns of thought among organization employees and the natural desire most people feel to conform. If everyone in the organization tends to view the tourism product, their visitor and the tourism industry in the same way, it is difficult for the researcher to argue against these beliefs. However, it is these common patterns of thought that cause the organization's problem and its solution to seem self-evident. These common thought patterns can also keep an organization from seeing opportunities that can be explored using research.

Making a correct assumption

Not all problems require extensive critical thinking. Sometimes the assumptions made about the cause of the problem are clear to everyone in the organization including the researchers. For example, if the owners of a local souvenir shop see its customers' cars across the street in the parking lot at the recently opened discount souvenir store, the problem is clear. Little questioning is needed to challenge the assumption that the customers are buying the competitor's product because of cost. The assumption might be made that research is needed to determine how much to lower prices. However, if the shop's owners, who take pride in their product,

> ## Case Study 3.1: Don't just sell a ticket – sell an event
>
> Concert promoters know that tickets to popular shows are bought by scalpers and then resold to people who want to attend but were not able to buy a ticket when they went on sale. The concert promoter and performers lose revenue while the ticket purchaser gets the same experience at a higher price. Pricing tickets is difficult. If the price is too high, it reflects badly on the performers as the public views them as ripping off their fans. This is true even if the fan would be willing to pay the same high price to a scalper. If the ticket price is set too low, there is an incentive for scalpers to buy up as many tickets as possible as they can make an easy profit when they resell them.
>
> The band A Perfect Circle decided upon a new approach to the problem. They packaged some of their tickets with extra benefits and services at triple the price. What did fans get? Besides the show they received octopus-shaped incense holders, silk-screened messenger bags and preshow wine tastings.
>
> Why don't the scalpers just buy the VIP tickets to sell? The fact is the price is high enough that they would be difficult to resell at a profit. Do fans like the VIP packages? They routinely sell out! What is included? It depends on the band. While Iron Maiden just provide beer, pretzels and t-shirts, they still sell out because one of the most prized VIP experiences is meeting the band (Karp 2017)!
>
> *Question: How could research be used to ensure that successful VIP packages are developed?*

instead conducted research on what benefits visitors desire when buying souvenirs they might find that visitors are also interested in products being locally made. This could then provide an idea for countering the competitive threat by promoting the local crafts people that produce their products.

Writing the research question

The research question might be very broad, such as what new visitor segment can be attracted to the organization's tourism services, to very specific, such as what hours should the visitor center be open on weekends. One common topic is gathering information on current, past and potential visitors. In addition, the marketing research question can focus on competitors to learn from their successes and failures. Ideas for product improvements or new product ideas are also reasons to conduct marketing research. The other issues commonly researched are the marketing mix components of price, promotion and place.

Sample research questions

- Price: Have visitor numbers for families decreased due to increased ticket prices?
- Product: Why do tour members aged 18–24 find the itinerary unappealing?
- Place: Do first time guests find the hotel location inconvenient because of traffic?

Figure 3.1 Clearly stating the research question is the first step in the process.

Photo Credit: 3D-creation

- Promotion: Are potential visitors aware of the organization's social media sites?
- Consumer: Why do older people not visit the beach?
- Competitor: Are our competitor's visitor numbers growing or declining?

Sources of information

Once the research question has been determined the next issue the organization will face involves deciding the source of the information that will answer the question. Information, or data, is referred to as either secondary, which has already been collected, or primary, which the organization will collect. Quantitative research studies gather statistical information and are conducted by another organization, a company or a government agency. Qualitative secondary data is also available through a number of different sources such as articles and online sources such as blogs and websites. The benefits of using secondary data include lowering the research costs, finding information that can help in the design of the research methodology and general background information on the issue of concern.

The term 'secondary' can be confusing as this is actually the first type of research that is conducted. As there is no reason to duplicate research, the first step in gathering data is to determine what is already known. The costs of conducting primary research include the time spent recruiting participants, developing the methodology, and collecting the data. Using secondary data rather than conducting primary research can help the organization lower the cost of research by saving both time and money.

Secondary data

Information that is already available as the result of some other organization conducting research is called secondary data. Since using already available data saves time and money, organizations should always first look for secondary data. For example, if the research question concerns what activities visitors attending bachelorette parties desire, a wedding website might already have conducted research and have the information. Even if the responses received from the research may not directly answer the organization's research question, it can still be used as a source of information and assistance in research planning. For example, the responses might not be directly applicable, perhaps because the research focused on bachelorette parties in beach locations while the organization in need of information is an urban community, but the survey questions might be useful as a model for what can be asked.

Benefits and examples of conducting secondary research

- Save time and money by providing answer to research question
  - ○ another organization has already conducted research on the same topic
- Help design research methodology
  - ○ find survey questions that can be added to the organization's questionnaire
- Provide background information on issue
  - ○ learn areas of concern to the public that need to addressed in research study

Of course, the organization is not going to find any data from external sources that directly addresses their organization. However, if the organization needs information on a general problem they face, the data may already exist. For example, a tourism agency may need to know what sports events are most popular. There is probably an organization that has conducted a larger regional or national survey. If the organization feels that the people who visit are similar to those surveyed, this data can be used.

Sometimes the research question needing to be answered is general in nature rather than specific to the organization such as, 'What type of activities are parents interested in for their children?' The tourism organization may want this information so that it can be used in an upcoming promotional campaign. Rather than conduct research themselves, they may find a website for parents that has already conducted research. For example, the data may show that educational content is of primary concern to parents. If the survey included parents in the organization's geographic area, they may decide that they have no need to conduct their own research.

Requirements of secondary data

The organization may find useful secondary data from tourism and economic studies conducted by government agencies, nongovernmental organizations, other nonprofits, and educational institutions. Unlike information obtained by research companies, which is often proprietary, research conducted by these types of organizations is often freely available.

The ease with which information can be found using online resources might lead an organization to believe that secondary research is simple. After all, there is a wealth of information available for free by just using an online search engine such as Google. In addition, other information can be accessed using online databases. If these resources do not provide enough information, databases only available through subscription can be found at public or academic libraries.

The fact that there are so many available resources to find secondary data puts the burden on researchers to ensure that the data they are using is a good source. There is so much information available that data can be found to support any research

Case Study 3.2: Secondary data shows how the Chinese traveler is changing

Anyone planning to provide tourism services to Chinese travelers would want to know what the Chinese visitors value in the travel experience. The problem is with a country that is so large and geographically diverse, how could a tourism organization afford research? Fortunately, because the country is of interest to many organizations and companies, marketing research firms have already conducted research that can be used. McKinsey & Company, which specializes in producing research reports, has the ability to conduct such a large-scale study. They interviewed 10,000 Chinese citizens living in 44 different cities about their consumption preferences.

What did the research interviews uncover? One fact is that there is a growing interest in international travel. While Chinese consumers are optimistic about the future they are aware of economic uncertainty. Therefore, they are borrowing less and saving more. They also are placing more value on spending time with family rather than simply purchasing products. This means that they are interested in lifestyle services and experiences, particularly ones that the family can enjoy together. When they do spend money on products, they are willing to invest in premium brands, rather than lower priced mass market brands. If they are buying a premium brand they are most likely to purchase a foreign brand name. This research would encourage a foreign company with a well-developed brand that sells premium tour packages designed for family travel to enter the Chinese market (Zipzer, Chen and Gong 2016).

Question: What other primary research would you recommend be conducted before the tour company enters the Chinese market?

issue. The researcher must not only find information, they must assess whether the information is useful because it addresses the research question. However, of equal importance is whether the secondary data is credible, which is determined by timeliness and its source.

The question as to how old data can be before it is too old to use, is not easy to answer. If an organization is faced with a problem that is the result of a new social issue, such as visitors wanting to vacation with their pets, the more recently the secondary data was gathered the more relevance it will have. However, there may be occasions when historical data is needed for comparison purposes. For example, an organization that sponsors concerts aimed at young people may want to know how technology has changed event expectations. Therefore, they may look for information that was gathered years ago. However, searching for historical data is an exception, as most organizations are looking for the most recently collected data.

If a problem is common and affects many people, the organization should be able to find current research. For example, a tourism organization that is researching trends in international tourism will not have a problem finding data. There are many websites and news sources that will provide the needed information. The researcher should use data from the most recent study.

However, if an issue is not that common, there may be less available data. For example, a tourism organization may have been formed to promote tourism to a small ethnic community and they need to know if potential visitors are interested. As there may be little information available any information would be useful, even if it is somewhat dated.

Once timely information has been located, the researcher must verify the source of the data. The most important question for the researchers to answer is who conducted the research. The research study should clearly state the name of the organization and the credentials of the person who gathered the data. While the names of the individual researchers may not be familiar, the organization conducting the research, whether a private company, a university or government agency should be credible.

If the information is contained in an article, and the researchers are unfamiliar with the author, they should check the publication's policies regarding publishing articles. Articles in academic publications are almost always peer-reviewed. The researcher will have to verify the credibility of articles in other types of sources, such as magazines and newspapers, by the reputation of the publication or the author.

Primary data

Sometimes available secondary data may be all that the tourism organization needs to answer the research question. However, it is more likely that primary research will also need to be conducted. Primary research involves directly asking those who have the needed information.

If the organization needs to conduct primary research the next issue will be to decide which research subjects have the necessary information. The information might need to be obtained from current visitors, potential visitors, or other people in the community. The research might even need to involve all three groups. Once it has been determined which group has the necessary information, the organization must be much more specific in determining the sample: how many, and what kinds of people should participate in the research study?

Types of marketing research

Marketing research can be divided into quantitative or qualitative methods. Understanding the distinction between quantitative descriptive research and qualitative exploratory research is necessary so the right method is chosen. They have different purposes and will result in different types of data that will need different forms of analysis. Of course, a research study can and, if possible, should use both methods as they complement each other.

Quantitative research

Quantitative research is useful for answering questions of fact involving what, where, when, who, and how often. For example, it can answer questions such as what hotel amenities visitors desire, where is the best venue to provide entertainment, when do guests like to eat breakfast, who is most likely to visit and how often do visitors go to an attraction. The organization may already have data that will help to answer some of these questions. For example, if a festival is trying to expand

Figure 3.2 Working collaboratively is the best way to design a research study.

Photo Credit: GaudiLab

geographic reach, knowing where visitors are from is essential. The organization may already have sales data that provides this information, but no other facts. In this case quantitative research can be used to discover the gender, age and other relevant demographic facts about visitors. It will also tell how often visitors attend the festival. Since repeat visitor is always a goal, knowing more about who attends frequently is essential to designing an effective promotional strategy. Finally, the question of what pricing level should be charged for festival tickets can be answered with a quantitative survey. All of this information can help an organization to determine if it is meeting its goal of increasing festival visitation.

If the organization needs to 'prove' a fact it should conduct a quantitative survey. If an adequate number of people are surveyed, the answer that is obtained can reliably said to be true for the entire group. For example, a hotel might have noticed a decline in the number of room service orders and believe that it is because prices are too high. They do not want to lower prices unless they are fairly certain that the result will be positive. A survey of current hotel guests might result in a finding that while 82 per cent of hotel guests were satisfied with room service prices, 18 per cent think that the prices are too high. Of course, it would be impossible to survey all guests, but if a sufficiently larger number is surveyed it can be determined that high prices are not the reason for the decline.

Qualitative research

If the organization needs opinions and ideas rather than facts, it will need to conduct qualitative research. The fact that 82 per cent of hotel guests are happy with room service shows that this is not the reason for order decline. Qualitative research methods allow research subjects to answer questions in their own words or even in ways that do not use words. Qualitative research answers the question of 'why', such as why are hotel guests not ordering. Rather than conducting a survey, qualitative studies use interviews, focus groups, projective techniques and observation to gather information. Such research methods might find that the problem is not price but instead the items on the menu or how long the order takes.

Descriptive and exploratory

Descriptive research is used when the research question is very narrowly focused and asks for facts that describe. Descriptive research is always quantitative and is usually conducted when the organization already has information about the research question. A survey is used when the organization decides to conduct descriptive research. For example, descriptive research is used when the organization wants to ask how many people are planning to attend an event, where they are from, what they buy, and who they are.

Exploratory research is used when the organization has little present knowledge on the needs and desire of their customers. Exploratory research is qualitative and is used when the organization needs to start from scratch by asking 'why' because there is not enough current information about the problem to write a quantitative descriptive survey. Instead the organization may hold a focus group or conduct interviews where an issue can be discussed in depth.

Research studies and their use

- Quantitative Descriptive
  - use when details and numbers are needed
  - research on customer demographics or purchase frequency
- Qualitative Exploratory
  - use when seeking insights on opinions and ideas
  - research on reasons for dissatisfaction or new service ideas

Combining methods

Sometimes the organization may develop a research plan that uses both approaches. For example, the organization may be faced with the situation of wanting to add new tourism services, such as guided walks, without being sure of what type would be desired. If they write a survey that provides as answers what they believe are possible types, such as historic or arts related, they will limit the responses of their visitors. However, if they first conduct qualitative exploratory research using interviews and focus groups they may find ideas, such as tours of local breweries, that they had not considered. Then to ensure that the ideas are valid, the organization can develop and administer a quantitative survey.

There are three reasons why organizations should consider combining qualitative and quantitative techniques. First, if the organization is unsure of the cause of a problem, research approaches should be combined to provide proof. Second, if there is a finding the meaning of which the organization is unsure of, a different research

Case Study 3.3: The hospitality industry is something, somewhere, someplace

Because it is so large, it can be difficult to categorize the hospitality industry. One way is to think of it as something to eat, somewhere to sleep, and someplace to go. Food service is the largest component of the industry and includes everything from fine dining to fast food. Accommodation, formerly only hotels and motels, now also includes Airbnb. Finally travel/tourism provides the someplace to go that isn't like home. This category includes both destinations and events.

While the services and products offered vary, one characteristic is true of all three, which is the need for excellent customer service. The higher the price the more customer service that is expected. Here are five rules of customer service that apply to hospitality.

It builds trust: While travelers may want adventure and new experiences they want consistency in service. Brand loyalty is built because why take a chance on an unknown service provider?

It makes price less relevant: Great service is more critical than the physical characteristic of a great product. When it is received, people are willing to pay more.

It builds brand awareness: It is service that differentiates one hospitality provider from another. The memory of great service will be associated with the brand name.

It reduces problems: If someone complains, considerable time needs to be spent correcting a problem. Excellent customer service saves time by reducing the need to make corrections.

It brings in new customers: A promise of excellent customer service helps reduce purchase risk for customers by making the choice easier to make (John 2015).

Question: How can an intangible such as the customer service experienced by visitors be researched?

approach may be needed to explore the issue more fully. Lastly, if insufficient information is obtained an additional method may be needed to learn more.

For example, a research study may have been planned with a simple question about what type of interaction visitors like when taking group tours of a historic site. A range of tour members, including a variety of ages, family status and income levels, may have been chosen for qualitative interviews on experience preferences. The interview questions may have asked about length of tour, type of transportation and subject matter. Surprisingly to the organization, many tour members stated that they wished the tour included the guides dressed in historic costumes. If the organization knows that the tour guides will not be happy with this idea, they must provide more definite proof that this is a desire. After all, the tour guides may argue that the people interviewed are not representative of most tourists. The organization could then conduct a quantitative survey to either prove or disprove the idea.

Sometimes an organization can find unexpected good news in research data. For example, a special event that is held each year to celebrate local folk culture may always conduct a quantitative survey to see who is attending. Each year, the results may show that the majority of the attendees are older visitors. If one year, a large percentage of younger visitors are attending, the organization will be pleased. The problem is that the organization does not know why they are attending. A qualitative focus group of the attenders can then be held to see what motivated the younger visitors to attend. Once this is known, promotional messages can be created to attract more such visitors.

A qualitative research method, such as focus groups, will allow the researchers to probe for information that can then be used in a survey. Sometimes the wealth of information can be confusing. If focus group participants are asked what type of food they would like served at a hotel's free breakfast buffet, the responses might range from basic cold cereals to expensive cuts of steak. They may even include local favorites from many countries. While all the information is valid, the hotel cannot provide such a range of options. However, the focus group has provided the menu options that can then be used to write a quantitative survey that will prioritize the choices.

New forms of research

Social media along with technology have resulted in new methods of conducting traditional research and entirely new research methods (Washington 2013). One of the ways that social media can be used is to find research subjects. Because of its reach subjects that cannot be contacted in traditional ways can now be invited to participate in a research study. In addition, social media can be used to post and distribute surveys. Finally, technology can be used to conduct focus groups and interviews without the research subjects being physically present.

The publics use of the organization's social media can also be used as a form of research itself (Martin 2015). Social media analytics of the organization's sites can be used by researchers to learn more about who is using the organization's social media. However, the process can also be used to determine the answer to research questions. For example, an organization marketing a destination may wish to learn what calls to action motivate a request for more information. Online messages on different benefits can be posted. One message might stress the upscale benefits of the destination while the another might promote inexpensive lodging. By analyzing which call to action for more information is clicked most often, the organization can learn if luxury or cost-savings has more appeal.

Online communities are now also an opportunity for marketing research. These communities are groups of people who while geographically distant share an interest or lifestyle. Using social media, they can now easily communicate to share ideas and opinions. If their interests are related to travel, a tourism organization can go online and become part of the conversation. By doing so they will be able to better understand potential visitors. This approach is often referred to as netnography as it is based on the traditional research method of ethnography, a research method used by anthropologists to live among and observe the behavior of dissimilar cultural groups.

Now this same approach can be used to observe the behavior of groups that might not be interested in participating in research. The tourism researcher may silently observe the online conversation about favorite destinations listening for relevant information. Another approach would be for the researcher to announce to the group that they are conducting research and ask permission to ask

Figure 3.3 Social media can be a source of research participants.
Photo Credit: Raxpixel.com

questions. Social media research can be a rich source of insights not available from using other methods.

Research methods available

Once the organization has decided upon the approach based on the research question and the type of information needed, the next step is to design the research method. Research methods can be divided into those used in quantitative descriptive research and those used in qualitative exploratory research. Almost everyone is familiar with the research survey used in quantitative descriptive research. However, surveys are not the only frequently used research tool in consumer marketing. Also commonly used tools in marketing research are qualitative exploratory focus groups and interviews. This is because most marketing research asks the question 'why'. Other qualitative research methods include intercept interviews, projective techniques and observation.

Research methods

- Surveys: administering the same set of predetermined questions
- Focus groups: applying group dynamics to draw out responses
- Interviews: conducting one-to-one in-depth discussion
- Intercept interviews: asking a few quick to answer questions
- Projective techniques: using creative techniques to get nonverbal responses
- Observation: watching people's behavior and actions

Surveys

Surveys are a quantitative research method that asks questions with predefined responses such as yes or no, often or never, or satisfied or unsatisfied. The survey might also provide a list of possible answers, such as benefits desired. The advantage of having predefined answers is that it allows a large number of responses to

Case Study 3.4: Happy (or maybe not so happy) Valentine's Day

Valentine's Day has now gone global. What was once considered just a Western holiday is now celebrated in many countries, including China. How important is Valentine's giving? A research study in the US found that 53 per cent of women would end a relationship if they did not receive a token of love on the day!

However, not everyone is involved in a romantic relationship. For these customers, the emphasis on romantic love can be a bit depressing. Here's how the hospitality industry can help!

Host special single events. But be sure to keep it upbeat! No one wants to come to a pity-party.

Market self appreciation: What better day to make a special offer at a spa! While everyone else is having dinner with their significant other, singles can enjoy pampering themselves.

Focus on others: Have a Valentine's event that focuses on love of the community. A charity event that provides for those less fortunate can put romantic disappointment in perspective.

Sponsor a seminar: A talk on goal setting can broaden the single person's perspective as to what is important in life. It will also provide an opportunity for singles to understand they are not alone.

And, hotel personnel please remember – don't ask *'only one?'* or *'are you alone?'* when a single person approaches. After all, no one asks a couple *'only two?'* or *'aren't there more of you?'* Single customers should be treated exactly the same as a couple (Houran 2017).

Question: What research question would you write to determine what your hotel should offer singles?

be quickly tabulated. The larger the number of survey responses received from the research subjects, the more certainty there is that they are true for the group as a whole. If enough surveys are conducted, it can even be said that the answer is 'proved'. While surveys can be administered in person or on the phone, they can also be self-administered, usually online.

The benefit of a survey is that once the effort has gone into writing the questions they can be easily reproduced and widely distributed. Even if the response rate is low, because of the large numbers sent a significant amount of information can still be received. The challenge in administering any survey is that people are increasingly reluctant to participate. This may be because people are too busy, receive too many survey requests or because they are becoming more sensitive to the issue of privacy. Members of some cultural or ethnic groups may be even more reluctant to participate. Because of this reluctance, the people that respond to the survey may not be representative of the people the organization needs to study.

Even when people agree to be surveyed they may not complete the form. To improve completion rates the survey should be well designed (Poynter 2016). The questions must be written clearly and simply since if the question is confusing, the research participant may not respond. The number of questions must be kept to a minimum, as if the questionnaire is too long, the respondent may lose interest. The survey should also be visually attractive to encourage completion.

Example of survey question

- Are any of the statements below reasons why you attended Folk Music Festival? (Please check as many as apply)
    - ○ I feel at ease with the other people here.
    - ○ I came to eat, drink and socialize.
    - ○ I might meet new friends here.
    - ○ I want to learn more about music.
    - ○ My friends or family wanted to come.

Focus groups

In a focus group, the moderator will have a list of questions and issues that will be introduced. Rather than just ask questions, the focus group moderator uses group dynamics to draw out responses from the participants. While the moderator has questions prepared in advance, the group will be allowed leeway in what they wish to discuss as long as it remains on the general topic.

The success of the focus group will depend on the skills of the moderator. Besides being a good listener the moderator needs be skilled in group dynamics. The moderator's task is to keep the group on topic and to make sure that no one participant dominates while also encouraging quieter respondents to participate.

If the organization does not have someone with the needed skill, it may be able to obtain the volunteer services of someone in the community. In fact, it is best if moderators are from outside the organization so that they can be objective if the focus group members express negative opinions. If this happens moderators who have a strong connection with the organization may take offence. If this feeling is communicated either verbally or nonverbally to the group, they will cease to provide information.

Example of focus group questions with follow-up

- Can you give me some idea how our town might attract more men to visit?
    - ○ Abdul, what attractions or activities motivate you to visit?
- What type of activities do you believe would attract more young people?
    - ○ Brita, how do you think folk music can attract younger visitors?
- How do we communicate to young people about the music offered?
    - ○ Sharon, you have been rather quiet, what do you think?

Interviews

Interviews may take less initial effort to design, however they will take much more time to conduct. Designing the interview requires deciding upon the questions to be asked and also finding the appropriate subjects. Designing the interview questions can be done relatively quickly as the number of questions is smaller than in a survey. However, interview research will require more time to conduct, as each respondent needs to be given sufficient time to respond. This additional time allows the researcher to explore in depth the consumer's behavior and motivation.

Besides the main interview questions, the interviewer will use probing follow-up questions to elicit additional information. The follow-up questioning is necessary because when first asked a question, many people will respond with what they believe to be the correct or appropriate answer. Many people want to be polite by answering in the affirmative and with positive praise whenever possible. Additional probing questions are needed before subjects may respond with their true feelings.

Because of the time required to conduct interviews fewer subjects will be involved. However, although there will be fewer subjects involved, interviews provide more in-depth information than any other research method. Obtaining this information is dependent on having the interview conducted by someone with the needed listening and questioning skills and choosing research subjects representative of the group under study. It is tempting for the organization to simply choose as subjects those people who can be easily convinced to participate. Unfortunately, the wrong subjects will result in the wrong information being obtained.

Example of interview question with follow-up

- Why do you think that the hotel fitness equipment is not used?
  - Tell me more.
  - Can you give an example?
  - What else do you think?
  - Please go on.
  - Do you have any other ideas?
  - Have you always felt this was true?

Intercept interviews

Intercept interviews involve many participants. However, each participant is only asked three or four quick open-ended questions. Intercept interviews are a useful technique when research subjects will not agree to a lengthy interview. Many more people will cooperate if they are told that the interview will only last two to three minutes. Another advantage of intercept interviews is that they can be conducted where the subjects can be found. This is why intercept interviews are often referred to as person-on-the-street interviews.

Intercept interviews can be conducted on site, such at the event, hotel or attraction. However, they can also be conducted in other venues as a means for the organization to obtain information from potential visitors. For example, a hotel that is wondering why young people are not booking rooms when attending a city-wide event, could interview people at the event about their preferences. Quick questions could be asked of young people regarding their knowledge of the hotel's rates and amenities to see if they are aware of what is offered.

Example of intercept interview questions

- Have you booked a hotel room for tonight or are you heading home?
- Did you research local options?
- Why did you or did you not stay?

Projective techniques

Projective techniques are research methods that gather information without asking for verbal responses. They are often used in focus groups to encourage communication or can be used on their own. Some simple projective techniques include word association, story or sentence completion and cartoon techniques.

Projective techniques were developed in the field of psychology but are now often used in marketing research. They are particularly useful when the research participant may be reluctant to discuss a subject. Even when there is no reluctance, projective techniques can create an increased level of interest and interaction in the research process. A research question of interest to the organization, such as how to redesign the visitor center or hotel lobby, may not be of interest to research subjects. In this instance the researcher could provide the participants with an outline of the space along with cutouts of various pieces of furniture and ask them to redesign using these materials. This technique will obtain much more information about the potential new designs than asking verbally.

Word association is asking the participant's first response to a name, photo or event. The idea is to obtain an emotional response to an issue rather than an intellectual opinion. If simply asked their opinion many visitors may not be able to verbalize their feelings and will think about what is the 'right' answer. Asking only for their first 'gut level' response results in participants responding with their true feelings rather than how they think they should answer. Someone at an event might be asked the first three words that come to mind to describe the experience.

Another projective technique is story completion. This technique provides a means for participants to respond with a concrete rather than an abstract answer. For example, participants might be asked to finish a story on what a typical tourist experiences at the attraction. This will allow an opportunity to communicate first hand experiences without labeling them as such.

Sentence completion is an even simpler projective technique. An example would be asking participants to complete a sentence regarding the reason for visiting. Cartoons can also be used where the participant fills in the bubble over the character's head. This might be a cartoon of someone attending an event saying, I'm glad I attended because.

Example of project word association technique

- Three words to describe your experience at our Local Food Festival are:
- When I think of Historic Downtown, the first word that comes to mind is:
- One word that I think of when someone mentions hotel pools is:

Observation

The observation research method records what visitors actually do rather than what they say they do. This is an inexpensive technique that can be easily used. For example, if the organization wants to redesign the hotel fitness center they might ask guests how they want it changed. However, it might be difficult for guests to respond because it is something to which they have not given much thought. Instead the organization might have researchers watch and record visitors using the fitness center. In this way they might find what equipment is most used.

Example of observation technique used to observe visitors to a community park

- Once at the amusement park mark your location on the map provided. Choose three 'subjects' to observe
- Please choose a variety of groups, couples and families
- Record in what activity they are engaged
- Repeat every 15 minutes

While simple to conduct, observation research still takes planning. Careful thought must be given as to the days and times the observations should be made along with what subjects to observe. In addition, as it is impossible to record all activity, the researcher must be provided with guidelines as to the type of behavior that should be noted.

References

John, D. 2015. 5 Reasons Customer Service Is Most Important [online]. Daymond John's Success Formula. 14 October. Available from www.daymondjohnssuccessformula.com/five-reasons-why-customer-service-is-more-important-than-anything-else/. [Accessed 13 February 2017].

Houran, J. 2017. To the Service-hospitality Industry, Holidays like Valentine's Day Often Make a Positive Contribution to a Company's Bottom Line [online]. 4Hoteliers, 14 February. Available from www.4hoteliers.com/news/story/16824?awsb_c=4hdm& awsb_k=nwsf. [Accessed 14 February 2017].

Karp, H. 2017. Musicians Hawk V.I.P. Concert Packages to Deter Scalpers, Boost Profits [online]. *The Wall Street Journal*. 13 January 2017. Available from www.wsj.com/articles/musicians-hawk-v-i-p-concert-packages-to-deter-scalpers-boost-profits-1484312401. [Accessed 13 January 2017].

Martin, R. 2015. How Social Media Data Is Enriching Market Research [online]. Infegy, 6 May. Retrieved 30 November 2016 Available from blog.infegy.com/how-social-media-data-is-enriching-market-research/. [Accessed 30 November 2016].

Poynter, R. 2016. Why the Long Survey Is Dead [online]. Vision Critical. 5 May. Available from www.visioncritical.com/the-long-survey-is-dead/. [Accessed 21 December 2016].

Washington, R. 2013. 5 Ways Technology Has Changed Market Research [online]. MarketResearch.com, 8 Oct. Available from blog.marketresearch.com/blog-home-page/bid/339928/5-Ways-Technology-Has-Changed-Market-Research. [Accessed 3 November 2016].

Zipzer, D., Y. Chen, and F. Gong. 2016. Here Comes the Modern Chinese Consumer [online]. McKinsey & Company, March. Available from www.mckinsey.com/industries/retail/our-insights/here-comes-the-modern-chinese-consumer. [Accessed 30 November 2016].

Chapter 4

Choosing research participants

Learning objectives:

- What criteria should be used when choosing participants for research to ensure they are representative?
- What is the difference between probability and nonprobability sampling methods?
- When should the quantitative methods of simple random, systematic, and stratified and the qualitative methods of convenience, snowballing and purposive, be used?
- How is the sample size determined for quantitative surveys?

Summary

- The tourism marketing researcher needs to know how to find the correct participants for both qualitative and statistically valid quantitative studies, which starts with developing a profile. Quantitative research methods use random selection techniques. Two of the critical criteria when choosing research participants are demographic and psychographic characteristics.
- Sampling methods can be divided into probability versus nonprobability. Probability sampling, which uses random methods, will result in a sample of participants that accurately represents the population as a whole. Nonprobability sampling selection methods are nonrandom where the participants are specifically chosen because they meet desired criteria. Qualitative research studies use nonrandom sampling methods of convenience, snowballing and purposive.
- When developing the participant profile for a quantitative study demographic, psychographic, geographic and visitor status may be considered. Everyone who is part of this profile is referred to as the population while the sample frame is a list of these potential subjects. Once the profile is developed probability sampling, where there is an equal or random chance of every person in the sampling frame

being chosen to participate in the research, will be used to choose participants. There are three probability sampling methods, which are simple random, systematic, and stratified.

- Quantitative studies attempt to support a hypothesis about the source or solution to a problem. These studies can provide 'proof' by using two statistical methods. The first involves statistical sampling to choose the participants who will be involved in the study. The second is the use of statistical tests to analyze the data.

Describing research participants

The quality of research findings not only depends on an appropriately chosen research question and methodology. Successful research also depends on choosing the right research participants. Even if the right research question and methodology has been chosen, if the wrong people are asked, the findings will be useless. Choosing and finding research participants in the tourism, hospitality and event management industries can be particularly challenging as most visitors do not reside in the local area. Even when they are visiting a tourist attraction, staying at a hotel or attending an event, they want to enjoy themselves, not take time to help answer a research question. Even if they can be contacted via email or text message after they return, they may not respond unless very unhappy with their experience.

Research participants for qualitative and statistically valid quantitative studies are chosen very differently. The tourism marketing researcher needs to know how to find the correct participants for both methods, which starts with developing a profile.

Developing a participant profile

Quantitative research methods use random selection techniques, which means everyone has the same chance of being included in the study. Once the researchers have developed a participant profile, they will randomly choose the necessary number of participants from this group.

There are four general criteria to consider when developing the detailed description, or participant profile, for either a qualitative or quantitative research study (Lee 2017). First the researchers should decide what demographic characteristics are important. Then they will consider what psychographic characteristics should be considered. In addition, the importance of geographic location should be thought through. Finally, for some research questions the potential subject's visitor status must be considered.

When developing the participant profile of who should participate in a research study, the marketing researchers should be as detailed as possible. The profile needs to provide a high level of detail on demographic, psychographic, geographic and visitor status, as it will be used to design a screening process for choosing participants. For example, the profile should describe all the important demographic characteristics of the potential participants. Just stating that the research will involve surveying young males is not detailed enough as too many questions are left unanswered. On the other hand, stating research participants should be aged 21–23, have

Case Study 4.1: Handling customers is a skill

It is often front desk employees who have the most impact on a service business, including those involved in tourism, because they are often the customer's first and last contact. In all businesses, management has two priorities: first to keep customers happy and, second, to maximize revenue. To do so, employees need to understand how to handle the following scenarios.

Call ins: Potential visitors will first check for rates and prices on multiple online sites. If they cannot find prices listed for the specific hotel they will check competitors' prices for comparison purposes. They will then call, email or text to verify the price. At this point an incentive for booking or purchasing immediately needs to be presented. If not, further research by the visitor might lead to losing the sale. Whether the visitor will respond best to a reduction in price or being treated as a VIP will depend on personal preference but also the cultural importance of status.

24/7 service: Many potential visitors are researching products and prices when their schedule allows, not during regular business hours. This might be late at night after the kids are in bed or early mornings at the gym. They may also be living in a different time zone. There must be an employee who responds to these inquiries whenever they arrive as being timely is important.

Up-selling: Many visitors are fixated on price. When dealing with visitors, their concern for finding the best deal should be respected. However, if they are informed that for an increase in price they can receive a much higher level of service, they may agree to pay more! The skill needed is to present the information attractively without making the visitor feel pressured (Kennedy 2016).

Question: What type of research could be conducted to ensure that these goals are being met?

finished at least two years of college, work part time, and live in their own home, is too specific as it would be too difficult to find enough participants that meet this profile.

Sample participant profile for study on use of visitor center

- Demographic: retired males age 65–80
- Psychographic: attracted to new experiences
- Geographic: resides outside of local area
- Visitor status: currently users of Visitor Center

Deciding on the criteria

For all research studies, one of the important factors when choosing research participants is demographic characteristics. Marketing research focuses on determining visitor travel experience desires, which are shaped by demographic characteristics such as gender, age, income, education, family stage, occupation, ethnicity, and religious affiliation.

Age, income, gender and family status may have the most direct bearing on the choice of destinations or events. For example, the demographic characteristic of family status is often part of a participant profile in tourism. The types of lodging and food services needed will be very different depending on whether the visitors are a solo traveler, a couple or a family. Including families in a research study on the desire for more fine dining opportunities would be wasted as they are not potential users of these types of restaurants. The types of tourism experiences desired would also vary. The opinions of couples for a research study to determine what activities families desired would be wasted. For example, a botanical garden might wish to know what it can do to motivate more divorced fathers to visit along with their children. They may develop a participant profile that includes divorced or never married fathers who have part time custody of their children.

It is much easier for the marketing researcher to determine a potential participant's demographic than psychographic characteristics. This is true because psychographic characteristics involve a person's attitude, lifestyle and opinions, which are not readily apparent. However, these characteristics are often more important than demographic characteristics in determining a person's tourism preferences. For example, a study of the use a water park might want to know why the sale of season passes has declined, as many families that formerly bought passes are no longer doing so. When designing the participant profile, the researcher might start with demographic characteristics, such as age, family status and income level. However, the reason that season tickets are not selling may have nothing to do with age, family status or income. Instead it might be psychographic characteristics such as a concern with safety issues that determine who will buy a pass. These psychographic characteristics cannot be as easily determined as demographic characteristics. Therefore the marketing researcher will need to develop screening questions to ensure that the participants match the needed profiles. By including families who are concerned about safety, the water park might learn how they need to promote differently.

Geographic location varies in importance based on the research question. If the question is based on a need to learn more about visitors from specific locations, then it must be included. In fact, the research question might be based on a need to find new visitor markets to target. Sometimes the tourism organization, hotel or event might want to know more about local residents who use their services. In this case, geographic location also needs to be part of the profile.

Another relevant geographic issue involves focus groups and interviews. For these the participant must travel to the location where the focus group or interview is being held. If the location is too distant or has inconvenient transportation options, the potential participant may decline. This is one reason for the growing use of conducting interviews and focus groups online. For observational studies, location is an important consideration, as the choice of location will determine who will be observed.

When developing the participant profile, whether the participant should be a current, potential or past visitor must be considered. For some studies, it may be important that the potential participant has no familiarity with the destination. For example, if the organization wants to develop a marketing message to convince people to visit, they will want to include people who have not done so. If a hotel wants to know why people do not make use of the on-site restaurant, they need to ask people who have visited, but chose not to dine.

For some research studies, the research participant must be a current visitor. These participants will be able to provide insight on why they are attracted to the destinations and events that are offered. They can also provide insight into how the tourism services or destinations can be improved. It might be difficult to find enough contact information to conduct a survey, but studies do not have to include a large number of participants. For example, a few interviews of people who visit competing destinations can be conducted online, either using social media or through online communities, and then interviewed.

Professional recruiters

Some researchers may feel they do not have the expertise or time to find the appropriate subjects for research. This is especially true if the research subjects are from a population that is ethnically or culturally different from that of the researcher. Another difficulty is if the participant profile specifies people who are not currently visitors.

Professional research subject recruiting firms can provide assistance in these situations (Saros 2016). These companies continually recruit subjects who are promised payment for participation. The company may already have potential research subjects in an existing database. If participants with a specialized profile are needed, they can be recruited by the company.

The major reasons for spending the money to use a recruiter are that it saves time, improves reliability and allows the researcher to stay focused. Finding visitors who fit the profile will involve personal or online outreach to many more people than are needed. It would not be unusual to have to contact ten potential participants to get one positive response.

Even when a positive response is received there is the issue of maintaining contact with the participant to ensure that they show up to participate. Even with the small percentage of people who agree to participate, some of these will not do so when the time comes. This may be due to a loss of interest or other responsibilities taking precedence. The job of a professional recruiter isn't just to find participants but to ensure that they are available and willing to participate when the date for the focus group or interview arrives. This is also an issue with survey respondents. The professional recruiter's role includes sending reminder emails until a sufficient number of responses are received.

An issue today is the emergence of professional research subjects. There are many websites that explain that to receive the incentive offered for participation, all a person needs to do is state that they meet the criteria. The websites then instruct how this can be done, even if the criteria are not met. Professional recruiters are skilled in weeding out these bogus research subjects.

Finding qualitative participants

Sampling methods can be divided into probability versus nonprobability. Probability sampling, which uses random methods, means that every person has the same chance (or probability) of being chosen. With this method, the researcher cannot introduce bias by choosing research subjects who will provide the answers they want to receive. An example would be research that asks if visitors like the organization's new website. If the designer of the website was part of the research team, they would prefer a positive response to the question so might be tempted to bias the results by choosing participants who are friends. Probability sampling will result in a sample of participants that accurately represents the population as a whole so no bias is introduced. However, it might be that the organization wants a professional opinion on the website. In this case nonprobability sampling would be used. By contrast, nonprobability selection methods are nonrandom when the participants are specifically chosen because they meet desired criteria, such as individuals who understand website design.

Qualitative research studies use nonrandom sampling methods. Nonrandom means that each potential research subject does not have the same likelihood of being chosen. However, nonrandom does not mean haphazard. Thought must be given to a process of choosing participants for any research study, even the smallest qualitative focus group or individual interviews. In fact, it could be argued that organizations conducting small qualitative studies must use extra care when choosing research subjects as so much weight will be given to the opinions of each. One participant in a focus group of eight has much more effect on the findings than one participant in a survey of 500.

The three basic methods that an organization can use when selecting participants for qualitative research studies are convenience, snowballing and purposive. After

Figure 4.1 Participants must be carefully chosen for research to ensure they are representative.

Photo Credit: Sira Anamwong

the participant profile has been developed the organization must choose which of the three methods is most appropriate. Convenience sampling uses the participants that meet the profile and are the most convenient or easy to find. Snowballing uses recommendations after the first participant is chosen. With purposive sampling, the participants that best meet the profile are chosen.

Qualitative sampling methods

- Convenience
  - find location where potential participants congregate
  - choose participants based on profile
- Snowballing
  - choose first participant to meet profile requirements
  - ask this participant to recruit others
  - confirm that recruited participants meet requirements
  - contact participants with needed information
- Purposive
  - develop participant profiles
  - create or find list of people who meet profile
  - choose names from list
  - invite to participate

Convenience sampling

Convenience sampling is used when researchers choose as participants any willing and available individuals who have the desired characteristics. The easiest way to use this method is to find participants at a location that will tend to attract those who will meet the profile. For example, if the research question calls for surveying the opinions of young females who attend music events, the best place to find them is at a concert. Once at the concert, the researcher will use their judgment when choosing which participants best fit the profile to ask to participate.

Convenience sampling is useful when potential participants may not be eager to be involved in the research process. Few young women excited about the concert experience are interested in the organizer's need to conduct research. With convenience sampling the researcher goes to a location where potential participants already congregate, such as a bar near the event venue. This makes the selection process much simpler as the potential participant does not need to respond to an invitation but is asked to participate personally. If an added incentive is needed, they may be offered the opportunity to meet a performer if they will take a few minutes to answer some interview questions.

One of the advantages of convenience sampling is that it is easy to conduct as it does not involve the time and expense of recruiting a sample. For this reason, it is useful when a quick research study is needed to gain a first impression of a problem or opportunity. The results of the study can then be used to conduct more detailed research. For example, if a hotel was considering the redesign of the breakfast area in the lobby, they might first conduct short interviews as guests are leaving the area after eating. If everyone responds that they are happy with the current arrangement, the hotel might reconsider the need for a redesign. The disadvantage of the method is that there is the possibility of error based on who is chosen. If by chance the group

Case Study 4.2: Golf, kangaroos and tourists don't mix

It is not uncommon to have kangaroos on Australian golf courses as they like to eat the grass and then relax under the trees. Golfers are familiar with sharing the course and simply wait till they hop on by before hitting their shot.

The problem is not the kangaroos but the tourists who come to see and photograph the animals. Viewing the kangaroos became so popular that tour buses would stop and 50 people would get out with picnic lunches. Many of the tourists were Chinese who were not familiar with the game of golf and believed a golf course is similar to a public park. As the game is not popular in China, they did not understand that getting hit with a golf ball can cause serious injuries. Not knowing how the game is played and trying to be helpful, if they found a golf ball on the green they would pick it up and return it to the player!

What is a golf course to do? Start a tour business! Now the Anglesea Golf Course outside of Melbourne offers Roo Tours. The tourists are taken to see the kangaroos in six-seat golf carts. The tours are given by club members who volunteer. During the last Lunar New Year holiday the course greeted over 100 tourists a day to see the kangaroos. The tourists are safe and happy and the golfers can get on with their game (Cherney 2016).

Question: What are three possible research questions that could be asked if the golf course wants to extend the tour business?

that is having breakfast happens to be very happy tour participants, the response will be biased toward the positive. If they are not feeling well because of late night partying, the response may be biased toward the negative.

The problem with convenience sampling is that some groups may not be found at a location. This is true if the organization is targeting a specific age group or ethnic community members who rarely attend events. There simply won't be enough potential participants at any one event to make the effort worthwhile. With groups that are hard to locate, the snowball sampling method should be used.

Snowball sampling method

As a snowball rolls down a hill, it becomes larger by gathering more snow. Snowballing as a sampling method works similarly. With this method the researcher first finds a single participant who closely meets the needed profile. This participant then recruits others with similar characteristics that also meet the profile. These participants will then recruit others and so on until enough participants have been found. Technology can now be used to track the invitations and responses, which simplifies the process (Sun 2015).

This method is particularly useful when recruiting participants from populations that may not be interested in participating in the research process as they are busy enjoying their holiday. If a garden tour group is staying at a hotel, they are occupied with their schedule. If the marketing researcher converses with one helpful group member and convinces them that the city would like to improve the tour and their

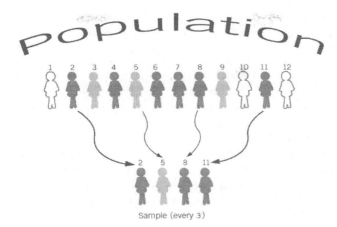

Figure 4.2 Probability sampling will result in a sample of participants that accurately represents the population as a whole.

Photo Credit: Iamnee

participation will assist in this effort, this group member may then convince friends to also be involved.

With snowballing, besides choosing the first participant to meet the profile characteristics, the researchers must also choose someone who is trusted and respected by the other members of the group. Once the participants have been referred, the organization will then confirm that they do meet the profile characteristics. The organization will then contact them with the information they need to participate in the research process.

There are several ways that snowball recruiting can be done. The first is linear where a relationship is established with one research participant who meets the criteria. This person will then recruit another who will find the third participant, and so on. Another method is to ask more than one potential participant to recruit a goal of several more without concern whether they meet the criteria. Using this method numerous potential participants can then be screened and only those who meet the criteria asked to participate.

Another method is to use social media sites to advertise for participants. This can include the use of the organization's own social media such as Facebook, Twitter and Instagram. Or, the tourism organization may purchase ads that appear on other social media sites to encourage people to participate in the research by offering an incentive.

Purposive sampling

There will be occasions when the research question might require that more than one group of visitors be involved in the research process. This might be true when the tourism organization is interested in the views of both younger and older visitors. The recruiting of research participants can become even more complicated when multiple groups need to be recruited based on different demographic, psychographic or geographic characteristics.

Purposive sampling methodology carefully designs these multiple participant profiles. The researcher will then create a list of potential participants in each category. For example, a list of visitors might come from a sign-in list at the visitor center. This can then be divided by geographic area in which the person lives. Event ticket sales can be divided by frequency of attendance. For some research studies, the organization may need to recruit participants who are not current visitors. Organizations or associations to which the people who match the participant profile belong, can also be used. Specific individuals from each list will then be asked to participate. This can be done based on the judgment of the researcher as to who most closely matches the profile or by who is willing to participate.

Purposive sampling can be useful when there is a limited number of possible potential participants. Because there is a limited number, having the sample be random is not an issue as it will most likely not be so. There are two specific types of purposive sampling that use the researcher's judgment. One is when the researcher is looking for a typical visitor to the type of venue or location. The criteria should be easy to determine such as a family with young children going to a zoo. Another situation is where the researcher wants to learn more about atypical visitors. In the case of the zoo example, this might be people visiting on their own.

Selecting quantitative research participants

Some of the issues with finding respondents for quantitative research methods are the same as with qualitative. There will be a need to determine what criteria need to be used when deciding who should participate in the study. While the process of developing a participant profile will be similar, the methods for constructing the sample will be different. In addition, if the researchers are using a quantitative method to prove a hypothesis, then the number of people who participate becomes critical and the researcher must decide which probability method must be used.

The population and sampling frame

At the beginning of the development of a quantitative survey, the discussion is focused on what needs to be known rather than on who should be asked. Before tackling the question of how many people need to be included in the sample to gain a certain level of accuracy, the concepts of the population and the sample frame need to be understood. At this stage in the research process the issue of not only who are the people who will be asked to participate, but also how many people, needs to be clarified.

The issue of geographic reach is more complicated for quantitative methods. With quantitative research the survey can be distributed widely online, by mail or by phone. Tourism researchers must decide if part of the participant profile will be where the desired participants live, rather than when they are at the destination. If this is the case, then there must be a way to determine the location of the participants. With physical addresses this is not a problem, but an email address does not provide location information and area codes for cell phones are not necessarily tied to the location where the phone owner lives. If geographic information is part of the profile, the participants must be asked where they reside using a screening question.

Because there may be no physical contact with participants when conducting a quantitative survey, the researcher may also need to add screening questions to determine if the participants belong to a demographic that is specified in the profile. If the participant profile was developed with psychographic characteristics needed, then screening questions on attitude, values and lifestyles will need to be added.

> ## Case Study 4.3: No one wants to read an email anymore
>
> A hotel, attraction or event understands that they must have a message that resonates with their targeted visitors. They may spend considerable time researching to get just the right words that describe the benefits they can provide so that potential visitors will click for more information. But what if no one reads the email that is then sent?
>
> Potential visitors want information and the hospitality industry makes the request process simple by embedding calls to action on websites and social media. It is quick and easy for even a just slightly interested potential visitor to click and request more information be sent. This usually arrives in the form of the email.
>
> The problem is that even though the information was requested it is not read. Why? First, people are busy. Second, the desire has passed. Third, no one wants to read. As we now increasingly rely on visual communication, people have less patience in the written word. The old saying that a picture is worth a thousand words has always been true, but now it is even more so.
>
> It is known that having the word video in a subject line increases the open rate. The new forms of video email marketing have the video play as soon as the email is clicked. The reader/viewer can immediately see smiling visitors, beautiful scenery and exciting action (Litt 2016)!
>
> *Question: If the email objective is to turn potential visitors into visitors, what subjects should be included in research to determine what video most motivates visits?*

The same goes for determining whether the participant is a past or current visitor to the destination. If any of these criteria are not used to determine the profile, they do not need to be part of screening questions.

Questions to clarify population

- Geographic: Where do the people we want to participate live?
- Demographic: Do their gender, age, income or other demographic traits matter?
- Psychographic: What attitudes, values and lifestyles should they share?
- Visitor status: Should the participant be past, current or potential visitors?

Once the profile is completed, the next step is to find a list of names of the members of the defined population. The term 'sampling frame' simply refers to this list of everyone in the population. If a research study is designed to include all hotel guests who stay frequently, the population might be described as guests who have stayed more than 20 nights during the past 12 months. The sampling frame will be the list of the names that have been found using the hotel guest database.

If a tourism attraction wishes to survey current visitors who arrived during the last six months, it may be possible to construct this list internally using the organization's own records of ticket sales. If the population the organization needs to study are people who currently do not visit, then getting the names is more difficult. It may be necessary for the tourism organization to purchase a list of names that can be used for research purposes. Another possibility is to use a professional research consulting organization to locate the participants. If the participants on the list are unknown to the tourism organization, the first questions in a survey will be screening questions that determine eligibility to participate.

Simple random probability selection

Once the list of population members has been created as a sample frame, the next task is to decide how to choose the individuals who will participate as the list may contain too many individuals. Nonprobability sampling refers to methods of choosing participants where the researcher uses their judgment to decide. Thus, every name on the frame does not have an equal chance of being chosen. However, when probability sampling is used, there is an equal or random chance of every person in the sampling frame being chosen to participate in the research. This method eliminates any potential bias when the researcher decides who to include. The three probability sampling methods are simple random, systematic, and stratified.

Statistical sampling methods

- Simple random: numbers chosen randomly from list using random number table
- Systematic: numbers chosen randomly from list using skip interval
- Stratified: certain groups chosen for specific characteristics

Using the simple random sampling method gives every name on the list of population members the same chance of being chosen. For example, the sampling frame that is used may be an alphabetical list of 1,000 past users of the visitor center's services. The organization may decide that they will survey a sample of 200 of the visitors. If everyone on the list meets the participant profile it would seem to be an easy task to choose the first 200 names on the list to be included in the study. However, this can lead to bias in the choice of participants. As family names of people can depend on ethnic background a bias toward or against an ethnic group may result. For example, many visitors to the destination may be Korean and therefore should have an equal chance of being included in the sample of 200. However, in Korea a common family name is Kim. There is a chance that they will not be chosen as participants in the same percentage as they are represented as visitors.

A method to avoid this dilemma is to choose the names from the sampling frame randomly. If a random sample of ethnic groups is desired and yet names can be determined by ethnicity, a low-tech method of solving this dilemma would be putting the names in a hat and then pulling out the first 200. However, a better means is to use a random number table. These tables can be easily found online. The researcher takes the first digit listed in the table, which might be 634, and includes in the sample the 634th name on the sampling frame list of 1,000 names. If the next number is 29, the researcher will do the same, and so on until all 200 names are chosen randomly.

Systematic sampling is easier than using a random number table and is almost as free from bias. With this method, every name in the sample frame is given a number. Then a skip interval is calculated by dividing the total number of names in the sampling frame by the number of participants needed, or 1,000 divided by 5, which is 20. The researcher then systematically goes down the list choosing every fifth name. To increase the randomness, an alphabetical list can first be scrambled so that people with the same list name will not be listed together.

Stratified random probability selection

A stratified sampling method is used when the researchers believe that people's responses to a research question will vary depending on their geographic, psychographic or demographic characteristics. For example the tourism researcher might want the random list of 200 names to include names from specific groups. Using stratified sampling will allow the researcher, once the survey has been completed, to isolate groups with specific characteristics and then compare the answers to the group as a whole. The groups might be stratified based on demographic factors such as gender, age or ethnic background. For example, a tourism attraction might have a special interest in knowing more about why young people and ethnic group members do not visit. When the sample is constructed the organization wants to ensure that enough young people or ethnic group members are included. The process can start with simple random or systematic sampling. However, once the participants are identified they will be reviewed and if they do not include enough young or ethnic group members, these names will be added even if that means they are not chosen randomly.

While this method is not truly random it is necessary in many situations because in the tourism, hospitality and event management industries, visitor motivation varies. Tourism is a complex experience that can be desired by different groups for different reasons. Clarifying the reasons by group is essential to most marketing strategies. In addition, with the increase in global tourism, knowing the benefits desired by international visitors is of growing importance. Rather than have a separate survey for each group, a stratified sampling method can be used to ensure that a sufficient number of each group is included.

Determining the sample size for surveys

Quantitative studies do more than simply gather information on consumers' attitudes and opinions. Quantitative studies attempt to support a hypothesis, or an idea, about the source or solution to a problem. These studies can provide 'proof' by using two statistical methods. The first involves statistical sampling to choose the participants who will be involved in the study. The second is the use of statistical tests to analyze the data.

It isn't necessary to understand statistics to use these methods. The following is a short summary of what is necessary to determine the size of the sample. If an organization decides to conduct a large-scale statistical study, there are many sources of additional information available in written or online sources.

Census or sample

If a researcher wants to prove with absolute certainty whether a fact is true of an entire group of visitors, it would be necessary to ask everyone in the group. For example, if someone wants to know with 100 per cent accuracy how many of the

50 people who are dining in their restaurant would use hotel delivery they would need to ask everyone. If they only asked 49, none of whom wanted the service, there is always the chance that the 50th person does want the service. The only way to be absolutely sure would be to ask everyone in the group, or population. When everyone in the population is asked, it is called a census.

If the number of visitors is large, it becomes too difficult and expensive to ask everyone. Instead a sample of the visitors would be asked. Using a sample of the population saves time and money and is the only reasonable alternative when the population is very large or when everyone in the population cannot be reached.

With a sample, an exact answer with 100 per cent accuracy is impossible. Two questions arise as a result of the impossibility of 100 per cent accuracy. The first question is, 'What level of accuracy is acceptable?' and the second is 'How many people will need to asked to get this level of accuracy?'

The answer to the first question is simple, as there are already established standards such as 90, 95 or 97 per cent accuracy that are used by researchers. The higher the level of accuracy that is needed, the more visitors will need to be included in the study. The answer to the second question is a bit more complicated and use of statistics will be necessary.

The hypothesis

A hypothesis is an idea or guess about the cause or solution to a problem. A statistically valid survey can be used to learn whether this hypothesis can be supported. Of course, the hypothesis can never be proved totally true without a census. Therefore, the researchers try to prove the hypothesis false. Because of this fact, the organization will state the hypothesis as the opposite of what it hopes to be true (since the organization is trying to prove the hypothesis wrong).

For example, an organization may be wondering if increased fees or ticket prices will result in fewer customers visiting an attraction. Of course, the organization is hoping that this is not true so that it can raise prices. The hypothesis will be stated as increased fees will affect visitor numbers.

Factors that affect sample size

Once a sampling procedure has been chosen, researchers must then decide upon the number of subjects that should be included in the research to ensure that the results are representative of the entire population. More is not always better when determining the number of research subjects to be included in a study. If carefully chosen, a small sample from the population can be reasonably representative of the whole. A smaller, but adequate, sample size will save time in finding participants.

While determining the sample size is done mathematically, there are a few general principles. For example, the more variation there is in a population, the larger a sample will need to be. When planning the design of a new fitness center a hotel will need to know the exercise preferences of its guests, such as whether they are into extreme sports, use fitness videos or just like to walk. If the hotel has a fairly homogeneous market segment of guests, such as elderly tourists, it can be assumed that their fitness preferences might be similar and it will take a smaller sample to confirm what they are. However, another hotel might have the same number of guests but

Snowball sampling

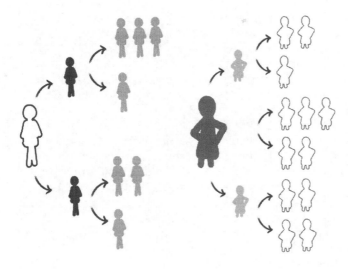

Figure 4.3 The snowball method is an example of a nonrandom where the participants are specifically chosen because they meet desired criteria.

Photo Credit: Iamnee

they cover many different age groups and lifestyles. In this case, it can be assumed that a larger sample will be needed as it would be expected that the interests of the guests will vary widely.

A second factor that must be considered in this example is the precision or size of the range between the survey results and the reality of the population as a whole. A survey question might ask how much of a fee each hotel guest would be willing to pay to use the new fitness center. From these responses, an average fee can be calculated. The hotel must then decide on how large a range or interval they are willing to tolerate between the average tabulated from the survey responses and the true answer that would be known only if everyone in the population was asked this same question.

A third factor that must be considered when determining sample size is the need for confidence that the research findings reflect the reality of the total population of all hotel guests. Total accuracy requires a census of all participants. Since this is not possible, the hotel must decide what level of confidence, for example if 90, 95 or 97 per cent, that the survey data accurately reflect the whole. The higher the confidence level desired, the larger the sample will need to be.

Determining the sample size

To calculate how many people need to be included in a sample, it is not necessary to know how many people are in the entire population. Nor is it necessary to do mathematical calculations, as a computer will take care of this. All that is needed for the computer to provide the sample size are the variation in the population, the acceptable range of the estimated answer from the true answer, and the confidence level that the calculated answer is correct. Most survey software will provide a template to make this calculation.

Case Study 4.4: What social media works?

Tourism organizations use social media along with traditional advertising to entice people to visit, book a room or purchase a ticket. They know that social media marketing works, but what they don't know is why it works. It might be thought that it doesn't matter as long as a person is enticed to make the visit or purchase. The problem is that if the organization doesn't know what social media is motivating people to take action, they won't know how to spend their marketing budget.

Attribution models try to figure out how a person becomes a customer. One method is crediting the last click that the person made. With this model if the last click was on a Facebook ad that brought them to the hotel website, it would get the credit. However, the same person might have read about the attraction in a blog, seen photos on Instagram or watched visitors on YouTube before they saw the ad. Which social media channel should get the credit? Here are some other attribution models provided by Google Analytics.

Multi-channel: How many conversions involved more than one channel.

Path length: How many interactions with each channel.

Time lag: The number of days in between channel use.

Top converters: Most common channel combinations used before conversion.

With this information, the organization will know where to put their social media efforts (Riffran 2017).

Question: How could social media conversion analytics be used in combination with quantitative research to improve conversion?

For example, an event venue might be very interested in determining what season ticket price would be acceptable for next year. There were 1,000 festival ticket holders last year to be surveyed about next year's price. The researchers know that the venue management would be happy for the survey answers to be 95 per cent confident that they represent the whole population. In addition, the range would be supplied by the venue management. They might state that they want the answer to be within a 10 per cent plus or minus range of the true answer.

With 1,000 people in the population at a 95 per cent confidence level and 10 per cent range, 88 surveys must be completed. If the confidence level is increased to 99 per cent, 143 people must be surveyed. If, additionally, the margin of error is dropped to 5 per cent, 400 people must be surveyed. The more confidence and accuracy, the larger the sample size required.

Normal distribution and variation

If a tourism researcher could conduct a census on how much people spent on travel last year, a true mean or average of the amount spent could be calculated. Of course, conducting a census is too expensive and time consuming so the researcher would survey a sample of visitors. From these data the average is calculated, which is used as an estimate for the entire population.

Perhaps the researcher wants to further make sure that this average or mean is an accurate estimate, so the survey is conducted a second time with a new sample. The same sampling procedure is chosen so the same number of subjects are asked the research question. However, the sample will now consist of different individuals. The researcher will again need to calculate the average. If the researcher were able to survey every possible sample in the population, this would result in a series of means. If all the resulting means were examined, it would be found that some answers will occur more frequently than others.

This similarity results from the fact that members of a population will have characteristics in common, which in turn will mean that many will behave in similar ways. However, there will also be some whose behavior will vary; some will spend little as they go camping, and some will spend more as they only stay in 5-star hotels. When these similarities and differences are shown visually they result in a graph where the most commonly resulting mean is in the middle with diminishing returns on either side for numbers that are higher and lower. This is the classic 'normal' or bell distribution curve.

Fortunately, most data will fit a normal distribution curve and, therefore, the variability within a population can be estimated. This is why a sample can be an accurate representation of the population as a whole. Normal variability is considered to be plus or minus three standard deviations away from the true value. Therefore, a researcher can take an estimated range of variability and calculate the variation. For example, the management of a tourism attraction may estimate that the range in acceptable yearly pass prices would be from $50 for those persons with limited incomes up to a high of $500 for the wealthiest visitors. This gives a range of $450. Since the standard deviation is plus or minus three on each side, the number 450 is now divided by six to get the variability of the population, which would be $75.

Using the example above, the sample size for the study of how much visitors are willing to pay for a yearly pass can be calculated. For the estimate to be at a 95 per cent confidence level, with a range of 25 each way and standard variability, only 35 visitors would be needed to participate in the survey. However, a total of range of 50 when the variation is 450 is quite large. Perhaps the tourism organization would like the answer to be more accurate. They may decide to change the range from 50 to 15. The sample size now changes to 96 visitors. If the organization narrows the acceptable range to only $5 each way, the sample size necessary changes to 864! Likewise, changing the confidence level will affect the sample size, as will a change in the variability.

References

Cherney, M. 2016. New Golf Course Hazard: Chinese Tourists Chasing Kangaroos [online]. The Wall Street Journal. 7 December. Available from www.wsj.com/articles/when-pelting-a-kangaroo-is-the-least-of-your-worries-1481128056. [Accessed 16 January 2017].

Kennedy, D. 2016. Hospitality Net – Train Your Hotel Sales Team to Tell Stories Not Just Quote Rates [online] Hsyndicate, 4 November. Available from www.hospitalitynet.org/column/global/154000392/4079186.html. [Accessed 28 November 2016].

Lee, K. 2017. Conceptual Foundation of Consumer Behavior. *The Routledge Handbook of Consumer Behaviour in Hospitality and Tourism*. Ed. Saurabh Kumar Dixit. Abingdon, Oxon: Routledge.

Litt, M. 2016. It's Time to Get Personal with Email [online]. Marketing Land. 23 May. Available from marketingland.com/time-get-personal-175529. [Accessed 20 February 2017].

Riffran, N. 2017. Attribution Models: The Secret Ways Guests Discover Your Hotel [online]. Northstar Travel Media. 20 April. Available from www.4hoteliers.com/features/arti cle/10304?awsb_c=4hdm&awsb_k=dnws. [Accessed 6 March 2017].

Saros Research Market Research Participant Recruitment Agency for the UK. 2016. Saros. Available from www.sarosresearch.com/. [Accessed 2 December 2016].

Sun, J. 2015. How to Find, Screen and Schedule Participants for User Research [online]. Field UX. 15 March. Available from www.fieldux.com/how-to-find-screen-and-schedule-par ticipants-for-user-research/. [Accessed 19 December 2016].

Chapter 5

Writing a visitor survey

Learning objectives

- What are the marketing mix issues that can be the topic of a survey?
- Why should a process be followed when writing and testing a survey?
- What are the formats that can be used when writing both survey questions and answers?
- Why should demographic questions be asked when conducting surveys, and methods of improving completion rates be considered?

Chapter summary

- Surveys may be the first research method that is thought of when research is considered. There are advantages in conducting surveys such as reaching a large number of participants and supporting a hypothesis. Disadvantages include the inability to probe an issue in depth. Surveys can be self-administered or administered by a researcher and used for topics related to customers and the marketing mix.
- The questionnaire development process starts with a meeting with stakeholders to review topics to be included. The survey is then written, reviewed and tested for question clarity and appropriateness. Answers need to be coded for a paper survey. The layout for the form should be designed to encourage completion.
- Time must be taken to carefully craft the questions so that they are understood correctly by research participants. Issues to consider when writing questions include reading level, translation and use of the active rather than passive voice. Both closed and open-ended questions can be used in a survey. The writing of the answers is even more critical than writing the questions. Different types of answers should be used depending on the type of knowledge that

is being sought. There are several answer formats including multiple choice, ranking and rating.

- What introductory demographic questions are asked, such as age, gender and income, depend on the purpose of the survey. In addition, questions may need to be asked about geographic location. The sequence of the questions, along with the design of the form, can either encourage or discourage completion.

Survey research uses

Surveys are used when the research question asks what, where, when, how many and how often. The questions used in surveys are most commonly closed with the participant asked to choose from a number of suggested answers. Occasionally some open-ended questions are included where participants are able to supply their own answer. While the survey can be administered by a researcher either in person or over the phone, most commonly they are self-administered using an online form. One of the challenges in getting people to complete an online survey is simply getting them to click on the link (Putnam-Farr and Riis 2016). When sending out survey links via email, giving the research subject the option of saying yes or no to the survey increases the likelihood of opening and completion of the survey.

Rather than focus immediately on writing survey questions, the organization should first consider how the findings from survey research can be used. Tourism, hospitality and event management organizations share research needs. All of them need information on current and future visitors and the products they prefer. Of course, all companies that make a product need information on their customers. With tourism and hospitality this need is even more critical because of the complexity of the product being offered. Tourism may offer some physical products, such as souvenirs, but mostly consists of services that provide an experience. The same tourism experience can provide different benefits as there can be many reasons for

Figure 5.1 The purpose of research is to obtain information that can be turned into recommendations for action.

Photo Credit: garagestock

visiting a destination or attending an event. Survey research can be used to discover these benefits.

Advantages and disadvantages of survey research

The most important advantage of survey research is that it can be used to disprove or support a hypothesis. To do so requires that the organization first construct a statistically valid sample by including a sufficient number of participants in the survey study. Once the survey questionnaire has been developed it can be easily reproduced digitally online and, using email or social media, distributed to many participants. In addition, a survey form has the advantage that it can be self-administered. Asking participants to complete the survey on their own saves the organization researcher time and, therefore, money.

Advantages of surveys

- Disprove or support a hypothesis
- Easily sent to numerous participants
- Can be self-administered

The disadvantages of survey research include the fact that the survey must be carefully designed with correctly written questions and answers. Writing a good question is not as easy as it may first appear. A poorly written question will result in obtaining information that is not useful for making decisions. If a survey is self-administered and the question is vague, the participant does not have the opportunity to have the question clarified.

Survey research results will also need to be analyzed. If survey design software is used the responses to questions will automatically be tabulated, but analysis that compares the responses still depends on the insights of the researcher. Researchers will need to have some basic understanding of statistical analysis along with the creative ability to see patterns so that they can understand the meaning of the tabulated statistics.

Disadvantages of surveys

- Must be carefully designed
- No researcher available to clarify confusion
- Analysis depends on researcher ability

Survey research and the marketing mix

Survey research can be used to answer questions about visitors to a destination, hotel or event, such as demographic facts or psychographic values, attitudes and lifestyles. They can also be asked about any aspect of the tourism product, including satisfaction with individual services or the entire experiences. Pricing can be explored to determine if it is appropriate for the targeted visitors. The place where the experience is held can be explored to see if it can be improved. Finally, the effectiveness of promotional ideas can be assessed.

Case Study 5.1: Why do customers walk out?

Every business in hospitality dreads the 'walk out', someone who won't even give the business a chance to make it right. A survey was conducted to ask what would make a person walk out of a restaurant, whether it was fast food or fine dining. Four items were most often cited. Surprisingly, food was not in first place. The four ranking from least to most serious were staff unfriendliness, poor quality of food, poor quality of service and, worst of all, lack of cleanliness.

Unfriendly staff: 21 per cent of those surveyed stated that unfriendly staff were a reason they would walk out. Staff attitude is critical. Staff can follow all the correct procedures but if their attitude reveals they don't care about the customers, it shows.

Poor food quality: 23 per cent stated that if the quality of the food disappoints they may not leave, but certainly won't be back. Diners understand that the quality will vary based on the type of restaurant. But they expect the level of quality that you said you would provide.

Poor service quality: 26 per cent would leave if the service is poor. This criterion is different from unfriendly staff. This has to do with how the service is given and also if the diner is given what they want when it is requested.

Lack of cleanliness: This is the biggest issue at 30 per cent. Those surveyed were not complaining about the kitchen, which they may never see. However, everything from the windows in the front of the restaurant to the restrooms in the back is taken as evidence of kitchen cleanliness. After all, if the restaurant doesn't keep the places customers see clean, heaven knows what the kitchen looks like (Gould 2017)!

Question: What survey questions would you write to explore these issues in more depth?

Use of survey research

- People
  - What are the age, gender and ethnicity of our current visitors?
  - What types of recreational activities do our visitors prefer?
- Product
  - What type of services do our current concert attendees want us to provide?
  - How can our tours of the military history museum be improved?
- Price
  - What price are people willing to pay to visit a botanical garden?
  - Would family pricing improve attendance at the festival?
- Place
  - How far are visitors willing to walk from parking to the event?
  - How can the hotel's fitness room be improved?

- Promotion
  - Which review sites are used by our target market segment of visitors?
  - What types of photos or videos most attract the notice of our customers?

Learning more about people

One of the most fundamental uses of survey research is to learn more about the organization's current customers including both demographic facts and psychographic values, attitudes and interests. Almost all survey forms will ask demographic facts such as the visitor's age, gender, income and education level. This information is needed so that the organization can better understand the needs of different segments of visitors. It is also needed so that the answers can be used to analyze the results of other survey questions. For example, if the survey asked about improvements to hiking trails, it would be helpful for the destination to know if there was a gender difference in what was desired.

The survey can also ask about the values, attitudes and lifestyles of customers as it is these factors that strongly affect the choice of destination and activity. Designing an experience without this information would be almost impossible. For example, an organization promoting tourism in a coastal area needs to know if visitors want to use the beach for active nightlife or for a time to quietly contemplate the sunset.

Another use of survey research is to discover more information about the person who is not attending or visiting. By doing so the organization may discover that there is a segment of visitors that could be attracted if changes were made to the experience being offered. Survey research of people who are not visiting is more challenging; they must first be located as they will not be onsite. Fortunately, social media can be helpful by getting the survey to people who may be interested enough to explore the destination online, but have not yet visited.

Learning more about the tourism experience

Another use of survey research would be to learn more about the tourism preferences of either current or potential visitors. The survey form may be designed to ask the visitor what destinations they visit or what events they attend. The form may then ask questions about the benefits visitors experience when visiting. They may also be asked what additional products or services they would like to see added. For example, the survey form might ask what type of snack should be available for hotel guests at check in or if a phone app with destination information would be useful.

Other product issues that could be researched using a survey form include the frequency of use. A questionnaire could be designed to ask how often the respondent travels and the frequency of event attendance. While this information is useful on its own, it is even more useful when analyzed with other information in the survey. For example, an organization that provides cooking classes to visitors might want to know if it is returning or new visitors who are most interested. The organization would also want to know if it is solo travelers, couples or families that are most interested in taking the classes.

The other use of survey research is to gather information on how the destination image is perceived by the public. Even destinations and events that currently have visitors should continue to research the public's opinion as perceptions can change, based both on what competitors offer and external events.

Learning more about price

There are also price issues about which a survey can be used to gather data. First the acceptability of various price levels can be explored in a survey question. The question could be written as open-ended, such as, 'What price would you be willing to pay for a guided tour?' Or, the question could give a price and ask if the price is too high, too low, or about right. They can also discover that people are willing to pay more than the organization anticipated for an added benefit. In addition, a survey could gather data on how visitor behavior would be affected by discounts. For example, a hotel might ask if a price reduction based on forgoing daily room cleaning would be attractive.

Learning more about place

Place, or distribution, can also be researched using surveying. For the tourism and hotel industries, the location is often a given, as it can't be moved. The questions would focus on what type of ambience or amenities would be desired by the visitor. For example, a survey form might be designed to ask how the lobby of the visitor center or hotel can be improved to better meet the needs of guests. Questions could be asked about seating, music, availability of refreshments and hours of opening.

The success of an event can be greatly affected by the experience the location provides. The experience of attending is based not only on the performance but also on the ambience of the venue. A music festival in a park is a different experience from the same music played in a hotel ballroom. The event management organization needs to know the preferences of different visitor segments.

An additional component that must be researched is the physical environment. For destinations, this would include the entire community. For hospitality, this would be the building and surrounding area and for events, it would be the venue. The organization may wish to survey visitor perceptions to learn what it is about the environment that they find attractive. This information can then be used in promotion. If the organization feels that visitors do not find the environment satisfactory, a survey can help determine what problem areas need to be addressed.

Learning more about promotion

Survey research can also be used to improve the effectiveness of the organization's promotional efforts. A questionnaire could ask what sources are used by current or potential visitors to find destination information. The answers would help the organization better place their content marketing, so that the information will be communicated to the target market segment. In addition, survey research can be used to help develop the marketing message, or the words that communicate the product's benefits to the visitor. For example, a survey question could ask which of several messages the current or potential visitor finds most appealing.

With so many people relying on social media, surveys should be used to determine which sites are most popular with different visitor segments. The survey can

Case Study 5.2: Crowdsourcing hotel design research

Why build a hotel and then find out if the rooms match what the guests want? Marriott decided that it would conduct crowdsource-based research for two of its hotel brands, Aloft and Element. They knew that business travelers have changed and so has what they want from the hotel experience. Marriott had plenty of ideas but didn't know which would resonate with the public. To learn firsthand which of their ideas they should implement they built a model of the room in Los Angeles. The public was invited to enter the room to see, touch, and hear how it is different. As guests walk through they will use a new swipeable survey tool to gauge their reaction.

What are some of the ideas that Marriott is pioneering? A different room configuration. Four separate bedrooms will surround a central living and kitchen area for teams that need to collaborate during their stay. A new food service of custom food pots. These feature dishes that reflect regional tastes. They can be ordered at a kiosk in the lobby and be delivered to the room in colorful containers with the chef's emoji. Finally, a high tech wine cart will automatically pour the wine of the guest's choice with a swipe of the room key. When the guest opens the door to the room, the wine will be waiting (Marriott 2017)!

Question: What other parts of the visitor experience could be crowdsourced for real time feedback?

also ask how often they visit sites and how they are used. The survey can also ask which review sites visitors find the most useful so that these sites can be linked. Because new social media sites come into existence and current sites evolve continually, if this information is needed, it should be surveyed frequently.

The survey questionnaire development process

Too often, organizations involved with tourism and events will simply decide at a meeting 'let's do a survey!' without adequately understanding the need to follow a process. This process includes choosing participants, developing the form, testing the form, conducting the research and analyzing the results (Brace 2004). When using online software to develop a survey, there may be a tendency to believe that it is an automatic process. Some online survey software will even state that they will write a survey on topics such as product improvement using already written standard questions.

The problem with this approach is that, while it is quick and easy, the questions will not address the specific information needs of the organization. If a survey is going to be effective in answering the research question, time and thought must be put into planning.

The planning process starts with a meeting between employees of the tourism organization who have knowledge of the research problem and stakeholders outside the organization who may also be involved, such as government agencies or local businesses. If no one has adequate staff to conduct the research, outside researchers may also need to be involved. At this meeting the questions that will need to be asked will be discussed.

After this meeting a draft survey will be written. This draft will then be reviewed by those responsible for the organization. Once the needed changes have been made to the questions and answers and any additional questions have been added, the draft will again be reviewed. After the draft is acceptable, the answers will be coded, if necessary, and the layout finalized. Then the survey will be ready for testing.

Questionnaire development process

1 Meet with management and stakeholders regarding topics
2 Write draft survey form and have management review
3 Researchers make adjustments and review again
4 Answers coded and layout designed
5 Survey tested, changes made if needed and retested

Meeting with management and stakeholders

Once the research question has been finalized, those who will be designing the survey form and those in the organization who have knowledge of the issue that gave rise to the research question must meet. Of course, in a small organization, these two groups may be the same people. However, whether the organization is large or small, it is critical that everyone discuss what topics need to be included on the questionnaire. It might be necessary to include external groups in the research process. There may be officials in city government who may wish to have input into what questions are asked. For example, they may ask that questions about parking availability be included. Local businesses might have questions about what hours they should be open to serve the needs of visitors. Community organizations that attract visitors may wish to add questions as they may not have the capacity to conduct their own survey research. Event management organizations may ask for questions about entertainment preferences to be added. Giving other groups the opportunity to include questions can build stronger relationships among all those involved in tourism.

For almost all survey research involved in tourism and events the questions asked would include some on visitors' demographic characteristics. Standard questions on behavior would ask if the survey participant is a first time or frequent visitor. Geographic information on home location may be needed to determine where visitors are from. Other questions will ask about the psychographic characteristics of the subjects, such as their values, attitudes and lifestyles.

After these initial issues, the next decision would be to break down the research question into specific topics that need to be covered. For example, the research question might be, 'Why is attendance declining at the local amusement park?' The questionnaire on the use of park attendance might be designed to address a number of issues, such as amenities desired, ticket pricing, food availability, hours open, entertainment options and parking issues. These must be prioritized so that only two or three remain. Each topic area will take more than one question, so if too many topics are covered, the final survey form will be too lengthy.

Sample survey topics

- Are people outside of the geographic region area aware of the local amusement park?
- What events would motivate visits to the amusement park during the off-season?
- What changes to dining options would increase park revenue from family groups?
- What type of season ticket pricing structure would sell best?

Writing and review of the draft survey

After this meeting it will now be time to start writing the questionnaire. At this stage the questions will be rough. It may take many repeated efforts before each question is stated in exactly the right words to obtain the needed information. Once the questions are written, a first draft of the suggested answers must be added. This means that suggested answers from which to choose must be written. The researchers may be surprised that what at first seems a simple task is actually quite difficult.

Once the questions and answers are written, they need to be reviewed by everyone involved in the process. Possible issues that may arise include having too many questions so that some must be deleted. A review may also disclose that an important topic area was not included and, therefore, new questions must be added. Any questions that are found to be confusing must be rewritten so that the research subjects will clearly understand the meaning. The suggested answers may also not be the ones that may most often be chosen by the participants. In this case, the answers must be improved.

Potential problems uncovered when reviewing drafts

- Too many questions so that some must be deleted
- Topic area not included so that new questions must be written
- Problem or confusing questions must be rewritten
- Improper or unclear answers must be clarified

Once the draft survey has been modified it must again be reviewed. It is not unusual for a survey to go through the writing and review process several times. However, each time there should be fewer modifications. The researchers may feel pressure to complete the writing process quickly so that the survey can be implemented. This pressure should be ignored. While the researchers may have felt the first draft asked exactly what was needed, they may be amazed by how much improvement will result from the review and rewrite process.

Answers coded and layout designed

Coding answers refers to the process of assigning a number to each answer in the list of choices. Because quantitative research findings will result in statistics, all answers need to be in numerical form and not words. This process is handled automatically when using online survey software. However, if a paper form is being used, some thought must be given to this process. For example, a question might ask the visitor to check whether they are unsatisfied, satisfied or very satisfied.

These words cannot be added numerically so the answers are given values of one, two and three. Survey takers do not need to be aware of the meaning of the number. When the data from the finished survey is entered into a computer, the number one will be entered when unsatisfied is checked, two when satisfied and three when very satisfied. The need to code answers only applies when data will be entered into computer software manually.

Questionnaire form testing

The survey questionnaire should be tested with participants who are similar to the research subject sample. If the sample consists of a variety of subgroups, at least some of the test participants should be from each group. During the first step in the testing process, a researcher should be present while someone with the participant profile completes the questionnaire (Vannette 2015). This way the researcher can make a note of any direction, question or answer that causes difficulty. If there are major problems with the survey form, the researcher should address these through changes and the testing should begin again. If there are only a few minor changes that result from testing the questionnaire, the testing can proceed to the next step.

The questionnaire should now be tested using the planned methodology, whether administered in person, over the phone, by mail, or online. The sample for the test can be small, with as few as five to ten individuals. The reason for testing the methodology besides the questions and answers is to determine the length of time that it takes for the survey to be completed. The amount of time it will take to complete will have an effect on the completion rate. In addition, this testing will confirm that all email or social media links work as planned.

Once the survey delivery methodology testing is completed, a final test should be conducted of the data analysis or entry system. The data analysis section of the online survey software should be checked to ensure that all responses are being recorded.

Writing effective questions and answers

The key to successful survey research is writing the questions so that they obtain the needed information. Even personal communication between two people can lead to misunderstandings over what was really meant by the words spoken. Because with a self-administered survey there is no one to clarify the meaning of the questions, they must be thoughtfully written and tested before use.

Another reason for taking care when writing questions is that small wording changes can make a large difference in the response received. A question such as, 'Do you want to visit a new destination this year?' may get a totally different response from one that asks, 'Do you plan to visit a new destination this year?' The first question asks about desire, the second asks about action.

Guidelines for writing questions

There are a number of general guidelines that if kept in mind will help the tourism researcher write better questions. These guidelines include only asking questions

Figure 5.2 A survey link can now be sent via text allowing participants to respond using a smartphone.

Photo Credit: Alizada Studios

visitors can answer, writing the question at the correct reading level, asking only one question at a time and avoiding the use of the passive voice. In addition, the researcher must keep in mind that the questions should be easy to translate into other languages.

Survey questions should be factual. They should ask the what, where, when and how of current visitor behavior. They can also ask the visitor to predict future behavior but only based on facts. When doing so, as much information should be provided as possible to help participants to assess their future behavior. For example, a question about the likelihood of visiting a new attraction should provide information on type, location and cost.

Factual question example

- Problem: Would you use a waterpark at our hotel?
- Improved: Would you be interested in visiting a new waterpark at our hotel if the cost was $50 for a family above the room charge?

The word structure for questions should be kept simple. Researchers who work in an organization will be very familiar with specific industry terminology. Even if they are not familiar with terminology when they start the research process, by the time they start writing the survey questions, they will have become

Case Study 5.3: Do you know what your employees really want?

Everyone is aware that the hospitality industry has high employee turnover, which costs time and money in recruiting, hiring and training. Knowledge of the current role and future goals of your employees can keep them on staff longer. How to discover these goals? Through research!

Of course, you should know the names of your employees. Even more important is to understand their title. It is the role they play each day at the hotel or attraction that gives them a sense of purpose on the job. Every role has value, those behind the scenes as much as those who have direct visitor contact.

What you may not know are the goals of your employees. What are their dreams for their professional future? Are they working toward promotion? Do they want to find a job in another department? Do they wish they had an opportunity for more training?

Perhaps you can find out this information through casual conversation, but this would be a very inefficient method. Instead an internal survey could be conducted to discover this information. Sample questions could ask about work site improvements that would make their job easier, preferred benefits and training desired. There are some managers who do not ask these questions, because they think that if employees aren't voicing complaints, then they are happy. This may be true, or more likely the employees may be quiet because they are busy looking for their next job!

A crucial point to remember is that it isn't enough to ask – you also have to deliver. A hospitality manager's job is to help their employees' dreams come true (Dihr 2016).

Question: What type of recommendations could result from conducting such a survey?

familiar because of meetings and discussions with others in the organization. However, the researchers must remember that the people reading the question will not be familiar with terms used on a daily basis in the organization. For example, a destination management organization might be concerned about parking issues in a city.

Confusing question example

- Problem: What means of transport did you use to visit the city?
- Improved: How did you travel to the city for your most recent visit?

The researchers should keep in mind the reading level of the participants who will be involved in the study. Reading level involves the choice of words, but also the number of words in the question and the question structure. Questions should be kept short and, if possible, not use any subordinate clauses.

Figure 5.3 Surveys can be administered personally where visitors can be found.

Photo Credit: Trong Nguyen

Reading level question example

- Problem: In terms of motivation and desire, how critical is the choice of bedding in the decision making process for hotel satisfaction?
- Improved: How important to you is the quality of hotel bedding?

In an attempt to limit the number of questions, and therefore the length of the survey form, researchers may be tempted to combine questions. This should be avoided as it can lead to confusion for the participant, which will result in inaccurate findings. A question that asks about ticket prices and reasons for not attending should be two questions. If written as one question it makes the assumption that if tickets are expensive people will buy fewer tickets. However this is actually two questions. Someone may consider prices too high but still be willing to attend.

Double question example

- Problem: Do you believe that the fact that event tickets are too expensive is the reason people are buying fewer tickets?
- Improved: Do you believe that event tickets are too expensive? Are ticket prices the reason you do not attend?

The passive voice does not use direct pronouns. Instead of using you, she, he or they, writing in the passive voice leaves the reader without any knowledge of who is the 'subject' of the question. A question such as, 'Should music festivals be cancelled if rain is predicted?' leaves the research subject wondering to whom is the question is directed. Instead the question should ask if they would attend a festival if rain is predicted.

Passive question example

- Problem: How does weather effect attendance for a music festival?
- Improved: Would you make the decision to attend a music festival even if rain is predicted?

When writing questions that will be translated, special issues need to be considered. Colloquial terms that have a meaning not associated with the literal translation should be avoided. Words such as 'vibe' might be fine when used in an English question asking if participants thought the current promotion was exciting. However, when the word is translated, it will not have the same meaning.

Translation question example

- Problem: Do you believe that our city's branding communicates the right vibe?
- Improved: Do you believe that our city's branding is exciting?

Answer formats

Not only do researchers need to understand the general guidelines for writing questions, they must also learn the different ways that the answers can be written. First, open-ended questions that allow participants to provide their own answer can be asked. While the advantage of filling in the blank answers is that the participant is allowed to answer in any way he or she chooses, each answer must be read, coded and entered into software. They should be used infrequently in surveys. Other ways that answers can be structured include dichotomous choice, forced choice, multiple choice, checklist, rating, and ranking questions.

Dichotomous choice answer structure forces the participant to choose from one of two possible answers. This type of question provides answers such as yes or no, or male or female. For example, an organization might ask if visitors are interested in guided tours during evening hours. They could ask if they are interested in more entertainment that is suitable for families. They can be simply asked if this is their first visit to the city. The answer in each case is either yes or no.

Dichotomous choice question and answer

Would you take a guided tour in the evening?

    Yes ___   No ____

A forced choice type of answer is similar to dichotomous choice but with the difference that the two possible answers are not opposites and, in fact, both might be true. The forced choice answer format forces the participant to state a preference. For example, it might be known that people at the hotel like the free breakfast but also the free evening cocktail hour. The organization knows that both are desired but needs to know which is preferred as they do not have the budget for both.

Forced choice question and answer

Which is most important when making the booking decision? (check one)

Free Breakfast ___   Free cocktail hour ___

Multiple choice is a term with which everyone is familiar. This format is used when the organization knows that the question has a number of different possible answers. For example, an organization that promotes a seaside resort knows that there are numerous reasons for visiting. The possible answers will be determined through information the organization already has, perhaps from conducting exploratory research. The list should not be so long that it is difficult for the participant to choose the best answer. The usual number of answers provided by a multiple choice question may be as few as three to as many as eight. Because even these might not cover all possible answers, a final choice of 'other' may be provided along with a line where the participant can write in her or his own answer.

Multiple choice question and answer

What is the most important reason you visited our city? (check one)

___ Beauty of nature   ___ Relaxation   ___ Nightlife   ___ Shopping

Of course, everyone knows the frustration of believing that at least two answers on a multiple choice question could be right but only being allowed to provide one response. A checklist choice question and answer is a way round this problem as it allows participants to check more than one answer. This type of answer also allows for the researcher to provide many more choices than multiple choice, as the participant does not need to do the mental weighing of which is the best answer.

Checklist choice question and answer

Which of the following were reasons you chose to attend Oktoberfest? (check as many as apply)

___ My spouse/partner made me come   ___ I love beer
___ I wanted to know more about brewing   ___ I love German food
___ I had guests visiting   ___ I had free tickets

A checklist choice can be modified so that even more information is obtained. A ranking choice asks the participant to rank their choices as to their importance in motivating their decision. The participant should not be asked to rank all choices as there are some that will not apply. Instead the participant should be asked to rank all those that do apply in order of importance. Or, the participant can be asked to rank the top three or five. A ranking choice provides more information for analysis. For example, a question might ask what three factors motivate their choice of destination. The checklist answers might range from 'inexpensive' to 'family friendly'. All of these answers are very different and the researcher doesn't know which to use as the basis for their recommendations. A ranking choice will let the researcher know which answer was most important overall. This can be accomplished by not just counting the responses but weighting each by importance.

Ranking choice question and answer

My choice of destination is based on: (rank from 1 to 3 the three most important motivating factors)

___ Cost   ___ Children desires   ___ Type of accommodation
___ Availability of shopping   ___ Sports activities   ___ Local food and drink

A rating question differs in that it allows the participant to choose how strongly they agree or disagree with each answer rather than just respond with a yes or no check or a listing of possible responses. For example, a question that asks about the motivation for visiting historic homes might ask whether the visitor is motivated by a love of architecture, the need for professional knowledge, the reputation of the guide, or a desire to discover decorating ideas for their own home.

Rating choice question and answer

Rate how each of these factors affected your decision to take the tour of historic homes:

	Agree	No Effect	Disagree
My love of architecture	_____	_____	_____
I need design ideas	_____	_____	_____
I heard the guide is great	_____	_____	_____
I heard they serve food at the end	_____	_____	_____

Demographic questions and response rates

The organization will write the survey to ask questions directly of the product or service provided. They will want to know what visitors like about the destination and what they want improved. They will be asked about the price they are willing to pay. Promotion questions will be asked about what motivated the visit and what media messages were heard.

All of the responses to these questions will be more useful if they can be correlated with demographic characteristics of the respondent. For this reason, standard informational questions should be added.

The first issue is the relevance of the age of the participant as tourism desires and behaviors often are affected by the visitor's age. Because young people will often want different activities than older people, the organization writing the survey needs to consider the relevance of age to its research findings. It might be enough to have broad categories, such as 20–34, 35–64, and 65 and over, for an organization such as a hotel, as it caters to a wide range of visitors. For an organization that knows it caters specifically to young people, they might want to break the first category into 20–24, 25–29, and 30–34 to determine if desires and behavior differ among young people.

Because another issue that determines the type of tourism experience desired is family status, the survey should ask the household type. These might be listed as living alone, living with another adult, living with children and a household with two or more adults with children. The survey might then ask if they are traveling with family members. This information will be helpful in determining whether this is a visitor segment that is being reached with promotional messages.

Other questions that might be relevant include income. While it is possible to list income ranges in the answer to the question, this is a sensitive issue. A better way to ask the question is to ask for total household income, which is less personal. Another way for this issue to be addressed is by asking for either education level or type of employment. Most college educated people make more money. The same is true of people who have professional employment.

Since tourism involves people traveling to new locations, another question that can be asked is about access to transportation, for instance whether the household includes someone who owns a car. Another question might be whether they have access to affordable train or air transportation, such as if they use car sharing services.

In addition, geographic location may need to be included. There are two ways this issue can be addressed. The first is to ask what distance was traveled. The second is to ask for their home location. Another piece of useful information is to ask if the destination is the sole focus of their trip. The destination, hotel or event needs to know if the trip was made solely for this visit or if the visitor is combining the trip with other destinations.

Response rates

The response rate for a survey is the percentage of people that start and complete the survey form. While it would be rare for everyone to complete a survey, the percentage who do so should be tracked. The percentage can be calculated by simply dividing the number of people who successfully complete the survey by the number of surveys sent. Doing so gives a percentage that is easy to understand, but more information is needed. There will be participants who start the survey but do not complete and this percentage should also be tracked. If it is large that can mean that these participants were willing to participate but found the survey either too long, too complicated or both (Poynter 2015). In this case, the design of the survey form needs to be reviewed.

Another rate that should be calculated is the number of people who did not even click to open an online survey form. If this percentage is high, the organization may need to consider a more attractive incentive. However, it might mean that the list of participants is at fault as they may not be sufficiently interested in the product to wish to participate

Using layout to increase response rate

The visual elements of a survey will affect whether people start and then complete a survey form. The visual elements that must be considered include the font size and

Case Study 5.4: How hard is it to get people onto an airplane?

Airlines have been transporting people for years. For all these years, people have been managing to get on a flight, take a seat and the plane has taken off. What was once considered standard behavior today has become much more complicated. Now getting on the plane is not considered standard but a perk that is to be rewarded or withheld according to the revenue model of the airline.

Finding a better model for boarding planes can be financially rewarding for airlines. It is estimated that saving 30 to 60 seconds on the time it takes to board a plane can save a significant amount of money for an airline that has thousands of flights a day.

But there is a secondary financial motive that developed when airlines started to charge baggage fees. After all, there is no need for a passenger to rush to board an airplane to get a seat; if they have a reservation and purchase a ticket they will get a seat. What impels people to jockey to get ahead in line is the need to get overhead space for their baggage. Since airlines started to charge for checking bags more people are taking their bags on to the airplane.

So, the airlines want to board planes as quickly as possible in an orderly manner while the passengers want to get on as fast as possible. The solution? Give priority boarding to passengers who pay more, have an airline charge card, are frequent flyers or pay for the privilege. It has become so complicated that American Airlines has nine categories for boarding preference. Oh wait, that would be ten categories if you count the group that is so privileged that it has no number that boards before Group One. What do passengers feel would be the best method? No one seems to have asked (McCartney 2017).

Question: What are five survey questions that could be written to research this issue?

style, the number of pages, the use of white space, the color of the paper and the use of decorative elements. All of these will affect the participant's first impression of the survey. This first impression may determine whether participants even attempt the survey or, if they start, whether they will complete.

Font size is important as it affects the perception of the difficulty of the material. Everyone is familiar with the term 'fine print'. This term usually refers to detailed information that may be deliberately confusing. While no one writes a questionnaire with this intent, if the font size is very small, the perception that many people may have is that what is written will be difficult to understand. Therefore the font should be large enough to convey the impression not only that the words will be easy to read but that they will also be easy to understand. Another issue with font size is that it should be large enough for older participants to read with ease. As eyesight diminishes with age, the ability to focus on small print becomes increasingly difficult even with corrective lenses.

In addition to size, deciding on the type of font used should be based on ease of reading. While it may be tempting to use an 'artistic' font, such fonts can be difficult to read. Artistic fonts should only be used in the title of the survey, if at all. The use of underlining, italics and bolding should also be kept to a minimum as they can make the survey seem too 'busy' and therefore give the perception that it will be confusing to complete.

The researcher in charge of the layout of the survey must achieve a delicate balance between the need to include all the questions to which answers are required and the need to limit the number of pages. A survey form with too many pages will be seen as requiring too long to complete and, therefore, will not be even started. The researchers may want to add to the directions the anticipated completion time. Online surveys can be built with a progress bar that shows how much of the survey is left to complete. This will let participants know that while lengthy, the questionnaire can still be completed quickly.

In an attempt to limit the number of pages of a print survey while not reducing the font size, the researchers may decrease the page margins or the spacing between questions. However, by cutting down on white space on the paper, the survey form will look more difficult to answer. White space is visually 'restful'. It gives the eyes of the participants a place to rest before moving on to the next question. White space should be thought of as the pause that naturally occurs between sentences when speaking. Its effective use helps the participant to more quickly finish the questionnaire.

While it is important that a survey form be easy to read, there is no reason for it to be boring. Adding visual interest can help attract and keep the participants' interest focused. For example, the organization's logo can be added to the first page. Images that correspond to the question can be added. The researcher shouldn't add so much decorative detail that the form will start to look confusing, but adding some interest will make it more appealing.

References

Brace, I. 2004. *Questionnaire Design: How to Plan, Structure and Write Survey Material for Effective Market Research*. London: Kogan Page.

Dihr, L.A. 2016. Core Values of a Professional Hotelier! [online]. *Hospitality Net*, 7 June. Available from www.hospitalitynet.org/news/4076469.html. [Accessed 27 February 2017].

Gould, B. 2017. Restaurant Guests: What They Really Want [online]. *4Hoteliers*, 16 March. Available from www.4hoteliers.com/features/article/10323. [Accessed 17 March 2017].

Marriott. 2017. Marriott's Pop-up Hotel Innovation Lab, Creating an Interactive Model Hotel Experience in Downtown Los Angeles to Crowdsource Real-time Feedback from the Public, Furthering the Company's Futuristic Vision [online]. *4Hoteliers*, 25 January. Available from www.4hoteliers.com/news/story/16764. [Accessed 26 January 2017].

McCartney, S. 2017. It Can't Be This Hard to Board a Plane [online]. *The Wall Street Journal*. Dow Jones & Company, 01 March. Available from www.wsj.com/articles/it-cant-be-this-hard-to-board-a-plane-1488378608. [Accessed 6 March 2017].

Poynter, R. 2015. Why the Long Survey Is Dead [online]. *Vision Critical*. 5 May. Available from www.visioncritical.com/the-long-survey-is-dead/. [Accessed 21 December 2016].

Putnam-Farr, E., and J. Riis. 2016. "Yes/No/Not Right Now": Yes/No Response Formats Can Increase Response Rates Even in Non-Forced-Choice Settings [online]. *American Marketing Association*. June. Available from www.ama.org/publications/JournalOfMarketingResearch/Pages/yes-no-not-right-now.aspx. [Accessed 25 April 2017].

Vannette, D. 2015. 6 Ways to Pretest Your Survey Before You Send It [online]. *Qualtrics*. 26 Aug. Available from www.qualtrics.com/blog/6-ways-to-pretest-your-survey-before-you-send-it/. [Accessed 25 April 2017].

Administering visitor surveys

Chapter summary

- Surveys can be self-administered or administered using a researcher. The advantage of self-administering is convenience for the research subject. The advantages of using researchers to conduct the survey include helping participants with the survey questions, motivating participation and reaching disenfranchised groups. Traditional self-administered surveys use mail and leaving forms to be picked up and completed. Distributing surveys to be completed online is now common.
- The organization may decide that it would be best if a researcher or other employee helped with administering the survey in person or over the phone. This method would be chosen if it was believed that the potential participants might not be sufficiently motivated to complete the survey on their own. The researcher will need training in how to conduct the survey.
- An advantage of using an online survey versus a mail survey is that the survey results appear immediately. This allows researchers to track the number of responses and send email reminders to those who have yet to complete the survey. The disadvantage of online surveys is that the participants must both be computer literate and have access. The links to online surveys can be sent out via email or posted on social media.
- Once the groups have been identified and participants screened, those that meet the profile and are selected to participate will be sent a letter or email that

provides both the name of the research firm and the name of the organization that is commissioning the research. People are willing to participate in research because they believe the results will help others, they have an interest in the research process or because of the incentive offered.

Self-administered survey methods

Survey distribution methods can be categorized as self-administered, where there is no contact between the researcher and the participant, and researcher administered, where the researcher guides the participant through the process. While online surveys may be the best option for many organizations, it shouldn't be assumed that this is the best method. There may be situations where conducting surveys using traditional methods will result in higher completion rates. The decision on which method to use should be based on the method preferred by the targeted research subjects.

Advantages of self-administered surveys

Traditional self-administered survey methods include mailing the form to the participant and paper forms that are left on site for visitors to pick up and online forms. There are several advantages to the organization if the decision is made to use a self-administered survey methodology, including cost savings. In addition, the participants can complete the survey at a time and place that is most convenient for them. Self-administered surveys also eliminate bias that might result from the researcher leading the participant to answer in a certain way or the participant answering the question with an answer they feel will be acceptable to the researcher.

There are cost savings that result from using a self-administered survey, such as not having to pay for someone to administer the survey. Particularly if a large number of survey form completions are required, the cost of hiring a researcher to lead the participant through the survey is just too large for many organizations. Such methods are used only when people will not respond in any other way. A self-administered survey can also be more convenient for the participant. Because they do not need the assistance of a researcher, they can complete the form at the location and time that is best for them. For example, a survey form that is placed at the reception desk for a hotel can be completed anytime during the stay, while an online survey can be completed during lunch break at work.

Besides saving money and convenience, another advantage of a self-administered survey is elimination from bias as there is no researcher to suggest an answer to the participant. While an ethical researcher would not do so intentionally, their body language or just the tone of voice they use when asking a question can lead the participant to answer in a certain way. Even when the researcher is scrupulously neutral, an advantage to self-administered surveys is that the presence of the researcher might result in the participant being less than truthful. For example, a question on how much money is spent at an event might be not answered truthfully if the respondent feels they spend too much money on bottles of wine. With a self-administered survey form, the participant has the privacy that will allow them to answer sensitive questions without concern for the researcher's reaction.

Advantages of researcher administered surveys

Traditional researcher administered methods would be calling the research subject and asking the questions over the phone. The researcher might also be on site where the participants can be found and ask the questions personally. There are advantages when an organization chooses to have researchers or other employees help participants with the survey questions. With a researcher assisted survey, someone will ask the questions verbally and then record the answers. A major advantage of this method is that participants can ask for clarification of any difficult or confusing questions. Even simple survey questions such as, 'How often did you visit our city last year?' may prompt questions. For example, the participant might ask if this includes the times they visited for business reasons or only for a stopover on the way to another destination. They might also need clarification on what is meant by last year: does it mean the preceding January through December of the proceeding twelve months? Without the researcher's explanation, the participant will have to guess what occasions should be counted as 'visits' and what is meant as 'a year'.

Having targeted research subjects complete survey forms is always an issue no matter what method is used. Researcher assisted surveys have the advantage of having someone present to encourage participants to complete the entire questionnaire. Even the most motivated research subjects starting a survey in their own homes, may then get interrupted by a family member. They may have started with good intentions of completing the survey to let the hotel know their opinions but never get around to finishing. Someone attending an event who is handed a form, may have every intention of completing it, but once they return home they have other distractions and never think of it again. A researcher-assisted survey eliminates these distractions and ensures the form is completed. Even when a self-administered survey form is completed, participants may completely skip questions they find sensitive or difficult to answer. A researcher assisted survey allows the researcher to encourage participants to answer every question.

A final advantage of using researcher assisted surveying is when working with disenfranchised groups. Members of these groups may feel that their views are not valued. Or, the members may not have the language skills or cultural knowledge to fully understand the research process. Whether the reluctance to participate is from a feeling of being outside the system or a lack of understanding of the process, it may take the persuasive skills of the researcher before participants will cooperate and complete the survey.

Comparison of advantages to survey methods

- Self-administered
  - cost savings
  - completion at convenience of participant
  - eliminate researcher bias
- Researcher administered
  - provides means of clarification of questions
  - researcher can motivate participant to complete
  - encourage participation by disenfranchised groups

Case Study 6.1: Motivating tourists to visit Iceland

If you had gone online in early 2008 looking for stories about Iceland, you wouldn't have found many. Iceland was not a popular destination and didn't often make the news. That changed in 2008 when the country endured a severe financial crisis. Then Iceland made the news! Social media research showed that in a seven-week period after the crisis hit, there were over 600 stories posted about Iceland, more than the previous 20 years combined. Then, in 2010 a volcano erupted in Iceland that was so large it stopped international air travel. Iceland was in the news again! However, the stories were again not positive ones that would encourage tourism.

As it is known that 92 per cent of travelers use online tools when making their travel decision, the country's tourism agency was concerned. What was needed was a way to convey positive stories about Iceland to motivate tourists to visit. So, the country's President announced 'Iceland Hour'. The country's schools, stores, and Parliament were closed for that hour and everyone was encouraged to use the time to post positive stories online. As a result of the effort 1.5 million stories about Iceland were posted by citizens on social media. Now, when someone searched online for Iceland there were plenty of positive stories (Markelz 2015).

Question: What type of survey could you conduct to determine if the posts were effective in motivating tourists to visit?

Traditional self-administered survey methods

If the organization opts to use a self-administered survey method, they must decide on the form of distribution. While the first thought might be some form of electronic distribution, there are still situations where mail and paper forms should be used.

Mail surveys remain in use despite the growing popularity of electronic delivery formats. There may be geographic regions or countries where customers do not use the internet either because of inability to connect or cost. In addition, not everyone can be reached via email. An advantage of conducting a mail survey is that nearly everyone has an address and they are usually easy to obtain. If the organization is surveying current or past customers, they will probably already have addresses in their files. For people who are not customers, the addresses will most likely be publicly available either from a phone book or by searching online. Mailing lists can also be purchased from companies that supply address lists. In addition, in some countries the government may be a source of addresses such as voter registration lists.

Mail surveys are usually mailed to the potential participant's home address. However, a work address can be used if appropriate. Work addresses would be used when the research question relates to the participant's work responsibilities, such as business travel. However, most surveys will be sent to home addresses. The survey form is usually sent in an envelope that includes the name of the organization so that the receiver will be motivated to open and read the material. A cover letter explaining the purpose of the research study with contact information will also be included along with a stamped return envelope.

Of course, with mail surveys, the completion rate will depend on the quality of the addresses. If the population that is to be surveyed moves often or lives with relatives, it will be more difficult to find current addresses. Another problem is that there may not be money in the organization's budget for purchasing commercially available mailing lists.

If the organization wants to survey current visitors, the forms can be personally distributed to the potential participants at the destination. The advantage of this method is that the person handing out the survey form can make a personal appeal to the potential participant to complete the survey form. For example, guests who have just completed a tour may be handed a form while listening to an explanation that completing the survey will help the city provide better tours in the future.

If it is not possible to hand out the survey form personally, the forms can be left at a front reception desk or placed on a visitor center table. In this case, information must also be provided as to the purpose of the research and any incentive for completion so that the customer will be motivated to do the survey.

The survey form should include clear instructions for its return once it is completed. They should be instructed to return the form to an individual such as the front desk attendant or to place the form in a designated box. The organization must also make sure that the person who has been designated to receive the forms retains them until they can be collected.

This type of distribution is mostly used to research people who are already visitors and meet the participant profile. If survey forms were just handed out in public or left at public places it would be difficult to ensure that the people who see the form and complete the survey are the ones that meet the profile. Without any direct tie to the organization, it would also be the rare person who would be motivated enough to take the time to complete the survey form.

Researcher administered survey methods

The organization may decide that it would be best if a researcher or other employee helped with administering the survey. This method would be chosen if it was believed that the potential participants might not be sufficiently motivated to complete the survey on their own. The questionnaire can be administered by the researcher personally or over the phone.

Researcher administered methods have the advantage of having someone personally persuade the individual to participate in the study. While the research study is very important to the tourism organization, potential participants may see no reason why they should stop what they are doing to give even five minutes to answer survey questions. It can take a personal appeal with the researcher explaining the reason for the survey and any incentive that is offered before participants are willing to participate.

Personal surveying

Personal surveying has the advantage of face-to-face contact. This allows the researcher to explain the purpose of the research and how participation will be helpful to future visitors by improving the tourism experience. Personal surveying can be conducted at a location where there are individuals who meet the participant profile. For current visitors this will most likely be at the tourist attraction, lodging or event. For individuals who are not users of the organization this will be at other locations. For example, if the organization wishes to survey families with children they may decide to conduct the survey at a local children's museum visited by tourists. If young women and men are the targeted population the organization may conduct the surveys at sports or music events where they may naturally congregate.

When conducting surveys the researcher can use visual prompts that can assist the participant in answering the question. For example, if the organization wishes to learn more about the effectiveness of promotional material, they can show participants sample website designs that have been produced. They can then ask the participants to rank them on their appeal. They could also show photos of art work, print ad copy, or even have them listen to short clips of music. All of these methods need to have a researcher present to explain how these prompts relate to answering the question.

When at the location where the survey will be conducted, the researcher must first ascertain that the potential participant meets the profile characteristics. Even if the survey is held at the destination, not all visitors may meet this profile. Some characteristics can usually be verified visually, such as gender, family status or age range. Others, such as lifestyle or religious background, cannot be so easily seen.

Figure 6.1 Not everyone is able and willing to complete a form online, so printed surveys are still used.

Photo Credit: Rawpixel.com

Case Study 6.2: Airlines use research to determine pricing

At first it might not make sense, but airlines can charge more for a ticket to travel from London to Dubai, than from London to Dubai and then on to Manila, which is a much longer trip. The reason is that the airlines know that people are willing to pay more to fly to some destinations, one of which is Manila. Research data has shown them that people flying from London to Manila buy expensive tickets so the airline does not want to lose a seat because someone booked a cheap ticket only going to Dubai.

What else do airlines know? People booking trips from London to sunny places are willing to pay more six months before their journey to confirm their plans. The fare gets lower as the date of the flight gets closer because most people have already booked their trips.

People traveling to Frankfurt are not going for the sunshine but rather business. They wait to book and will pay more. So, six months out, prices are cheap and then rise.

While this model has worked well in increasing revenue, airlines are looking at a new pricing model, called bundled pricing. Airlines would love to price like Amazon with every customer getting a personalized package of services, such as free baggage, food service or amenities at the airport, for which they would be willing to pay more. To do so, they will need to learn more about what customers really want (CNN 2016).

Question: How would you define the segments of customers that airlines should research to start getting this information?

The researcher must first ask the potential participant screening questions to see if they fit the profile.

Before asking these questions, the researchers should introduce themselves and quickly explain the purpose of the survey research. They then should explain what type of participant is needed and why. For example, the survey research may have been designed to determine whether a wine tasting event is meeting the expectations of visitors or if the experience should be changed. However, the researchers will have no way of knowing which visitor enjoys drinking wine. By explaining the purpose of the study first, the potential participant will not be offended when, after having stated that they do not drink, they are not asked the survey questions.

Technology has provided a means to discard the paper questionnaire form traditionally used when conducting personal surveys. Instead, a computerized tablet is used by researchers to read questions and record answers. A researcher or assistant would still be present but the answers would be recorded electronically. There are important advantages for researchers in using this form of electronic data collection. Researchers will save money as there will be no data entry costs and the recorded answers can be downloaded directly into a computer program for analysis. Besides the cost savings, direct downloading increases reliability by excluding data entry errors. Complex survey forms will often be written with directions for a participant to skip ahead to a specific question based on their response to a previous question. With an electronic form this will happen automatically, minimizing confusion. In addition, the sequencing of questions can be randomized. This is an important consideration if there is any concern that question sequencing might be influencing the resulting answers. Of course, there will be the cost of buying the technology and training people in its use.

Telephone surveying

The disadvantage to personal surveying is that the researcher must be at the same location at the same time as the research participants. This is not a problem when the potential participants can be found at an event, hotel or attraction. However, this is often not the case. While telephone surveys have long been one of the most popular methods of surveying, there is a growing concern whether this method will survive. While it is difficult to conduct phone surveys of the general public because of call restrictions, telephone surveying can work with visitors with whom the tourism organization has an established relationship.

Telephone surveying has the advantage of the researchers being able to motivate the individual to participate and complete the survey even though they are not physically present. While a mail survey may be automatically thrown in the trash, a friendly voice on the phone may motivate a research subject to participate. Just as with personal surveying, a telephone survey allows the survey taker to explain the reason for the survey and sort out any confusing questions. An advantage of telephone over personal surveying is that the participants can be geographically dispersed as almost everyone has a phone number. Another advantage that telephone surveying has over personal surveying is privacy. With a telephone survey, the participant may be more willing to reveal sensitive or negative information. For example, a survey conducted by an organization of customers who have complained about the service they have received at a spa may ask if the participant for more details. The participant may be more willing to answer the question if they are not face to face with the researcher.

When conducting phone surveys it is best if the researcher has a script from which to work. The script will ensure that the correct information is given as to the sponsorship of the survey. After an introduction using their name, survey takers will then inform the research subject who is sponsoring the research. They will then explain why the research is being conducted. They will then inform the subject why they are being contacted. This may be because they were a past visitor or their name was randomly chosen. Finally, if appropriate, an incentive will be offered. The survey taker will then read through the questions and possible answers. The same language must be used for each question so that no bias will be introduced. The survey taker needs to be trained to provide assistance with leading the research subject to answer in a particular way.

Sample script

- Hello, my name is Maria and I am conducting a survey for the Convention and Visitor Bureau of Tourist Town. The results of the survey will be used to improve the services offered by our visitor center.

- As a past visitor to our town, will you please give us five minutes of your time to answer questions about your experience?
- If you complete the survey, I can provide you with a code that when used on our tourism website will provide you with a discount coupon.

Training survey takers

The success of a researcher administered survey depends on the skill of the survey taker. Large tourism organizations can use the services of a commercial call center. However, survey takers do not need to be professional researchers. Small tourism businesses that only occasionally conduct surveys can hire hourly employees. This type of part time job could be attractive to college students or the retired. However, because these employees will not have experience in conducting surveys, they need to be trained before the survey process begins.

The training should inform the survey takers of the purpose of the research. Survey takers will be more motivated to have participants complete the survey if they understand the rationale of the research question. The second step in the training is to explain the structure of the survey and the reasons for each of the questions. The role of the supervisor or lead researcher should be explained, which is that they are there to assist with difficult participants and to provide general support. The survey takers should also be taught general rules for conducting successful surveys.

If the survey is to be conducted with communities that are culturally different from the survey takers, additional research needs to be done (Jong 2016). For some communities, survey takers will need to use a more personal approach than working strictly from a script in order to build trust. With some ethnic and religious groups the gender of the survey taker will impact the ability to motivate participation.

Once the training has been completed, the survey takers should first administer the survey on each other. In addition, the supervisor should role-play uncooperative or rude potential participants so that the survey taker learns how to defuse these situations. Once the survey taker is on the phone, the first surveys should be supervised and monitored.

If the survey takers express interest, and the information is not private, they can be provided with a summary of the data. Knowing that they will be informed of the results can better engage the survey taker in the process.

Online survey forms

Survey forms are not usually embedded in emails because of practical issues. An email attachment that is large enough to contain all the text and formatting for a questionnaire may be too large for a potential participant's computer to handle. In fact, such a large attachment may be screened out as SPAM. However, electronic delivery using email is appropriate for short questionnaires targeted at small groups that are familiar with the organization and therefore likely to respond. This allows the respondent to quickly answer the questions in the body of the reply email. Links to short surveys that can be completed on a smartphone can also be sent via text message (McGeeney and Yyan 2016). It has been found that people respond and complete a survey faster than when notified by email.

Figure 6.2 A survey that is being administered via smartphone must be designed to work on many systems.

Photo Credit: dennizen

Most electronic survey forms though will be on separate websites and email will only be used to send the relevant website link that provides access to the form. There are many types of online survey software sites that will assist in the design of a survey, collect the responses and tabulate the results. The newest products are free or relatively inexpensive for surveys sent to a limited number of participants. While the fact that the form is electronic does not change the survey questions, it can change the way the questions and answers are presented. Visuals can be incorporated and the sequence of questions can be easily varied.

Advantages and disadvantages with online surveys

A major advantage in using an online survey versus a mail survey is that the survey results appear immediately. This allows researchers to track the number of responses and send email reminders to those who have not responded. It also allows researchers to change any of the questions that seem to be causing confusion or to reconsider any of the questions that are not being answered. The question order can also be designed so that a response to a question will automatically result in the next appropriate question being shown.

There are also disadvantages to online surveys. First, respondents must have computer access and feel comfortable responding online. It should be remembered that not all types of jobs require people to be in front of a computer. In addition, not everyone enjoys being online. For those individuals who are not online every day because of their job or personal interests, completing an online survey will mean that they must go online specifically for that purpose, which is not as easy as picking up a pen or answering the phone.

Case Study 6.3: It's not the wait time, it's the people at the front of the line

Tourism is a service business. Everyone knows, including the employees, that how you treat your customers is critical. How critical? When a research study at a major airport was conducted of travelers' views of security procedures it was thought that a shorter length of wait time was the factor that determined customer satisfaction. The assumption was wrong. Survey research found that the critical factor was how the passenger was treated when they got to the front of the line. People could forgive the long wait, if they were treated well, which depended on employee morale. The researchers interviewed employees and found they treated customers badly because they were treated the same way by their managers.

Observation research was also conducted at the airport. Researchers watched employees going about their daily routine. What they noticed was that as they walked through the airport they avoided eye contact with travelers. Again, it might have been thought that employees were just simply rude. Not so! When employees were asked, it was found that they avoided contact with passengers because they knew that they would be asked questions for which they did not have answers. After all, why should gate attendants know answers to such questions as where is the closest restroom or where they should go to rebook a missed flight, when they don't use these services? Only if they are given the information needed, even if it is not immediately relevant to their jobs, can they provide service.

The answer to ensuring good customer service in tourism businesses is to treat them well and give them the tools they need to service the public (Boyarsky, Ritter and Enger 2016).

Question: How could you research what type of information is needed by hotel front desk clerks?

Another disadvantage is that the potential participants who wish to respond to online surveys in some countries may be skewed toward younger, better educated individuals. If a research sample calls for responses from a quota of specific demographic and psychographic types, online may not be the best methodology to get the responses needed.

In some countries, the income level of the research subjects may mean that they cannot afford to be online because of the costs. They may have access to a smartphone instead of a computer, but may not be willing to use their data time to complete a survey.

Advantages of online surveys

- Results appear immediately
- Survey software widely available
- Electronic survey questions can be customized

Figure 6.3 In some countries, personally administering a survey will work best.

Photo Credit: Iakov Filmonov

Disadvantages of online surveys

- Subjects may not have computer access
- Challenging to reach some segments

Choice of survey software

The type of software available for designing and conducting surveys varies as to the complexity of data analysis that can be performed. Using the software will vary by price as the more technically sophisticated online survey software products will cost more. Pricing may also vary based on the number of surveys that are sent. If the tourism organization is new to conducting surveys, it might be best to choose one of the many available free products that can be used to design and conduct surveys. This is true if the list of subjects that will be sent the survey is small and the questions relate to a single topic. As the data received from the first surveys is analyzed, it might be found that a more sophisticated survey product is needed.

Free products limit the number of survey forms that can be sent. If the organization has a very large number of emails to which the survey will be sent, they can purchase a paid version of the free product or select another.

An advantage of purchased online survey software is that it will allow more sophisticated analysis of data, such as analyzing answers for sub-segments. For example, a hotel may send out surveys to a wide range of respondents. They may want to analyse the data separately based on demographic factors such as age group or geographic location. More complex would be the need to analyze response correlations. For example, if a high percentage of respondents were unhappy with the hotel pool facilities, the software will then correlate these responses to determine if the answers varied by demographic or geographic factors. This will help determine if it was a single group who responded most negatively.

Purchased online survey software products will also vary as to what type of media can be added to the survey form. For example, a tourism attraction may have produced three different promotional videos based on the potential guests' lifestyle. They would want to use survey software that would show all three videos to ask for a reaction.

Finally, a paid version will allow for more design options that can help with the completion rate. A short ten-question survey may not need enhanced graphics to encourage completion. A long survey that is visually uninspiring may not be completed. Finally, the charts and graphs that are produced by a purchased product will also be more sophisticated and interesting.

Technical requirements

Most online survey software is very intuitive and does not require extensive training. The software usually provides tutorials on the use of the program. The tourism organization will still need to consider carefully the questions and answers, but writing each into the software is easy as templates are provided. While the software will provide statistics showing the findings of all research participants, it is still necessary for the researcher to have a basic understanding of what the statistics mean.

Posting survey links on social media

Surveys can be disseminated to research subjects using email. This allows the marketing researcher to individually choose each potential participant. The body of the email is used to explain the reason for the survey and the link to the survey site. To motivate participation a well written email should explain that the results of the survey will assist in producing a better tourism experience for future visitors. The email can also be used as a screening mechanism by describing what type of person should participate. The problem with this method of distribution is that it is limited to people for whom the organization has an email address. These are most likely people who have already visited or at least have requested information on the destination.

Another means of obtaining research participants is to send out text messages to the research sample with a link to the survey. This method works well with participants who already have a close relationship with the organization. The text message does not allow the researcher to communicate any information that would motivate participation based on altruism. It can work by including a message that the first 100 people who respond and complete the survey will receive a discount.

Social media is a third technology that can be used as a means to distribute the survey to a wider range of research participants. The difference with this method is that the marketing researcher cannot control who will respond. However, if the research is to gather opinions and not to provide a quantitative answer to a research question, then posting the survey link on social media is an option. This method has the advantage of getting a wide variety of respondents, particularly if participants are asked to share the link with friends. If there is an incentive for participation, then people are more likely to share the link.

The organization should only post on social media sites on which it is already active and has a following. These followers have demonstrated that they are interested in what the destination has to offer. If the survey is going to be posted or tweeted it should be short. Even if the link brings the research participant to the survey software, people on social media are rarely interested in spending time answering questions. It may be necessary to offer an incentive for completing the survey form. As the people who are on the organization's social media sites are interested in the destination, providing a discount should motivate completion. Another idea is to enter all those who complete the survey into contest where the prize is a free trip.

Inviting and incentivizing

Another issue that the marketing researchers must consider is the potential participant's willingness to participate. Of course, just because the organization has targeted a certain group of people as being necessary to include in the study, does not mean that the people will be interested in participating. Some motivators for participating in studies include a desire to help improve a product or experience. Some people also receive satisfaction from providing their opinion and enjoy the research process. If these are not sufficient motivators, a financial incentive can be used.

Nonprofit community organizations involved in tourism have an advantage in motivating people to participate in research studies, as the organization can explain how the research will help it fulfil its mission, which in turn helps the community. For example, an organization may want to learn how to more effectively motivate a visitor to hike a local trail. They will be able to explain to potential participants how participating in the research will improve people's health through more frequent hiking. This is not a claim that can be made by an amusement park that wants to know which amusement park thrill ride people prefer.

Some people will be willing to participate in research just because they are interested in the research process. They may enjoy the fact that the organization is seeking their opinion. For a person who may feel overlooked in everyday life, it may be flattering to have their opinion recorded. While interest in the research process is an acceptable reason for participation, the organization must be careful that a participant is someone who does not repeatedly participate in surveys. This type of participant may be more interested in expressing their own opinions than in giving careful thought to answering the survey questions.

Motivating participation with incentives

There will be occasions when the organization may want to consider providing an incentive to participate. The amusement park manager may need to provide a financial incentive to have people participate in a survey about thrill ride preference, such

Case Study 6.4: Why are they always complaining? Not all complainers are the same

Everyone knows that one bad online review may be read, and believed, by many potential visitors. As a result, all tourism related companies do their best to provide excellent service so bad reviews don't happen. And yet people do complain. It is helpful to consider the type of person who complains as the response to the complaint should fit the motivation. Below are some categories of frequent complainers.

Free stuff seekers: Unfortunately, there are people who complain in order to try to get either a price reduction or a free product. These people will always find something of which they can complain. While this happens infrequently, it is good to be aware that sometimes, the problem is not really a problem.

Consistently negative sorters: These are the people for whom not only is the glass half empty, rather than half full, they don't even like the glass. These people need to be listened to, but they don't really expect the problem to be solved.

Righteous world changers: These guests complain a lot but they view the experience of complaining as positive. They will explain that the problem doesn't bother them, but they worry about other guests. They need to be earnestly thanked for bringing the problem to the attention of management.

Simply stressed outers: These are the people who are running late, just got bad news, or wish they were at home. Traveling is not always a fun experience. These guests may complain loudly but what they need is understanding. They may come back and apologize later (Kennedy 2017).

Question: What type of research should be conducted to determine what type of complainer is most frequent?

as free tickets to the park. However, a nonprofit organization involved in tourism may not have the funding available to pay participants. In addition, they may hesitate to provide payment, feeling that to do so would be in contradiction to their organizational mission.

Incentives should not only be thought of as a form of payment. Instead they should be considered as a way to say thank you. The nonprofit tourism organization might consider offering something as simple as a t-shirt with the organization's logo that they normally sell or give away to people who make donations. If the organization sells tickets to events, they may wish to provide free attendance. These are inexpensive ways of acknowledging that the participants' time is valuable and that the organization appreciates their participation.

One issue is that to gain the incentive, the research subject will need to provide contact information. This needs to be done in a way that does not compromise anonymity (Wolff-Eisenberg 2016). One way to do so is that once the survey is completed online, the research subject can be directed to a separate form to provide an email or postal address where the incentive can be sent. In person, the research subject can be handed a separate paper form to complete.

Why people are willing to participate

- Belief research will help others
- Interest in research process
- Financial or product incentive

Using advertising to invite participation

Participants can also be found by advertising an invitation to participate. This method is used when potential participants are needed who do not have a current relationship with the organization. For example, researchers in a tourism organization may need to conduct a survey of skateboarders to determine how to attract young visitors to a local skateboard park. The researchers could tell a local skate shop that they are looking for research participants. However, this would only reach local residents who do not reflect the profile of the targeted visitor. Instead the tourism organization could purchase an online ad that will appear on websites that attract skateboard enthusiasts. The researchers may need to provide an incentive to encourage participation. The incentive, perhaps a prize of skateboard equipment, should be communicated in the advertisement.

The list of potential participants who have responded to the ad should then be asked a few short screening questions. These questions will verify if the potential research subjects meet the profile determined by the researchers.

Using social media as an invitation to participate

Another way to invite participation in the research study is to use social media. A first step would be to post the information on the organization's own website and social networking sites. If the organization uses Twitter, the information about the research study can also be tweeted. This information will reach potential participants who already have some contact with the organization as they are users of the sites. The organization may also wish to find participants who are not already involved the organization. In this case, they may also ask users of their social media sites to repost or retweet the information to their friends or others who may be interested.

If the organization wishes to reach further beyond those already involved with it, one way to do so is to use bloggers. They can blog about the need for research participants in the hope that the blog will be picked and shared by others. If research participants all share a common interest, a Meetup group may be formed. These groups meet to share the subject of interest, such as travel or leisure activities. Their group members could be approached online to ask if a researcher could attend a meeting to recruit research participants.

Crowdsourcing to find participants

While letters and emails have been the traditional means of inviting potential research subjects to participate, because people are inundated with information they may never be opened. Technology provides new means of recruiting participants. Crowdsourcing of online communities is a cheap and fast way to find research subjects. However, it tends to result in younger, computer-savvy participants, which may not be appropriate for the study. Another way that technology can be used is approaching online forums for potential research participants. The cost is low and the response is usually positive if the topic is of interest to the group. Facebook ads can also be used to find people that are willing to participate.

Providing information to participants

Once the groups have been identified and participants screened, those that meet the profile and are selected to participate will be sent a letter, email or text message. The letter or email should provide both the name of the research firm, if one is used, and also the name of the organization that is commissioning the research. In the interests of transparency, a short description of both the research firm and the organization should be provided. A webpage link, email address or telephone number should also be provided so that the participant can contact someone if they want more information on the purpose of the research.

In the letter or email the reason for conducting the research should be clearly described without using any research terminology. For example, the methodology and sampling process should not be described in technical terms. Instead, if the invitation is to participate in a focus group, the information sent should simply describe how a focus group functions, the time it requires and the place it will be held. If the invitation is to participate in an interview, the potential participant should be informed of what subjects will be discussed.

The details as to time and location should also be included in the letter. Any email should include a map link and transportation and parking options. This will ensure that the participant is able to commit to the scheduled date and location. The letter should assure the potential participant that the information obtained is confidential and that their participation will not be disclosed. The letter should provide the potential participant with a number to call or an email address if they are interested in participation. However, it may take a personal phone call, in addition to the letter, to get a commitment to participate in a focus group or interview as these take more time than a survey.

Invitation letter or email components

- Name and contact information of organization commissioning the research
- Name and contact information of research firm if used
- Name of researchers if a qualitative technique
- Purpose of research
- Research details as to when and where
- Incentives for participation

The quality of the final research recommendations depends on the quality of the research participants. When the wrong people participate in the research, the wrong strategic decision may be made. This not only loses the company money, it means that it will take longer to develop the correct strategy. Meanwhile, a competitor may have already done so. It is for these reasons that an organization may wish to use a professional recruiting firm to find participants.

References

Boyarsky, B., R. Ritter, and W. Enger. 2016. Developing a Customer-experience Vision [online]. *McKinsey & Company*, March. Retrieved 30 January 2017. Available from www.mckinsey.com/business-functions/marketing-and-sales/our-insights/developing-a-customer-experience-vision. [Accessed 30 January 2107].

CNN. 2016. How Airlines Decide What Fare You Pay [online]. *Cable News Network*, 16 September. Available from www.cnn.com/2016/09/16/aviation/airline-pricing-secrets/. [Accessed 19 December 2016].NAQ

Jong, J. D. 2016. "You Are Here." Cross-cultural Survey Guidelines [online]. *University of Michigan*. Available from ccsg.isr.umich.edu/index.php/chapters/data-collection-chapter/telephone-surveys. [Accessed 28 Apr. 2017].

Kennedy, D. 2017. Conquering Complaints – Part Two [online]. *4Hoteliers*, 11 January. Retrieved 30 January. Available from www.4hoteliers.com/features/article/10200?awsb_c=4hdm&awsb_k=dnws. [Accessed 30 January 2017].

Markelz, M. 2015. How Iceland Rode a Social Wave to Tourism Success [online]. *American Marketing Association*. July-August. Available from www.ama.org/publications/MarketingNews/Pages/how-iceland-rode-a-social-wave-to-tourism-success.aspx. [Accessed 31 January 2017].

McGeeney, K. and H. Y. Yyan. 2016. Text Message Notification for Web Surveys [online]. *Pew Research Center*. 7 September. Available from www.pewresearch.org/2016/09/07/text-message-notification-for-web-surveys/. [Accessed 28 April 2017].

Wolff-Eisenberg, C. 2016. Survey Administration Best Practices: Using Incentives Effectively [online]. ITHAKA S+R. 27 February. Available from www.sr.ithaka.org/blog/survey-administration-best-practices-using-incentives-effectively/. [Accessed 28 April 2017].

Chapter 7

Moderating focus groups

Learning objectives

- What are the benefits of conducting focus groups along with the disadvantages?
- What process should be followed when conducting a focus group in person or online?
- Why are logistical issues, an understanding of group dynamics, and techniques for encouraging interaction necessary for a successful focus group?
- How can a moderator encourage group interaction while preventing group conflict?

Chapter summary

- Focus groups are used when organizations need to answer the question of why that includes visitor behavior and desires. The advantage of a focus group is that it allows the exploration of issues in depth. In addition, the interaction between focus group members can spark new ideas. The disadvantages of a focus group are that the results cannnot be used to prove facts and their analysis depends on the skill of the moderator.
- A focus group is not just a conversation but must follow a process. Obtaining useful information requires advance preparation and a skilled moderator. The focus group process involves three stages of preparation, conducting and analysis. Each stage includes a method followed by prepared questions and techniques. Focus groups can also be conducted online where technology is used to replicate personal interaction.
- Researchers need to address logistical issues, such as venue, that will help ensure focus group success. In addition, the stages of group development – forming, storming, norming and performing – need to be understood so as to minimize

conflict. Tools for increasing interaction, such as projective techniques, will also need to be planned.

- The moderator of a focus group needs personal skills and the ability to resolve group conflict. The personal traits that are necessary in a moderator include interest in the research process, curiosity about people's ideas, adaptability and empathy. The skills of a successful moderator include knowledge of research methods, the topic under discussion, group dynamics and the ability to analyze and report the findings.

Using focus groups

Focus groups are a qualitative research technique that uses participant interaction to uncover consumers' attitudes, opinions and values. Because an issue or problem is being explored, focus groups are considered exploratory research. They are often used when little is known about external trends, consumer preferences or the cause of a problem. Once focus groups have been used as a first step in exploring an issue, the findings can be confirmed using a quantitative research technique such as a survey.

Focus groups are sometimes misunderstood as mere discussion groups where people just talk while a moderator listens. However, a focus group conducted by a trained moderator can encourage participants to go beyond their first response to the issue being discussed. Interaction between the group members is used to uncover deeper insights which can result in new and creative ideas for the marketing mix. The insights revealed by a focus group can then be used to build support within the organization for the new ideas.

Focus group research questions

Because the employees of a tourism, hospitality or event management organization can only see a problem or issue from their own viewpoint, it is extremely helpful to get the opinions of current or potential visitors. For example, if attendance is falling at the annual heritage fair, the organization might consider the problem to be lack of promotion of the event. Rather than decide this assumption is correct, it would be more helpful to ask the opinions of potential attendees. By conducting a focus group, the organization might learn that people are aware of the event but do not attend as there is limited opportunity for participation. Using this information, the organization could then improve the visit experience.

While the organization might think in terms of targeting groups demographically, there is a growing trend to target psychographically based on shared lifestyles, attitudes or values. Focus groups can be used to learn what psychographic groups might be interested in the tourism experience. For example, a focus group of visitors to a community might discover that they are interested in wellness. The tourism promotion organization could then decide to target a visitor segment that has a healthy lifestyle. To do so they can promote their hiking trails not only as a way to see the local natural beauty but also a way to exercise. Healthy local food options would also then be promoted at this segment of travelers.

A focus group can help the tourism organization package a destination or experience to make it more appealing to visitors. To do so an in-depth conversation needs to take place on how visitors experience a destination or event. By using insights from potential visitors, the organization has a better chance of having their tourism product or service be successful. For example, an arts organization may have decided to offer painting classes to visitors. A focus group with visitors could be used to learn visitor preference as to the time and day of the classes, where they should be located, how long they should last and what other inducements, whether dessert and coffee or wine and cheese, should be added. The focus group participant input will be used to package the product so it is as appealing as possible.

A final purpose for having a focus group is to gain new insights as to how the tourism organization can best communicate with the current and potential visitors. The organization cannot know what marketing message to use and with what media it should be communicated without input from those in the target market segment of visitors it is trying to reach. After all, only those who are on the receiving end of the message can know what words and visuals should be used to describe the benefits in a way that will motivate a visit.

Purposes of conducting focus groups

- Exploring the cause of a problem or issue
- New psychographic market segments to target
- Enhancing the product to increase its appeal
- Developing effective promotional campaigns

Advantages of focus groups

Quantitative research methods answer the questions of who, what, how many and how often. Only qualitative research answers the question of why. Focus groups are particularly useful when wanting to get beyond a participant's first answer by asking probing follow-up questions. Because tourism organizations often offer experiences that have an emotional meaning, it is important to understand people's reaction to the destination, attraction or event.

For example, a local yoga studio may want to know how to attract tourists. If they surveyed visitors they might receive the response that people are not interested because they believe taking a class would not be an exciting experience. This information does not solve the problem. Only in a focus group can the moderator ask probing questions to discover how the yoga classes could be made more exciting for visitors. The moderator might explore whether the location of the class, such as being outdoors, would change the perception. Continually probing for additional responses may uncover the fact that people feel intimidated by attending as they believe that yoga is only for a certain type of person. The moderator can then explore how to make people feel less intimidated.

An additional advantage of conducting focus groups is that they can be combined with other research methodologies such as projective techniques, which will be discussed in detail in the next chapter. The organization may have thought long and hard over what questions to ask research participants. However, to the participants the question comes as a surprise and they may have difficulty providing a response. A focus group can be combined with projective techniques that provide the participants with a nonverbal means of answering a question. For example, the focus group

Case Study 7.1: How many robots are too many?

Guests already expect hotels and attractions to use technology. They demand free Wi-Fi and want to check in online. They like keyless entry and text reminders of upcoming stays. Now technology is being used to replace people with standard tasks. Hotels are starting to use robots to provide services such as cleaning rooms and room service delivery. A 'Maidbot' can be rented for $2,000 a month to clean hotel rooms. This is cheaper than hiring an employee and the Maidbot does not need to be paid overtime or won't call in sick. (Although it might take time off for a systems failure!)

Robots are also being used as butlers for room delivery of small objects such as bottled water. The time from request to delivery is only four minutes. It is thought that such robots will become standard in the next five years.

The question is how much human interaction should be replaced? With online check-in and check-out and now robots doing the delivery, a hotel guest might never interact with a real person. People are enjoying interacting with the robots as they are often showing up online in selfies. (Taken by the guest, not the robot – at least so far!) The question is, do hotel guests still want to interact with human staff (King 2017)?

Question: What type of method should be conducted to research this question?

participants might be asked to list on a card the first three words that come to mind about the destination. An even more creative, and fun, task would be to have the participants help design the information that should be on the website. In addition, these techniques will help participants to think creatively and should result in more thoughtful discussions.

Advantages of conducting focus groups

- Probes issues in depth
- Interaction between participants can spark new ideas
- Combine with projective techniques

Disadvantages of focus groups

The data that a focus group collects are words and sometimes images, but not quantitative data that can be statistically analyzed. The researchers should also understand that while the information collected in a focus group can be very helpful in making decisions on what visitors to target along with product and promotion ideas, they should not be the only basis for such decisions. If a focus group has provided input that suggests a drastic or expensive change to the current marketing mix, this idea should be further researched using a quantitative technique before proceeding with the change. The number of people in a focus group is too small to generalize the findings to the entire population. For example, if focus group participants feel that visitors would be willing to pay more for admission to an event, this should be confirmed with a large-scale survey before a price change is implemented.

Another disadvantage that is inherent in the focus group methodology is the fact that the results that are obtained depend on the skill of the moderator. A well moderated focus group can provide useful information. However, an unskilled moderator will be unable to use follow-up questions to move beyond the participants' initial responses to uncover underlying ideas. Worse, a poor moderator may result in a group where disagreement turns into conflict and the participants will leave with a poor impression of the organization based on the choice of moderator.

Disadvantages of conducting focus groups

- Can't be used to prove facts
- Results depend on skill of moderator

Focus group process

A successful focus group that provides insightful information for the organization requires preparation. A focus group conducted by a skilled moderator may seem effortless. However as with many skilled activities, the sense of effortlessness derives from the fact that a great deal of time has gone into the design and planning of the group. The focus group process involves three stages of preparation, conducting and analysis.

Focus group process

- Preparation
  - discuss issues
  - decide participant profile
  - choose moderator
  - write focus group script
- Conducting
  - prepare facility
  - prepare materials and techniques
  - moderate proceedings
  - collect and organize data
- Analysis
  - transcribe information
  - organize written data and code for themes
  - write report with recommendations
  - make presentation

Preparation

The first step in preparing to conduct a focus group is to hold a meeting with everyone, both in the organization and external stakeholders who have an interest in the research findings. By having everyone who has a stake in the outcome of the

Case Study 7.2: They say they want it but then don't use it

The hospitality industry knows it needs to conduct research and many organizations do so. In fact, a hotel organization conducted a survey on what amenities people want when they visit a hotel. A majority of survey respondents stated that they wanted to be able to work out while on a trip so hotels have been installing fitness centers. These centers are costly not just for the initial outlay of design and equipment but also the ongoing expense of staffing and maintenance.

However, it has been found that while 46 per cent of guests said that they would use the fitness centers, only 22 per cent did so. The higher end the hotel, the less likely people are to use the equipment even though they said they planned to do so.

The report's conclusion? That hotels would be better served by observing the guests' actual usage behavior than relying on survey results. People do not always act the way they say they are going to (Stein 2017).

Question: What other guest behavior could be observed so that hotels make the right investment in amenities?

research involved in the planning, they will be motivated to act on the recommendations that result from the research.

While the research question may already have been determined, it is now necessary to decide exactly what issues should be discussed in the focus group. For example, a focus group on attitudes toward establishing a local carnival might be designed to address the research question on what would motivate visitors to attend. This general question then might be broken down into subject areas of perceptions of carnival as a family experience, the type of activities that should be included and what promotional message should be used. As many issues as possible should be developed as these would be the bases for the focus group script.

After the focus group discussion topics have been chosen, the next step in the process is to develop the participant profile. Because fewer participants will be involved in a focus group than in a survey, it is especially important that the correct participants be chosen. A focus group needs to have participants that have some similar characteristics to promote interaction.

Choosing an appropriate moderator is part of the preparation process. A larger tourism organization may have an employee who can perform this function. If not, it may be necessary to recruit someone from outside the organization to act as moderator. If the funds are available, the organization can hire a professional moderator. If these options are not available, the organization may wish to contact a nearby educational institution to determine if they have someone on staff who is willing to provide assistance.

The final step is to write the focus group script. Stakeholders involved in design of the focus group may want to include more topic areas than can be covered in the session. However, only a few topics should be covered as an hour-long focus group session with eight participants does not result in eight hours of discussion, but only one. In addition, the focus group topics must be related. If a focus group is to be successful, it cannot jump from one topic to another. It takes time to develop the rapport that makes the participants willing to discuss challenging issues.

A focus group script should follow the three stages of building rapport, probing and closing. The first stage is used to introduce the members to the subject and then present them with an easy to answer question. The focus group moderator will then ask more challenging questions. The focus group will move on to a concluding question. Once the script has been prepared, it will be reviewed by management to ensure it adequately covers the topics under discussion.

Sample focus group script for visitor center project

- Building rapport: relax and bond group and connect group to subject
  - Method: welcome and general discussion
  - Question: What is your experience of using Visitor Centers?
  - Technique: hand out cards asking participants to write down the first three words that come to mind when they hear 'Visitor Center.'
- Probing: uncover information useful to answering research questions
  - Method: general discussion followed by projective techniques
  - Question: If you could design the services offered, what type of services would you include?
  - Technique: ideas generated by participants will be listed on large pieces of paper. Each participant will then be given a gold, silver and bronze sticker to use to vote for their favorite ideas
- Closing: move group towards closure
  - Method: general discussion followed by projective technique
  - Question: How should the Visitor Center promote to tourists?
  - Technique: ask participants to complete an advertisement for the Center by listing the benefits

Conducting

Once the preparation is completed, the organization will be ready to conduct the focus group. To ensure that the moderator will be able to focus on what is being said, all the materials should be prepared in advance. The materials for any projective techniques, such as cards, pens, and poster paper should be stocked. A means of recording the proceedings should be ready so that the moderator does not need to take notes during the session. A focus group may even be videoed if all the participants are comfortable with this method. While a video is helpful in reviewing, not only what people said, but also their body language, some people may feel constrained if they know they are being videoed.

Of course, the process includes moderating the focus group. The task is challenging, as a skilled moderator has to be aware of what people are saying at the same time they are planning their next question. After the conclusion of the group, the moderator must collect and organize the data. This includes making sure that the digital tape is properly labeled as to date, time and purpose of group. In addition, all written material will need to be labeled.

Analysis

After the focus group has been completed, the tapes must be transcribed. While there is software that will turn an audio recording into a text file, there is a significant advantage to listening to the tape. It is often the tone of voice and speed of speaking that reveals the emotional content of words. Any written information on cards and paper should be either typed or scanned for analysis. All of this information is then coded for common themes. With this information as a reference a written report with recommendations will be prepared. In addition, a presentation must be prepared.

Online focus groups

Technology has been successfully used to conduct quantitative research. Using software to write and distribute a survey online is now considered standard procedure. Digital methods of communication are now also being used to conduct qualitative research, such as interviews and focus groups. In fact, when holding focus groups to discuss the benefits of digital products or the effectiveness of social media promotion, online might be the preferred option (Carpenter 2014). People targeted with digital products and promotion will already be comfortable interacting using technology. They might view the necessity of all being in the same physical location at the same time to share opinions as unnecessarily constricting.

Digital methods of conducting focus groups using website chat rooms of existing groups or links created expressly for the occasion take the place of person-to-person communication. When using this approach the researcher and subject can communicate in real time or the researcher can leave the questions for participants to answer to a time of their convenience. Using webcams or other video technology people will be able to see and interact with each other and the researcher.

Asynchronous online focus groups are sometimes referred to as bulletin board focus groups. The advantage is that the participants and group moderator do not need to be present at the same time. Using methods, such as Google Hangouts, the moderator posts questions to which the focus group members respond (Stewart and Shamdasani 2017). The members also respond to the comments of others, duplicating the interaction that would take place when conducting a focus group in person. Online focus groups can also be conducted synchronously using Skype or some other form of video chat program. This has the advantage of enabling people to see each other's body language. The disadvantage is that if the focus group participants live in different time zones, scheduling can be difficult.

Digital methods try to replicate as closely as possible the personal interaction that takes place face to face. There are advantages to using online methods for focus groups and interviews. First, there are no geographic limitations to who can be involved. Second, people can interact from the comfort of their own home or office. Because they are in familiar surroundings, their reactions may be more natural and honest. Having the focus group or interview online allows the researcher to include photos, images and video clips for comments. There is also a cost savings because focus members will not need to be paid for any travel or meal expenses. However, the disadvantage is that the participants are limited to those who have, and are comfortable using, the necessary technology.

Managing focus group interaction

Once the planning of the focus group has been completed, the researchers can move to addressing logistical issues that will help ensure success. A marketing research firm may have a special facility just for conducting focus groups. This facility would have a reception room where participants would be greeted, with a separate room with projective equipment for showing video clips, electronic whiteboards and other high tech equipment. Attached to the focus group room would be an additional room that would be used for viewing the focus group through a one-way window. This room would be used by management to watch the focus group as it is being conducted.

However there is no need to have such a specialized facility. In fact such a facility, by being so professional, may intimidate some participants. A focus group can be held in any location where eight to ten people can be comfortably seated. In fact, the researchers should consider holding a focus group at the location that is most convenient for the participants. This could be a hotel conference room, at a visitor center, or even at a restaurant. If any technical equipment is needed this can be brought in from other locations.

Besides convenience, another reason for conducting the focus group at a location that is familiar to the participants is that it builds trust and acknowledges that the participant is taking time from their busy holiday to be a research subject. For example, research about branding of a community would need to be conducted using visitors as participants. The tourism organization needs the ideas of these visitors much more than the visitors need to be involved in the research. Conducting the focus group at a nice restaurant where refreshments are provided demonstrates to the participants that their views are important and will be taken seriously.

Figure 7.1 Focus groups should be held in a location that is convenient for participants.
Photo Credit: Pack-Shot

The moderator should arrive early to ensure that seating is available. The seating should be placed around a table if the moderator will be using projective techniques that require writing. Refreshments should be available even if it is just something to drink. Offering refreshments is a way of welcoming the participants and also provides a common activity that helps to bring people together. The researcher should have a supply of writing paper, various markers and also pens. Large pads of self-stick paper should be available that can be placed on any wall surface, written on and then easily removed. If any special materials are needed for projective techniques there should be adequate supplies available. Lastly, the researcher should have a recorder for taping the proceedings.

Once the room has been prepared the moderator is ready to greet the participants. Making the participants feel both welcome and at ease is critical to the success of a focus group. The welcome should be sincere as without the involvement of the participants, the research would be impossible. Although the moderator might have been through the focus group process numerous times, it may very well be a new experience for the participants. The moderator should inform them of the seating arrangements, the availability of refreshments and the location of any needed facilities.

Once all the participants are seated, introductions should be made. Depending on the situation, only first names or both first and last names, may be used. The moderator should now explain the purpose of the research and the topics that will be covered. The moderator should also explain that the proceedings will be taped, but that the tapes and any other material produced will only be used by those involved in the research. In addition, participants should be reassured that no names will be used in the final report so all information will be held in confidence. Finally, the moderator should inform the participants that they can receive a summary of the findings of the research if they are interested.

Stages

The moderator is now ready to start the focus group. A focus group usually lasts from one hour to 90 minutes. The first few minutes will be the used in building rapport. Most of the time will be spent asking probing and follow-up questions. The focus group will then move to the closing stage.

The first part of the focus group is used to build rapport between the moderator and the participants. After introductions, the first questions asked should be easy ones that pertain to experiences or knowledge all of the participants share, such as where they are from, as they will all be visitors to the area. Starting the focus group with challenging questions, such as whether they plan to return to the destination, may intimidate the participants and result in less interaction throughout the remainder of the group session.

It is the moderator's responsibility to encourage active participation while at the same time not making any of the participants feel pressured to speak. This is the 'art' that the moderator performs that may not be understood by others. The moderator must watch and assess the facial expressions of any quiet group members to gauge when will be the right time to encourage them to speak. By keeping the early questions easy to answer and non-threatening and encouraging everyone to speak, the moderator prepares the participants for more challenging questions later in the focus group.

After the initial stage of the focus group, the moderator will move to more probing questions. These are questions that ask the participants to explore more deeply their

Case Study 7.3: Is it a bar? A travel agency? Or both?

In the past the only way to book a trip was to use a professional travel agency who had the knowledge and the tools to make the airplane reservation. Today it is hard to imagine a world where the only way to find out information was from a travel professional. The number of travel agencies peaked in the United States in 1997. Less than half were in business in 2012 because people could find information and book everything online.

Why then are some travel agencies making a comeback? Because now there is too much information! Travelers no longer have the time to wade through it all to create their own individualized travel experience. The busy Millennial does not have time to do their own taxes, shop for their groceries or clean their home. They rely on professionals for these tasks for which they either are not equipped or do not have the time. Now it is time for the resurgence of the travel agency!

Called by different brand names, but often referred to as Departure Lounges, it is a travel agency that looks like an upscale bar and sells craft beer, wine and cocktails. They also have travel consultants who will take over the task of designing a personalized itinerary. These new types of travel agencies also hold special nights to learn about travel to exotic locations. In addition, family events are held where dolls and books from other countries are available. Does it work? Eighty per cent of clients who come in to meet with a travel consultant end up booking a trip. The average cost of the trip is $10,000! There are no fees for the traveler, but the departure lounges do make money on the high priced drinks they sell. If you are going to book at $10,000 trip you are not going to complain about the cost of a drink (McCartney 2017).

Question: What questions would you ask in a focus group if you were exploring the possibility of opening such a lounge?

attitudes, opinions and ideas. For example, they may be asked about their motivation for a visit. In addition, probing questions ask participants to imagine a reality different in some way from what they experienced. For example, visitors may be asked if they would like timed tickets to an attraction that would help avoid crowding but that limit flexibility. These questions don't just ask 'why', they also ask 'what if'. This probing stage will take up most of the time of the focus group. These questions, because they are challenging, may require follow-up questions to clarify the participant's meaning.

Sample probing questions:

- Tell me more?
- When did you start to feel this way?
- Can you clarify what you mean when you say 'boring'?

During the focus group, not only will the moderator interact with the participants, the moderator will also encourage conversation between members. The moderator can do so by asking participants to respond to each other's questions.

Sample questions to encourage conversation

- Do you agree with what Kim has just said about the hotel front desk staff?
- Have you also had this experience when waiting for the visitor trolley?
- What do you think of the idea of using virtual reality for promotion?
- Do you have a different solution than Sean's to the lack of affordable activities?

The moderator will use these techniques to encourage everyone to become involved. However, the moderator should never push participants to speak when they seem uncomfortable. Even though the conversation should always be nonthreatening, a question may have resulted in an unpleasant memory that the participant does not wish to share. A moderator is not acting as a psychologist trying to have participants share thoughts and memories that are troubling or painful. The purpose of a focus group is research, not therapy.

The moderator should also be aware of the possibility of conflict between the participants. While a conversation may become intense, it should never be allowed to cross the line into anger. It is the moderator's responsibility to watch for signs of personal animosity between the participants and defuse it immediately. For example, someone might mention in a focus group that they find the presence of so many young (or old) visitors on the beach unappealing. This might result in a strong response from other participants. The moderator first should acknowledge that the participants have strong responses to the topic. The moderator should then remind the participants that the purpose of the focus group is to provide helpful input. If the moderator does not defuse the anger, the other participants will feel uncomfortable and stop participating.

With about ten minutes remaining in the focus group, the moderator will move to the closing stage. The moderator will use this time to gather final thoughts or ideas. The closing stage also allows the participants to disengage from what may have been an intense experience. This time should also be used to thank the participants for their assistance. Besides just general thanks, the moderator should mention one or

Figure 7.2 Focus groups can include conflict when strong opinions are shared.
Photo Credit: Stella Levi

two of the ideas that were generated during the group that the tourism organization may find particularly useful. The participants should leave with the feeling that the time and effort they have contributed has been helpful. Finally, the moderator will remind the participants that they may get a summary of the research findings if they so wish. The only task remaining is for the moderator to collect and label any written material that was produced during the focus group process.

Interaction

During the probing stage the moderator may use various methods to help the participants articulate their ideas. If the focus group is discussing the image of a destination, the moderator may have photos to view. If the focus group is being asked to address how to increase bookings for local walking tours, one issue that might be discussed would be what type of promotion should be used. Having sample website home pages available for the participants to examine will help prompt answers.

If the issue being discussed is layout of the hotel's business center, showing a visual of the proposed layout would be helpful. Another example is when a focus group is being used to judge the visitor reaction to a controversial new art gallery show. A short video clip of the art the gallery will display could be shown to the participants rather than have the moderator attempt to explain the work

When ideas are being discussed during the focus groups, they can be listed on large sheets of paper for everyone to view. The reason for this technique is so that the participants have a reminder of what has been said. The lists can then be organized to summarize comments by themes. The moderator can then ask if anything of importance is missing. Another useful technique is for the moderator is to ask the participants to prioritize what is listed. This can be done by giving the participants different color labels to place by the items they consider first, second and third in importance. This not only provides valuable insights; it also gets the participants up and moving. If the participants cannot or do not wish to move, the assistant can

Figure 7.3 It is the interaction between focus group participants that provides the best information.

Photo Credit: Stella Levi

123

place the stickers on the items. Finally, these lists will be useful for the moderator when using analyzing the proceedings.

Simple projective techniques, such as asking the participants to write down the first three words they think of when the city's or attraction's name is mentioned, are excellent ways to have everyone participate and start the conversation flowing. However, the moderator can develop her or his own task. Using the example of the focus group on redesigning the hotel's business center, the participants could be give a blueprint and cutouts of various types of furniture and asked to create their own floor plans.

Managing conflict

The success of a focus group is dependent on the skill of the moderator. Even with the right questions and participants, if the moderator is unskilled, the focus group will not obtain the needed information. The characteristics of successful moderators include both innate personal traits and skills that have been learned. The personal traits that are necessary in a moderator include interest in the research process, curiosity about people's ideas, adaptability and empathy. The skills of a successful moderator include knowledge of research methods, the topic under discussion, group dynamics and the ability to analyze and report the findings.

Personal traits

Some of the characteristics that determine whether a person will be a successful focus group moderator are inborn and can't be learned. It is easy to be interested and enthusiastic the first or second time someone runs a focus group to discuss the branding of a hotel, event or destination. However it becomes progressively more difficult for the remaining groups. For this reason the moderator must be interested in the process of research as it will provide useful information for the tourism organization. If this is true, the moderator will approach each focus group with enthusiasm.

Successful moderators are interested in people's ideas. This is actually a different trait than being interested in people. The moderator is not a therapist who is going to explore the life stories and feelings of the participants. The personal life of participants is only relevant in regard to how it affects their attitudes and opinions about the destination or event. Instead the moderator wants to learn more about their ideas. In fact, too much emphasis on the emotions of the participants can lead moderators into situations they are not trained to handle.

Successful moderators need to be adaptable to whatever situation arises during the research process. While moderators must come to the session with a script prepared, they must also be able to change their approach as needed. For example, a focus group might have been planned to discuss what activities families would enjoy during a visit. However, the focus group members might stress that teens need additional separate activities. The moderator must then focus the discussion on the type of activities that would interest teens while on holiday.

Finally, moderators must have empathy with the focus group participants. Empathy includes both understanding and compassion. At times the focus group participants will be from a community or practice a lifestyle with which the moderator is unfamiliar. The moderator must be able to look past the differences to understand the common elements that bind all people together. For example, if the focus

Case Study 7.4: It started with a TV show

Potential visitors might have known that the city of Nashville is the home of country music and the Grand Ole Opry. The TV show Nashville, about attractive young musicians struggling to make it big in the country music industry, changed all this image. Filmed in Nashville, it showed iconic sites such as the honky-tonk bars on lower Broadway and the Bluebird Café where singer songwriters perform. The TV show is now seen in over 100 countries.

Since the TV show introduced this new image of a youthful, fun city, Nashville has seen a 45 per cent increase in visitors and has become known as a destination for bachelorette parties. But are they coming because of the show? Survey research of visitors found that 20 per cent of visitors who watched the show said it was the motivating factor for planning their trip to Nashville. It also found that these visitors stayed longer and spent 23 per cent more money during their visit. While in Nashville they want to see the sites that were shown in the TV show and special tours have been developed to help them do so (Hodak 2015).

Question: How could a focus group get participants to discuss their motivation for visiting?

group is of older visitors, a moderator who is young must still be able to appreciate them as individuals.

Personal traits of a successful moderator

- Interest in research process
- Curiosity about people's ideas
- Adaptability during the focus group
- Empathy for members of all groups

Needed skills

Successful focus group moderators should understand the uses and limitations of all qualitative and quantitative techniques. This knowledge is necessary so that focus group moderators will know when they are being asked to conduct research that is better handled by another technique. For example, a restaurant might decide they need a focus group to determine what food items are preferred. However this task, which does not require in-depth discussion, can be handled best by use of a survey. If the restaurant wants to understand people's attitudes toward genetically modified food, a focus group is appropriate.

Successful focus group moderators will familiarize themselves with the research topic under study. This knowledge will help ensure the success of a group because the moderator will be familiar with any terminology used by focus group participants. For example, a focus group on carnival attendance should be familiar with the different types and cultural meanings of carnivals. They will also be better able to explore any underlying issues that the participants may be avoiding. For example, a focus group on carnival festival attendance might find the participants stating that they don't attend because they can't afford the ticket price. The moderator should already be aware that the festival has low priced tickets and also that most people will give a high price as a reason for nonattendance. With this knowledge, the moderator will continue to probe, even after receiving the first response, to get at the underlying reason for nonattendance.

It is essential that the moderator be skilled in group dynamics. A successful moderator will understand that disagreement is part of the focus group process. If everyone during the focus group session is in agreement, nothing new will be learned. Successful moderators are not frightened of conflict. Instead they know how to use disagreement to discover ideas without allowing disagreement to degenerate into personal insults. The moderator will keep the group focused on the ideas and never allow personal attacks.

Finally, in addition to the skills necessary to conduct a group, the moderator must also have the ability to analyze and report the findings. With other methodologies, the tasks of conducting the study and analyzing the findings can be separated. The person who writes a survey form does not need to be the person who analyzes the statistical results. However, with focus groups it is not enough to have someone else listen to the tapes and analyze what was said. The insights of the moderator are critical to understanding the findings. How people respond to a question, even their silences, provide critical insights that help to answer the research question.

Skills needed by a successful moderator

- Knowledge of research methods
- Knowledge of the topic under discussion
- Skill in group dynamics
- Ability to analyze and report

Managing group conflict

While a focus group moderator should not be afraid of disagreement, it is their responsibility to never let disagreement cross the line into conflict. A source of conflict is inappropriate behavior by group members. This might include participants who try to dominate the group by continually talking and participants who believe they are experts on the topic. This type of conflict results from the personality of the participant. The second source of conflict is inherent in the group process itself.

Difficult participants

While it would be wonderful if every participant was an emotionally mature adult whose only purpose in attending the group was to further the cause of research, this will not be the case. In every focus group there will be participants who will require extra attention. Two of the most common sources of conflict are the incessant talker and the group expert.

Incessant talkers usually have a strong need for attention. If not controlled, they will tend to dominate the other participants and cause feelings of resentment. A skilled moderator will become aware of the presence of such a participant early in the process. These participants usually tend to spend more time talking even when first introducing themselves to the group. During the group they will insert themselves in the conversation even when others are making important comments. Once moderators become aware that a participant is an incessant talker, they must step in to redirect the conversation when necessary. They will need to kindly but firmly interrupt the talker with a simple statement such as, 'Thanks for the interesting idea for tourism promotion but I am going to ask Maria to first finish her comment. And then let's hear what others think.' The moderator will need to continue to use this technique as incessant talkers rarely have the self-awareness to understand they are dominating the conversation.

Sometimes participants will take on the role of group expert. They will assume that only they know the right answer to any question, perhaps because of their background. For example, because they work in marketing, they will feel they have the only good idea on the type of social media that should be used to communicate a marketing message. This type of participant will even tend to correct the ideas of other participants. If the expert speaks in a knowledgeable manner, the other participants may defer to their judgment and stop providing their own insights. Or, the other participants may start to feel resentful and argue with the self-proclaimed expert. The moderator's responsibility is to provide support that all participants' opinions are equally welcome and valid. A statement such as, 'Joe thanks for your thoughts on marketing, but Maria's opinions are also important; Maria can you tell us more about your social media idea?' may need to be used.

Group formation

All groups go through predictable stages. The stages in this process are inherent to how people communicate and interact socially and can't, and shouldn't, be avoided. For this reason the moderator should have some knowledge of group dynamics. One of the most common theories was developed by studying the formation of work groups. However it is also useful in understanding how focus group dynamics work. The Tuckman model describes four stages of group development; forming, storming, norming and performing (Priestly 2015).

According to this model all groups start with the forming stage. During this period the group members, who are strangers, make quick judgments about each other. This is a predictable and necessary step so that they can make decisions on how to treat each other. During the forming stage, each participant will decide who they like, who they dislike, who they trust and who they don't trust. These decisions are based on past interactions and may have no bearing on the present reality. For example, participants who have children in the same age group tend to immediately bond.

The moderator can help the group through this stage by relating a positive characteristic about each participant and why they were chosen to be part of the group. The goal would be to reinforce the legitimacy of each participant's involvement in the process while still allowing people to form their own opinions of the other participants.

During the storming stage the group members will state strong opinions that may be in disagreement with the opinions of others. For example, a participant may state that children should not be allowed in the hotel pool as they are too noisy and rude. Participants who have children may immediately react negatively as they feel their children are being attacked as rude and noisy. In fact, an argument may ensue about the proper behavior of children. That participants have strong feelings and opinions is a positive sign that the focus group could result in new and interesting findings. All participants must feel that the moderator is in charge of the situation and will defuse any disagreement that may escalate.

Moderators handle this stage by not getting caught up in the conflict themselves. The moderator handles the storming stage by acknowledging and even thanking all arguing participants for their ideas. The moderator then reminds the participants of the larger purpose of the group, which may be to ensure that all hotel guests have a positive experience and refocuses the discussion at the proper emotional level. They use their skill to move the group to the norming stage where everyone understands the limitations that will be placed on individual members.

Once all the participants understand that the moderator will not let the conversation degenerate into personal animosity, the group enters into its performing stage where the real work of the focus group can be accomplished. It is in this stage that the idea might be developed of separate pool hours for families that would include fun activities.

Stages of group dynamics

- Forming: participants meet and make snap decision about each other based on past experiences.
- Storming: snap decision can result in argumentative behavior.
- Norming: moderator establishes behavior limitations.
- Performing: group can now get to work on task.

References

Carpenter, R. 2014. Focus Groups in a Digital Marketing Age [online]. *Digital Current* 3 October. Web. 2 May 2017. Available from www.digitalcurrent.com/digital-marketing/focus-groups-in-digital-age/. [Accessed 2 May 2017].

Hodak, B. 2015. The Real-Life Impact of ABC's 'Nashville' [online]. *Forbes Magazine*, 29 October. Available from www.forbes.com/sites/brittanyhodak/2015/10/28/the-real-life-impact-of-abcs-nashville/#1e2d1b3c1e2d. [Accessed 28 March 2017].

King, D. 2017. Robots the Talk of Tech Innovations at Hospitality Summit [online]. Travel Weekly. *Northstar Travel Media*, 2 February. Avaiable from www.travelweekly.com/Travel-News/Hotel-News/Robots-the-talk-of-tech-innovations-at-hospitality-summit. [Accessed 3 February 2017].

McCartney, S. 2017. No, Really, That's a Travel Agency [online]. *The Wall Street Journal*. Dow Jones & Company, 15 February. Available from www.wsj.com/articles/no-really-thats-a-travel-agency-1487174530. [Accessed 17 March 2017].

Priestley, D. 2015. Forming, Storming, Norming and Performing: The Stages of Team Formation [online]. *Venture Team Building* 11 August. Available from www.ventureteambuilding.co.uk/forming-storming-norming-performing/. [Accessed 2 May 2017].

Stewart, D. and P. Shamdasani. 2017. Online Focus Groups, *Journal of Advertising*, 46:1, 48–60.

Stein, J. 2017. Using the Stages of Team Development [online]. *HR at MIT*. Available from hrweb.mit.edu/learning-development/learning-topics/teams/articles/stages-development. [Accessed 03 February 2017].

Chapter 8

Managing projective techniques and observation research

Learning objectives

- What are the advantages and disadvantages of using projective techniques alone or with other methods?
- How can creative tasks be used to get nonverbal responses from research participants?
- Why does observation research obtain more accurate information than other techniques?
- What methods can be used to conduct observation research?

Chapter summary

- Projective techniques can be used to obtain emotional rather than rational responses from research participants. They also have the advantage of allowing the participants to provide information anonymously. While they can be used on their own they can also help to make other research techniques more interactive and engaging.
- Completion projective techniques, which ask the participant to complete a task started by the researcher, include sentence, story and cartoon completion. Creative tasks are more challenging and include word association, drawing, and program or ad creation. Other projective techniques can be created by the researcher.
- Observational research is used to watch what consumers actually do, as against asking them what they do. This research method works well when participants do not recall behavior or it is inconvenient to ask people. Another use of observational research is when the potential participants would not be willing to provide verbal information. Observational research can be conducted as complete observer, participant observer or complete participant.
- To conduct observations, the researcher must first decide upon the behavior to observe and develop a participant profile. The researcher must then find a site

where these participants can be found and then determine the best times to conduct the observation. An observation form must be prepared and observers must be chosen and trained.

Projective techniques

Projective techniques allow the participants to provide nonverbal answers to research questions. Instead of responding with the spoken word, the participant answers through writing or drawing. The method is based on the psychological concept that people may be willing but unable to describe in words their emotional state (Furnham 2014). These tasks are creative tasks that research participants may enjoy. Projective techniques can be used on their own or they can be used in focus groups to enliven interaction. Both completion and creative tasks can be used in focus groups or in-depth interviews.

Advantages and disadvantages of projective techniques

There are three advantages for considering using projective techniques either alone or with another research methodology. First, they obtain emotional insights rather than factual information. When participants answer a question verbally they have time to consider a rational response. Projective techniques tap into feelings at the emotional level. For example, when asked a verbal question about the image of a city, the participant might have trouble trying to explain their reaction, but choosing from among images would be easier. The information that is written or drawn may reveal feelings or ideas of which the participant is unaware or would have difficulty verbalizing.

Projective techniques also allow participants to respond anonymously to sensitive issues. Rather than have to speak up in front of other participants, their ideas can be written on a card. All the cards can then be collected by the researcher who lists them for the participants to see without attributing the comments to any specific individual. For example, many research visitors may not wish to be rude by stating a negative reaction to a destination. Projective techniques allow participants to express themselves more freely. This is especially important when participants are expected to reveal negative information about their own behavior. For example, if participants are asked verbally how much they tip at hotels or restaurants, they may all answer with a high estimate, while on paper they may write the true figure. It is not that people want to be dishonest; it is just that they have trouble admitting the truth that they are cheap tippers. If everyone responds in writing and the researcher reads the responses, everyone can feel comfortable discussing the reason why they don't tip.

The third reason for using projective techniques is that they are interactive. Technology allows people to multi-task by providing many sources of instant access to information and entertainment. People can listen to their choice of music or watch television while also performing other tasks. Their smartphones allow people to access information in small bits that are quickly read and they can then move on to the next topic that strikes them as interesting. As a result, people have short attention spans. The idea that participants will be able to stay focused simply discussing a topic for an hour or an hour and a half is unrealistic. This is

Case Study 8.1: Hotels with technology just like home

The use of technology continues to increase in hotels for a number of reasons. First, although there is the initial investment cost, personnel costs are lower. Second, people want a personalized experience which technology can help deliver. Finally, hotels have always tried to be a home away from home and nowadays, home is full of technology.

- You don't need a key to open your car door, why should you need one to open your hotel room door? Some hotels now allow you not only to check in on your phone but then also to use your phone as your key. Just wave the phone at the door and in you go!
- You are not limited to broadcast channels at home, why should you be in a hotel? TVs in hotel rooms can now be used to stream whatever service the hotel guest uses at home.
- Your home is wired to remember how warm or cool you want your room at night and what type of lighting you prefer, can't a hotel room do the same? High end hotels are experimenting with Bluetooth technology that will recognize the guests as they arrive and have all the room settings to their preferences.

At the same time, those check in kiosks hotels installed? Guests walk right by them to check in with a real person (Stokes 2017)!

Question: What type of research should be conducted to determine what guests really want technology to do?

true no matter how skilled the researcher. People are simply conditioned to expect a high level of stimulation and may find engaging in 'only' a conversation 'boring'. Projective techniques help the researcher engage and maintain the interest of the participants.

Advantages of projective techniques

- Obtain emotional rather than rational responses
- Allow privacy when discussing sensitive topics
- Engage and maintain interest of participants

Of course, there are situations where projective techniques might not work. Some participants might find the idea of drawing a cartoon or completing a story too challenging. Other participants might be reluctant because they believe that they will be judged on their creative abilities. These reluctant participants might be encouraged to participate by reassuring them that projective techniques are not to be taken too seriously. They should be reminded that it is simply a fun way for the participant to provide information. Of course, any participant who objects should be told that their participation is entirely optional.

Disadvantages of projective techniques

- Tasks may be considered too challenging
- Concern about lack of creative ability

Completion tasks

Many projective techniques involve completion tasks, such as giving the participants the task of finishing a sentence, story or cartoon. Completion tasks, which are a useful means for starting conversations, can be used in focus groups but they are also useful with other forms of research methodology. For example, a researcher may feel that an in-depth interview on what would motivate visitors to attend a foreign film festival is off to a difficult start as participants seem uninterested in the topic. Giving the participant a task to complete, such as sentence completion on why a person chooses not to attend, can help the conversation get started as the task provides the participant with more structure. This structure can help relieve any pressure the participant might feel to say the 'right' answer and allows the participant to feel more relaxed.

Sentence completion tasks are easy for the researcher to create and can be used alone or with other types of methodology. The sentence can be used to gain information on the visitors' opinions of the destination's image. It can also obtain information on the pricing, promotion or location of the tourism product. An advantage of sentence completion is that using the same sentence for all participants allows comparability. While the words provided by the participants may vary, the researcher will almost always find common themes.

For example, a sentence completion task on cruise lines might focus on participants' perceptions of who takes a cruise. The sentence might start with 'People who take cruises are ____ The sentence might also gauge their opinion of the product such as 'The activities available on cruises are ____.' Even information on price can be obtained with sentence completion using a sentence such as. 'I think the cost for going on a cruise is ____.' These sentences should not ask for factual information such as what price the cruise line should charge as this is a simple survey question. Instead the sentences should be aimed to obtain information at an emotional level. Sentence completion tasks can easily be used in focus groups and in-depth and intercept interviews. This technique is also appropriate for use on social media. The sentences can be posted and the users of the site asked for a response. The issue is that there is no way to know the composition of the sample of people that will respond.

Examples of completion topics and sentences

- Customers: People who have destination weddings are...
- Participant: I want a destination wedding because...
- Product: Guests attend destination weddings because it...
- Price: Destination weddings cost...
- Place: The best location for destination weddings is...
- Promotion: I notice information about weddings on...

Story completion tasks require more time during the research session and also more effort on the part of the participants. To complete this task the participant will need to have information on the destination, lodging or event so that they have enough ideas to finish the story. The participants need to have a high level of familiarity so that they can relate to the start of the story, which should be constructed so that the circumstances and names used are familiar to the participants. For example, an event management organization whose target attendees are young college students from Germany would construct a story using German names and city setting. The names in the story can then be changed when working with a different ethnic group.

Example of story completion task

- Amelie is a corporate attorney in Frankfurt. One evening she decides to have pizza with Lina, an old friend from her university. Lina asks her if she is planning to attend an upcoming music festival in Berlin. Amelie answers that she stopped going to festivals because the people who attend are _____.

Cartoon completion has the participant write words in a thought bubble above a character drawn in a cartoon. The advantage of cartoon completion over sentence or story completion is that it provides more information to the participant, making it easier to complete the task. The cartoon picture helps the participant visualize the situation as it shows the context, such as the people and surroundings, in which the comment is made. This context can be changed based on who is participating in the research.

For example, a new tourism business in Italy that was formed to provide wine tours might show a cartoon with one young person saying to another, 'I'm spending part of this weekend tasting wine, why don't you?' The other character in the cartoon might be saying, 'I don't go on wine tours because ____.' Another cartoon might show older people having the same conversation. The ethnicity and gender of the cartoons can also be changed so that the participant can more easily imagine what is being replied.

Of course, participants will most likely reply with their own feelings which they will assign to the cartoon character. This method allows participants to express negative comments without feeling that they are being rude. One of the challenges in getting honest replies is that most people want to say something positive. If they cannot do so, they then tend to be quiet.

Creative projective tasks

Word association is a verbal creative task that is easy to implement and quick to use. Tasks that take longer include drawing exercises that can be used to gather details that are difficult to verbalize. Program or ad creation is a way to get people to participate in the design of the tourism organization's product or promotion. Besides the established projective techniques, researchers can create their own techniques to obtain information.

Word association allows the participant to respond on an emotional level by asking for the first one, two or three words that come to mind. Word association attempts to get at a 'gut' level emotional response from the participant. The stimulus for this response might be a destination name, hotel brand, or a photo of an attraction. What is used will depend on what is being researched. For example, the

Figure 8.1
Projective techniques
include cartoons
where participants
can add comments.
Photo Credit: Inspiring

local botanical garden might want to learn more about the perception of their organization. To do so they can simply ask participants to say the first three words that come to mind when the garden is mentioned. If it is thought that people may not want to say what they are thinking in front of others, the responses can be written down on cards that are then collected for later analysis.

If the answers recorded include boring, old people, dull, and dreary, there can be two potential findings. First, if the negative responses are being received from people who have visited the garden, then the organization may need to redesign what it is offering. If people who are not familiar with the garden have a negative response, then the organization knows that it had better create more effective promotion to communicate that it is a destination for all ages that offers interesting and fun activities.

Word association can also be used to get an emotional opinion of new city souvenirs by showing the product and then getting a reaction. If the organization is planning to order 1,000 t-shirts as a promotional giveaway to tourists this is an effective and easy method to make sure that the design is one the potential visitors will like. Word association can also use photos. This might be a photo of a historic site that cannot be physically shown. Or it could be a photo of the outside or inside of a hotel building or lobby.

If this technique is used alone as a research methodology, it is important that a sufficient number of responses are received. However, these tasks are most effective when used along with other methodologies as the researcher can then ask the participant additional questions about the reason for their response.

This is a method that can be used on a social media site. The hotel, event or destination photo can be posted and people asked to post their responses. The images

Case Study 8.2: Millennial traveler myth vs. fact

Everyone in tourism seems to be focused on attracting the Millennial traveler. They are the children of the digital age, born between 1982 and 2004. Because they spend so much time online we might think we know all about their preferences. We do know that these travelers are confident and goal oriented. We know that they view travel as a necessary part of their lifestyle and not a pleasure to be earned, the view of previous generations. Because they travel frequently, they are targeted by many in the tourism industry. Here are misconceptions about this group:

Myth: All that is needed is social media marketing.

Fact: It is the content, not the media, that gets their attention.

There is nothing new about social media with this group. Ninety-seven per cent are already posting their own travel stories online. What they want is to find stories of peers traveling that have a human connection. Over 50 per cent of Millennial travelers were inspired to take their last trip because of something they saw on social media.

Myth: They are online bargain hunting.

Fact: They are online experience hunting.

Of course, while price is considered, this group has money to spend if they can be convinced that what they will get is a personalized, authentic experience. Sixty per cent of Millennials would rather spend money on an experience than a possession. To them, travel is a social experience and what they want to do is interact both with other travelers and local residents. The lesson learned, sell peer to peer using stories of local experiences (Pixlee 2017).

Question: How would research what tourist stories motivate travel?

can even be texted for a quick gauge of people's emotional response. The advantage of using a social media site is that people can see, and be inspired by, the responses of others.

Sample word association exercise

- What are the first three words that come to mind when you hear the name Our Town Historical Tours?
  - possible answers: interested, hate history, no way
- What are the first three words that come to mind when you hear free t-shirt?
  - possible answer: excited, not another, cheap

A creative task that can be used to add a little fun to a focus group is asking the participants to draw. This is usually a way of getting at underlying perceptions about the destination by asking the participants' view of the current visitors. Many adults when presented with sheets of paper and a variety of colored markets wish to participate. For example, the Smithville Walking Tour Company might understand that they have a problem with the perception of their current customers. If they decide to conduct a focus group on this issue, they might ask participants to draw a picture of a tourist who joins the tour. Artistic ability is not required as participants will be asked to explain their drawing. At this time the participant can explain that the stick figure is bent over because he or she is old.

A projective technique such as drawing is used to get people emotionally involved with the topic. The researcher should create a relaxed setting that communicates to the participants that the exercise will be fun. This atmosphere will help alleviate any concern the participants may have that they will be judged on their artistic ability.

Even more creative is to ask the participant to help in designing the tourism organization's promotional visual. As tourism is often intangible, the participant can be asked to design a list of amenities and services. If the researcher asks verbally for this information, the request might be met by silence as the participants have not given the subject much thought and may be at a loss as to where to start. A creative task gives the participant a chance to consider their response.

An organization that provides entertainment events might ask the participants to create the program for one evening. To get them started a list of various performers should be provided. The participants can be asked to rank by preference who they would like to see or hear at the event. After choosing the performances the participants could then be asked what else they would like to see happen that night, such as lobby entertainment or the availability of special menu items or special drink offers. A blank program form could be created that the participants working alone or in groups would complete.

Sample program creation

- Enjoy the music! Tonight's program will include:
  - ○ _____
  - ○ _____
- Lobby entertainment provided by
  - ○ _____
- Don't forget to stop by the café for
  - ○ _____

After the participants have finished each person or group will share what they have created, which should result in a lively discussion as people will agree or disagree with each other's choices. This same technique could be used to create a list of hotel services that could be offered or a schedule of classes that could be held at a spa.

This technique also works well with promotional ideas with the participants being asked to create an ad for the organization. The participants are responsible for developing a 'message' that would head the ad and the visuals the ad would contain. The researcher will provide large pieces of paper, colorful pens and pencils and even photos that can be cut and pasted on the ad. By creating such a stimulating environment, the participants' inhibitions should be lowered and they will be able to provide more creative ideas than if they just answered with words. Again, sharing the created ads will help spur conversation among the focus group members. For example, the participants would be asked to design an ad that would encourage more families to visit the State Park.

Sample ad creation

- Mountain State Park:
  - Our _____!
- Visit Mountain State Park:
  - The place for families because _____
- While at Mountain State Park:
  - Be sure and _____
- Draw the visuals that should be used in the ad.

Process of conducting projective research

Successfully using projective techniques will take planning. While projective techniques are sometimes used alone, the researcher might plan to use them while using another research method. Even when a focus group or interview is planned without any interactive activities, researchers may want to consider having contingency plans for adding projective techniques if the participants are not responding well to questions. For example, a researcher who is conducting a focus group or interviews may have difficulty getting the participants emotionally involved in the discussion of the promotion of a new hotel. It is useful to have a projective technique, such as having the participants design a webpage, ready to liven up the conversation.

The steps involved in using projective techniques include deciding upon the method, preparing the materials and testing the procedure. When deciding upon the method researchers should consider how the participants will react to tasks that are unstructured and creative. If the researcher feels that the participants may experience more anxiety than excitement with such a task, simple word association can be used. The cultural background of the participants should be understood as this will affect whether the use of the technique will be successful (Roller 2013). If, on the other hand, the participants would enjoy the interaction, drawing or ad completion can be used to gain additional insights and spark conversation.

Social media can now be used as a projective tool (Ipsos 2015). Because of the popularity of image uploading sites, there is already an abundance of images online. If a resort wants to know what type of ambience is desired by the target market of potential visitors this resource can be used. Participants can be asked to start their own page on the posting site and then upload the images they feel represent the destination ambience they would find attractive.

Before using the projective technique it should be tested on people with similar characteristics. The test is not only to determine if the technique works, but also to practice the directions that will be used by the researcher. If the directions are too specific, the projective technique will not be useful in obtaining the participants ideas and opinions. However, if the directions are too vague, the participant will be at a loss as to what is expected.

Observation research

Observational research is one of the few methodologies that does not rely on any form of direct communication between the researcher and participant, either verbal or written. Instead of asking participants about their consumer behavior, with this

Case Study 8.3: Hotels rediscover and redefine hospitality

The hotel industry continues to evolve as society changes. Some of the trends to watch for are co-everything, experience beyond the hotel and local means serving locals. All revolve around the concept of hospitality rediscovering its roots. Hospitality is not just about serving the people who need a bed for the night. Hospitality is being redefined as serving all the needs of the guests and reaching out to local residents to also serve their needs.

Co-everything: It seems that every day a new company gets into the co-workspace business. These co-working spaces are of interest to people who work remotely and don't have a company office. But they are also popular because people like the energy that results from working together. Hotels are responding by adding more communal spaces rather than assuming that people want to work in their rooms.

Experience beyond the hotel: people want local experiences when they stay in a community. Rather than just have a concierge who tells people what to see and do, hotels are starting to create their own experiences that they can then sell to visitors. Local isn't just using local art for decoration and local food in the kitchen.

Serving the locals: while hotels provide additional services to guests to gain more revenue they have traditionally ignored the local community. The only service they may have provided to local businesses is booking meeting rooms. Now hotels are considering the hundreds of business people who work in nearby buildings and the services they might need. This includes use of a hotel room for freshening up before an evening event, use of the gym facilities or package delivery (Ting 2017).

Question: How could observational research be used to discover the co-working needs of hotel guests?

methodology the researcher watches and records what they actually do. Observation is used by researchers because what people say they do, and what they actually do, is not always the same. This is not because people intentionally lie. Instead people's words and actions differ because they may not remember the details of their behavior. For example, when people check into a hotel they may be too tired or preoccupied to remember all the details after the process is completed.

A tourism attraction, such as an amusement park, may wonder how people spend their time when visiting. Conducting a survey of visitors after they have returned home will not be the best methodology as people will have forgotten the details of their visit. They may remember the highlight of the trip, such as the roller coaster, but few other details. Conducting intercept surveys as people leave the amusement park will be more successful. However, while they may recall more, they will be tired and in a hurry to leave. Only observational research, where the actions of visitors are watched and recorded, can answer the question of what people do when they visit the park.

Uses of observational research

Observational research is used to gather data on consumer behavior rather than feelings or opinions. The researcher can use the data gathered as a means to provide insights into visitor preferences and trends. Observational research is used because it is often too difficult for individuals to recall behavior when surveyed later. It is also used when it would be inconvenient to stop and ask people about what they saw or did while at an attraction or event.

For example, visitors to a festival may not be able to provide verbal information on what they experienced. To do so they would have to be both familiar with, and be able to recall, the names of artists and musicians they saw perform. Another example of participants' inability to recall behavior would be to ask people how they spent the time waiting for their hotel room to be ready. This question would probably result in an answer describing the length of the wait, rather than what they did. People may say that the wait was very long and inconvenient. Observation research may find that it was actually 15 minutes, which they spent comfortably seated while on their phones.

Another use of observational research is when asking people questions about behavior close to the time it takes place would not be possible. For example, a theatre company that attracts tourists might want to know how people spend their time during intermission. However, right after intermission, everyone is hurrying back to their seats and there is not enough time to ask questions.

Another situation where observational research is useful is when people may be inclined to give what they consider the correct answer to a question. Visitors to a history museum, when asked how they spent their visit, might respond by mentioning exhibits they remember seeing. They will rarely respond that they spent most of their time in the gift shop and café. After all, everyone knows that one should visit a museum for educational reasons.

Advantages and disadvantages of observational research

The main advantage of observational research is that it obtains information on what people do rather than what they say they do. Another advantage is that it can be less costly than other forms of research such as interviews, focus groups or surveys. With this methodology, there is no need to hire a professional moderator or interviewer. There are also time savings because there is no need to recruit participants.

An additional advantage of observational research is that the organization does not need to gain the permission of the participants as long as the observation takes place in public. For example, a tourism marketing organization may need to know more about how young tourists attending an extreme sports event spend their time. These young people are unlikely to willingly participate in a research study. However, their behaviour can be observed while they are at an event.

Advantages of observational research

- Learn of behavior without verbal input from participants
- Cost and time savings
- Involve participants who may not be willing to participate in a study

There are also disadvantages to the observational research methodology. While there is no need to hire professionals to conduct the research, there is a need for patient and observant researchers to faithfully record the data. Even with supervision they must be vigilant if they are to accurately record details.

Another significant disadvantage is the inability to ascertain if the participant meets the required profile. While the profile for observational research is usually broadly defined using observable demographic characteristics, such as families with preschool age children from a specific ethnic group, there may still be problems with observation. It will be left to the skill of the observer to determine people's ages and ethnic background. It is even more difficult to use psychographic characteristics when defining the participant profile. Sometimes lifestyle can be guessed by clothing or hairstyle, but this is very weak evidence.

Lastly, the research methodology is dependent on who happens to be at the public place. A research study on what types of visitors attend free concerts in the park across the street from a hotel can be meticulously planned. However, the research effort might be wasted if the night is cold and rainy and the crowd is sparse.

Disadvantages of observational research

- Findings depend on accuracy of observations
- Difficult to profile participants
- Success dependent on who is present

Types of observations

The organization can choose from three approaches to observation research: complete observer, participating observer or complete participant. The choice will depend on the behavior that needs to be studied.

For some research tasks, it is important that the researcher is not noticed by the participants. This is because seeing the researcher observing might change the behavior of the participants. For example, researchers might want to watch families interact at a museum to see if the children become bored. Fidgety children would mean that the exhibits need to be made more child friendly. If the parents see that the behavior of their children is being observed, they will likely insist that they 'behave' and the true reaction will not be known. With the complete observer method, the researcher will station themselves at a location where they cannot be seen. This is not because the organization wants secrecy, but rather because the act of being observed may change the behavior of the participants. For example, researchers standing at the side of a hotel lobby with a clipboard making notes on the behavior of the guests might find that everyone is avoiding where they are standing.

Complete observation can be conducted when the behavior is videoed so it can then be studied. Of course this would not be appropriate in any public setting. In fact, videoing behavior at any organization for reasons of conducting research should not be done without the permission of those being videoed. However if organizations have security video cameras that are used in public places such as lobbies, the tapes can ethically be used for research. Such tapes might be used to determine if there is a need to redesign the seating in the lobby based on how easily people can find somewhere to sit.

While observation research has been used to record behavior, technology is providing a way for it also to be used to gather emotional information. Software has been designed that recognizes common facial expressions (Lawlor 2017). Two major challenges still remain with the use of such programs. First, cultural differences affect the amount of emotion that will be displayed visually. Second, the software needs appropriate lighting and video angles to be able to distinguish the facial expressions that reveal emotions.

Most observational research is conducted with a participant observer. With this technique, the researcher does not aim to be hidden from view, but tries to mix in with those being observed. While the observers do not intend to hide from view, they will try to make their observations as unobtrusive as possible. For example, the tourism organization of a city may want to know what people do when they visit an historic site. Observers while at the site would be asked to record who comes to the site, how long they stay and what exhibits caught their attention.

The observer would not try to hide at the historical site, which might be impossible. Instead they could sit on a bench looking at their phone while at the same time observing. If the researcher has a good memory, they can watch for a few minutes and then record at another location. This method could also work well for observing what people are doing at a festival. The observer would be dressed similarly to the festival attendees and observe while casually strolling around. Or, an observer at the festival might station themselves by one stage and record who stops and how long they view the performance.

If someone questions what the observers are doing, they should explain that they are trying to learn more about visitors without bothering them with questions. If researchers are observing in a public place they should have with them a letter from the organization conducting the research explaining the purpose. This letter should also contain contact information for someone in the tourism organization who can verify the researcher's identity.

Sometimes the observer is also a participant. With this type of observational research, the observer participates in the same behavior as the research subjects. For example, if the researcher wants to know more about how people interact during a bus tour the observer can be a tour member. This not only allows the researchers to observe behavior, it also allows them to overhear comments. The researchers do not identify themselves; they simply participate in the activity under study.

Observation research process

As with other methodologies, to successfully complete observational research takes advance planning. While watching behavior seems simple, without preparation no useful data will be recorded. It is too easy to forget what was observed or to confuse the dates or times. The steps involved in planning include deciding what behavior to observe, preparing a participant profile, choosing the correct site, choosing the dates and times, preparing the observation form and training observers.

Deciding on behavior and participants to observe

Research always starts with a question or problem whose answer depends on input from current or potential visitors to the destination, hotel or event. Because

Figure 8.2 When conducting observations, the researcher can pose as another member of the group.

Photo Credit: Fotos593

observational research can only obtain answers through watching behavior, the researchers must first decide on what behavior they need more information. While the analysis of the recorded behavior might provide insights into attitudes, this cannot be the purpose of the research. Instead the research must focus on people's actions. For example, an inappropriate research question for observational research would be, 'Do guests enjoy sitting in the hotel lobby?' An appropriate question would be, 'Do guests use the seating in the hotel lobby?'

The participant profile developed by the researchers must only describe characteristics that can be determined visually. The profile starts with describing the visitor segment, such as event attendees, hotel guests or city visitors. The profile should not ask the researcher to observe participants with psychographic traits, such as happy hotel guests, as there is no way for the observer to know an individual's emotional state. Instead the profile should describe demographic characteristics such as age and gender. Other easily observed characteristics that can be used are whether the individual is alone or with others or whether they are disabled or infirm. Some demographic characteristics, such as ethnicity, are more difficult to ascertain.

Observation logistics

A critical step in designing the observation research methodology is to choose the site or sites where the research will take place. Sometimes this decision will be easy, such as hotel swimming pool or a local historic site. Sometimes the answer is not so clear, such as when the task is to observe visitors to a destination. Choosing a site is

Case Study 8.4: A library at sea

Cruise ships are now trying to cater to more than the sun and fun crowd. While some cruise ships in the past may have said they had a library, most only had a few popular paperbacks. Silversea Cruises was planning its launch of a new ship for spring 2017. The target market segment was a more upscale and upper income cruise line passenger. To appeal to this segment an onboard library that would reflect the atmosphere of a private library in a wealthy home was planned. The library would have hardcover books, magazines and reference materials.

The company wanted the ship to have a real library, but did not have the expertise to choose the books. Rather than conduct research themselves to determine what titles their customers might want, they asked Heywood Hills, a bookstore located in London to develop the titles for the onboard library. The bookstore, founded in 1936, has created libraries for individuals, hotels, and private jets. Since the bookstore already has customers from 60 countries they should know what anybody and everybody wants to read (Stieghorst 2017)!

Question: What focus group questions should have been asked before the cruise line decided to hire an outside expert?

much more difficult when trying to observe the behavior of people who are visitors to a city as they could be at many different sites. Sometimes the location chosen is one that is commonly used by people for the behavior the organization wants to observe, such as a public square where visitors are known to stop and take photos.

Once the correct site is chosen, the researchers must decide what are the best days and times to observe the behavior. Using the hotel example, there might be a difference in behavior between how the lobby is used during the day and evening. The behavior of weekday and weekend guests will differ as more business people will be there on weekdays. If a festival organizer wants to know more about how all attendees interact at the concession stands, they should make sure that they observe both before and after a performance. If researchers want to know more about families, they should then concentrate their observations on daytime.

The best method for choosing both location and day and time is for the researcher to scout the location. The researcher should visit the site to determine if it is frequented by a sufficient number of people who meet the participant profile. Then the researcher should visit at various days and times to determine when the observations will be most successful. There is no purpose in scheduling observations when no behavior can be observed.

Event versus time sampling

There are two approaches that can be used when recording observational data, which are event and time sampling. With event data recording, the researcher is watching for specific behavior. For example, at a resort the research question might deal with the ability of families with several small children to get on and off company shuttles that move people between the hotel and beach. With event sampling, the observer will wait until they see such a family getting on to the shuttle and then record any difficulty they have in doing so. On the data form they will record the number of people in the family group, the behavior they observed and the time of the observation. The observer will be given instructions as to how many families they should observe before the research session is considered complete.

Time sampling is often used when the frequency rather than the type of interaction is being researched. In the example above, the researchers may want to know how many families board the shuttle each morning and afternoon. The observation schedule will ask the observer to record each time a family loads onto the shuttle and the number of people in the group. It may also ask to record any difficulties they have in boarding, but the main purpose of the research is to know the number of families within a certain time period. If the schedule calls for observations between 7:00am and 10:00am during which no families board, this is still valid research as the answer to how many has been obtained.

Preparing the observation form

Because even the best observer can only remember a limited amount of detail, the researchers will need to prepare an observation form where data can be recorded. For some types of observations, the form can be filled out while the observation is taking place. Other times, the researcher will first observe and then later record the data. This method will be used when recording data at the same time as observing would draw attention to the researcher.

The form should display the date, time and place of the observation and also the name of the observer. The form should then have a place to record details on who is being observed. At a crowded location, observers cannot possibly note the behavior of everyone. Therefore, they must choose which participants to observe and then record their characteristics. For example they may note that they are observing a family with two adults and three children, a same gender couple or single elderly male.

The form will provide time slots where observations will be recorded. Most observation periods will be from 15 minutes to as long as half an hour. The time will depend both on the time period in which the participants engage in the behavior and the comfort of the observer. Because the research is dependent on who happens to be at the site when the observation takes place, more than one observation period will be needed. It is best that a number of observations at different days and times be planned. This is to ensure that the research will adequately record the behavior that is needed to answer the research question.

Choosing and training observers

Like other research methods the success of obtaining the needed data depends on the skills of the researcher. The research will take time as a number of observations will need to be made to ensure that the behavior was adequately observed. This time commitment could be costly except for the fact that conducting observational research does not require a high level of skill. A tourism association may wish to consider using volunteers from their own organization.

The observers should be unknown to the participants. A hotel should not use staff members who are already known to guests. If they are known, the participants

Figure 8.3 Observation research can be conducted without changing visitor behavior.

Photo Credit: Michele Vacchiano

might come over to strike up a friendly conversation which will end the research. Another idea is to hire college students to conduct the observations. In fact, if the students are in a program where they are studying research methods, they might find the research not only an educational experience but also something they can put on their resumé.

The skills needed by observers are an attention to detail and patience. Observers must use their own judgment as to whether a person meets the participant profile, so they must also be able to make an informed guess as to the observable demographic characteristics of the person. In addition, they can observe whether the person is alone or with someone else. During the observation process, they may need to be able to discern whether the person being observed seems to be having difficulty, is unhappy or confused.

The observers also must have patience. They must observe the same people over a period of time and then be willing to start the observation period all over again. The behavior they observe will often be similar. Repeatedly they may record comments such as 'father and child playing in swimming pool' and 'parents with baby unable to find place to sit'. Alone these observations may not seem all that exciting. However, after all the observations have taken place and a researcher analyzes the data, it may be found that the pool, which is mostly used by families, does not have enough seating. These findings can then be used to improve the visit experience for families.

Once the observers have been chosen it is important to train them properly. The observers should first be instructed on how to identify the proper participants. They then should be trained in the use of the form. To ensure that the observations are successful, the researcher should accompany the observers during the first observation period. This will help the observer with any unanticipated difficulties and also reassure the researcher that the observer will be able to perform the task. It is recommended that the researcher check on the observers occasionally during later observation periods just to ensure that everything is going well.

References

Furnham, A. 2014. Projective Techniques [online]. *Psychology Today*. 10 March. Available from www.psychologytoday.com/blog/sideways-view/201403/projective-techniques. [Accessed 4 May 2017].

Ipsos. 2015. Leveraging Social Wisdom for Better Community Insights [online]. Game Changers. Ipsos, 1 October. Available from www.ipsos.com/en-us/leveraging-social-wisdom-better-community-insights>. [Accessed 10 May 2017].

Lawlor, T. 2017. Is Facial Recognition in Retail Market Research the Next Big Thing? [online]. Chain Store Age, 14 February. Web. 4 May 2017. Available from www.chainstoreage.com/article/facial-recognition-retail-market-research-next-big-thing. [Accessed 1 May 2017].

Pixlee. 2017. Welcome to The Travel Marketing Guide to the Millennial Traveler; A Handbook for Tourism Marketers Looking to Reach, Appeal To, and Build Lasting Relationships with Millennial Guests [online]. *4Hoteliers*. 18 January. Available from www.4hoteliers.com/features/article/10212?awsb_c=4hdm&awsb_k=dnws. [Accessed 7 February 2017].

Roller, M. 2013. Projective Techniques: Do We Know What They Are Projecting? [online]. *Research Design Review*, 16 November. Available from researchdesignreview.com/2013/11/15/projective-techniques-do-we-know-what-they-are-projecting/. [Accessed 4 May 2017].

Stieghorst, T. 2017. Silversea Hires London Bookstore to Create Library [online]. Travel Weekly. *Northstar Travel Media*, 31 March. Available from www.travelweekly.com/Cruise-Travel/Silversea-hires-London-bookstore-to-create-library. [Accessed 1 April 2017].

Stokes, N. 2017. At Hotels Around the World, the Friendly Face of a Concierge Who Remembers Your Name Could Soon Be Replaced by Technology That Aims to Do Just the Same and When It Comes to a Great Hotel Stay, That Personalized Touch Is Often the Defining Feature [online]. *4Hoteliers*, 8 February. Available from www.4hoteliers.com/features/article/10248?awsb_c=4hdm&awsb_k=dnws. [Accessed 8 February 2017].

Ting, D. 2017. 10 Hotel Trends That Will Shape Guest Experience in 2017 [online]. *Skift*, 13 January. Available from skift.com/2017/01/03/10-hotel-trends-that-will-shape-guest-experience-in-2017/. [Accessed 5 May 2017].

Chapter 9

Conducting visitor interviews

Learning objectives

- What are the uses of interview research and its advantages and disadvantages?
- Is there a difference between in-depth, expert and intercept interviews?
- Why are there different types of interview questions?
- What are the issues involved in recruiting and screening participants?

Chapter summary

- Interviews allow the time to probe deeply to find the true cause of a problem. They provide a researcher with time to search for answers without distractions while research subjects have time to consider their answers. Conducting a successful interview requires a skilled researcher. Because of the time needed for an interview fewer research subjects will be involved.
- The interview process consists of an opening to build trust followed by prepared questions, the answers to which will lead to probing questions. The interview is closed with thanks. The length of time spent on each stage will depend on the type of interview. In-depth interviewing of visitors is only one of the possible methods. In addition, expert interviews of competitors and stakeholders can be conducted. Finally, intercept interviews can be used to get quick feedback from visitors.
- Interviews use open-ended questions that do not provide the participant with any already selected answers from which to choose. Descriptive interview questions ask the participant to describe their behavior. As long as the question is not perceived as invasive or threatening, these are the easiest questions for the participant to answer. Causal questions ask the visitor why a behavior takes place.
- The fewer participants involved in a research study the more important it is to find the correct participants as each participant's input into the study is heavily

weighted. It is harder to recruit participants for interview research. The researcher should develop a participant profile that includes the visitor status along with the desired demographic characteristics.

Uses of interview research

Most tourism, hospitality and event organizations will be aware that surveys and focus groups can be used to conduct marketing research. Some organizations that provide tourism services will also know that much can be learned about the needs of their visitors by informally asking about their experiences. However, most tourism organizations have not considered using interviews in a more formal way for marketing research. They should reconsider this attitude as marketing research interviews can be very useful and worth the investment in time, effort and money when the organization is faced with a serious problem, such as a lack of visitors or a recent uptick in online bad reviews for which they do not know the cause.

Interview research consists of the researcher asking questions of a single participant. Some of the questions will be predetermined while follow-up questions will be added when needed during the process. The three different types of interviews, in-depth, expert and intercept, are used for different purposes.

In-depth interviews conducted with visitors are often used to uncover the source of a problem. In-depth interviews are also used when the researchers need to explore visitor behavior and attitudes in depth. The longer time spent with the subject will allow the researcher to gain insights that having only a short conversation would not be able to produce. The insights from interviews can be used to better understand a current problem confronting the organization. For example, a hotel that is seeing a decline in visitors may use interviews to get a deeper understanding of the reason for this decline than can be obtained from survey responses.

Expert interviews are used with subjects other than visitors. Instead expert interviews are usually conducted with competitors or stakeholders and provide a means of gathering factual information. This includes information from other organizations that have faced a similar difficulty. For example, if marketers for a music festival know that there is lower attendance at other festivals they may want to interview the competing marketing managers to determine their understanding of the problem.

While in-depth interviews can be used to gain insights from visitors into the cause of a problem and expert interviews are used to learn factual knowledge about the problem, intercept interviews allow the researcher to quickly gather impressions from many visitors of a tourism product or service. For example, a tourism organization may conduct intercept interviews as visitors are leaving a historic site. The participants may be asked why they visited and if they plan to return. Many may state that the cost of tickets is too high for a return visit, while others may state that there is little to do at the site. These reasons could then be further explored using survey research.

It is true that an in-depth interview takes a skilled interviewer and, therefore, might not be a methodology that is available to small organizations. However, all organizations can have their own personnel conduct expert interviews to learn more about their competition and then adjust their marketing mix accordingly. In addition, intercept interviews can be conducted by anyone with an outgoing personality and these will provide the organization with insights that can be confirmed with other research techniques.

Learning more about problems using interviews

- In-depth: gaining insights into visitors' behavior or attitudes
  - What would motivate you to use our hotel's spa services?
- Expert: obtaining factual knowledge about the source of a problem
  - Is the number of people purchasing spa treatments declining elsewhere?
- Intercept: developing ideas for use in further research
  - Why do you not use the hotel's spa services?

Advantages of using interview research

All research methodologies have their own advantages that make them useful for specific situations. Each also has disadvantages of which the researcher should be aware. One of the skills a researcher must have is the ability to choose the methodology that will work best for obtaining the answer to each research question.

One of the major advantages to interview research is that it gives the researcher time to get at the underlying reasons for visitor behavior and attitudes without the distraction of comments by other participants. The questions should not simply be asking what visitors want. Instead the time can be used to explore the problems that visitors face (Liu 2015).

The advantages of interview research include the ability to probe in depth a single topic without distraction by the comments of other participants. Some participants may be hesitant to speak up at a focus group for fear that their ideas will be criticized. For example, a destination management organization may wish to research the perception of crime in the area. It may take repeated probing questions to get at the real reason that people feel the area is unsafe. It might have nothing to do with their personal experience but with news stories they have read. The interview process gives the researcher the time needed to explore in depth a single topic to get at the real reason for an attitude.

It may be that participants are willing to take part in research but may need time to develop their answers. The interview process gives the participant time to consider an answer. For example, a small regional theatre may wonder why tourists

Figure 9.1
Interviews can be
conducted using
phones or computers.
Photo Credit: Alissa
Kumarova

Case Study 9.1: Hostel takeovers – you get art with your bed

Hostels were originally designed to provide an inexpensive place for traveling young people to stay while they discovered the world. While there are still backpacking young people willing to settle for a bunkbed in a shared room, there are now new guests at hostels who want a better experience. First there are more young people with access to the funds to travel in style. Second, older people, and even business travelers, who want a local connection are staying at hostels. These new types of hostels that provide a more upscaled local experience are a global phenomenon and can be found in Europe, the US and Asia.

What is really driving the use of hostels for both groups is the connection to a local area. To keep costs down most hostels are located in neighborhoods outside the main city core. This gives guests a chance to explore where the locals live. One way that hostels are using this connection is by promoting local art. Hostels that are in refurbished older industrial buildings are using their wide-open spaces for the display of large-scale contemporary art. They are not focusing just on traditional visual art forms but also local comic books and even tattoo art.

Not content just to display art, many hostels are going one step farther by having artist in residence programs where guests can watch local artists produce new work. They are even giving hostel guests the chance to join in and help produce the art (Mohn 2017).

Question: If you were interested in opening such a hostel, with whom should you conduct expert interviews?

do not attend even though the performances are heavily marketed and are enjoyed by local residents with similar demographic and psychographic characteristics. The first response a visitor might make is that they didn't have time in their schedules. Participants might need time to think about why they found time for other activities but did not attend the theatre. The underlying reason might be an attitude that attending a play is not a holiday experience. The researcher can then explore what would change this perception.

Because an interview only involves one researcher and one participant at a time and does not need any specialized facility or equipment they can be held at the location that is most convenient for the participant – the local tourism office, a hotel or restaurant. An interview can even be held in a public place, such as a park. Finally, intercept interviews can be held in any public place where the visitors can be found.

Expert interviews are conducted to gather background information on the organization's problem. These experts might be personnel from competing organizations. This research is not designed to gain insights into behavior but to gather facts. Interviews work well as an expert is more likely to respond to the request for information in person than through a written survey. After all, the expert has nothing to gain from the research process other than helping a colleague with a problem.

Advantages of interview research

- Provides researcher time to probe insights free from distraction
- Provides visitors time to express themselves
- Can be conducted at many types of locations
- Can be used to gather factual data

Disadvantages of interview research

Of course, there are disadvantages to any research methodology. For interview research these include the need to have a skilled researcher conduct the interview. Another disadvantage is that comparability of findings is difficult. As the interviewer is exploring the reasons for behavior, each interview, just like each participant, will be unique. Since interviews take longer to conduct, the researcher will have findings from fewer participants to analyze. Because of these limitations, interviews are not used routinely to conduct research but saved for when the organization faces a critical problem for which they have no idea of the cause.

An interview is a useful research technique when the organization knows little about the cause of a problem. Because it is difficult to obtain information on the underlying causes of behavior, a skilled interviewer is needed. This person must have previous experience in interviewing from working either in the social sciences or marketing. An interview is not just a conversation, rather the interviewer is acting as a detective looking for clues and then, when they are revealed, probing more deeply. To find these clues the researcher must repeatedly ask for clarification of statements without frustrating the participant. In addition, the interviewer must be careful not to lead the participant to any specific answer. A skilled interviewer keeps the conversation on the research topic while at the same time following up on ideas presented by the participant. This is a skill that must be learned.

The researcher may find that after conducting a number of interviews, different reasons have arisen in each. This does not mean that the research has failed, but does make comparisons of the data difficult. It will take additional analysis to find a common theme when the individual reasons differ. For example, a restaurant may be exploring why they have such a high number of canceled dining appointments. Interviews with guests might have revealed a problem with transportation, a discomfort with the neighborhood, or difficulty with parking. While different, additional analysis might reveal that all of these reasons relate to the restaurant's location.

While interviewing can provide valuable insights, the requirements of the methodology will limit the number of interviews that can be conducted. First, the potential participant must be willing to give up the time to be questioned on a topic which might not be of much interest personally. Apart from the constraints of finding willing participants, using a skilled interviewer, if the organization does not have one on staff, will be expensive.

Disadvantages of using interview research

- Requires researcher skilled in interview techniques
- Unable to make comparison between findings
- Fewer participants means less findings to analyze

The interview process

In-depth, expert and intercept interviews each have a distinct process while also containing some common elements. All interviews have an opening, questioning, probing and closing stage. The opening stage involves the researcher explaining the reason the interview is being conducted. During this stage there will also be a conversation about the logistics of the interview including the time it will take. This stage of the interview process will also be used to explain that all information will be held confidentially and while findings will be reported, no names of interviewees will be divulged. This opening stage of the interview is used to build trust and establish rapport. The length of the phase will vary. With in-depth interviews, it will be a few minutes, while for intercept interviews it will be a few seconds. While the researcher might be eager to start to pose questions, this stage should not be rushed (Steber 2016). Only if the research subject is at ease and trusts the researcher will useful responses be obtained.

The questioning phase of the interview process will use predetermined questions designed to elicit information that will help answer the research question. There should only be a short list of questions so that the participant will have enough time to answer each. The length of this stage will be determined by the type of interview. Because some research subjects will be less talkative than others, enough questions should be prepared so that the time is used productively

The probing stage is where the researcher will develop and ask questions based on the answers to predetermined questions. The interview may actually move back and forth between the questioning and probing stages as new topics are introduced. The probing questions do not add a new topic. Instead they ask for explanations of what was said during an earlier answer if it is unclear. A probing question might also ask for more detail on a suggestion or opinion that was given. Even a short intercept interview will have a probing stage as a final question asking if there is anything else they would like to add.

The closing stage is where the researcher thanks participants for their time, again reassures them about confidentiality and asks for any questions the participant might have about the interview process that has just been completed. Adequate time for this stage should remain so that the research participant does not feel rushed out the door. After all, they have provided useful information and should be treated with respect.

Interview research process

- Opening
  - explain purpose of research
  - describe logistical details
  - assure participant of confidentiality
- Questioning
  - ask a series of prepared questions
  - number depends on length of interview
- Probing
  - ask follow-up questions based on responses
  - ask for clarification or additional information
- Closing
  - thank participant for participation
  - reassure participant of confidentiality

Case Study 9.2: Ski resorts want more than slopes and gravity to excite skiers

Now they also want phone apps. While socializing at ski resorts has always been a group activity, going down the slopes was a solitary experience. This may be one reason that interest in skiing was declining with youth. Now a new group of ski apps are changing how skiing is being experienced. The first generation of ski apps were designed to simply communicate snow and weather conditions to skiers. While helpful, they did not change the skiing experience. The next generation allowed app users to share images and videos they had taken on the slopes. This allowed skiers to share socially what they are experiencing.

Since then, ski apps have become much more sophisticated and focus on people's interest in both cooperating and competing. As no skier enjoys standing in lift lines, a crowdsourcing app now exists that allows all skiers to upload real time lift waiting periods. This not only helps the individual skier avoid long lines, it helps even out the load over the slopes. Competition is made possible by the ability of the app to track the miles skied so that it can be compared with that of friends. The app than awards prizes. Besides competitions based on miles, fun competitions include riding every chair lift in a single day, time airborne and calories burned. The next round of apps will use geo-locators to provide skiing hints based on the skier's location and share speed calculations to impress friends. After skiing is done, the app provides a map of the lodge and area with suggestions for what to do next. Now, even on the slopes, you never need to be alone (King 2017).

Question: What interview questions could be asked to develop an app for those who like to travel to run marathons?

In-depth interviews

An in-depth interview is conducted by a researcher with a single participant. The interview will be held at a location that is free from distraction so that both the researcher and the participant can concentrate on the research question. The interview will open with the interviewer thanking the participant for arriving and explaining the purpose of the interview.

After the opening stage, the interviewer will first ask prepared questions. The prepared questions will be written to specifically address different aspects of the research question. For example, an organization may have recently seen a decline in attendance at a Mardi Gras celebration. The research question might be: 'How can the visitor experience at the annual Mardi Gras celebration be improved?' A meeting of the organization management may reveal a number of issues. The organization may know that its marketing message on the Mardi Gras is being communicated to potential visitors and yet they are not attending. They may guess that potential visitors are worried about safety having heard news stories about crime. As a result, the organization may want to know what would reassure visitors that the experience is safe. A direct question as to whether a visitor feels safe is a simple question that can be handled with a survey. Instead the questions prepared for the interview will cover why visitors don't feel safe. They will also be asked what changes would increase their feeling of safety.

Only a few questions will be prepared. At first it may seem as if these questions will not fill an hour-long interview. However, each prepared question will lead to additional probing questions. The prepared questions are general in nature with the probing questions being more specific. These probing questions cannot be prepared as they will depend on the answer received from the participant. For example, if an interviewee mentions that they don't feel safe because of insufficient lighting, probing questions would explore where lighting is needed. If another interviewee answers that they don't feel safe because of all the warning signs regarding keeping their personal property safe, they might be asked what type of message would be an effective reminder without emphasizing crime. Enough time should be left as participants may suggest interesting ideas such as using videos to promote the Mardi Gras showing all ages engaging in fun, safe activities.

As a result, each interview may discuss in depth a different topic, which is why interviews are not comparable. After the probing questions, the interviewer will close the interview by giving the participant a chance to offer any additional comments on topics that were not previously addressed.

In-depth interview process stages and questions

- Opening
  - ○ researcher thanks participant and explains purpose of interview
- Questioning
  - ○ Why do you feel unsafe when you attend Mardi Gras?
  - ○ What changes could be made to make you feel safer?
- Probing
  - ○ if answer to question one is 'it's too dark' ask: Where is lighting needed?
  - ○ if answer to question two is 'less signs about crime', ask: What type of message would remind people to be careful without making them fearful?
- Closing
  - ○ researcher asks for any additional comments

Expert interviews

Expert interviews are usually used early in the research process when the organization needs information that the visitor cannot provide. For example, the tourism organization sponsoring Mardi Gras may wonder if other organizations are having the same problem attracting visitors. While answers could be found to this question using secondary research, the organization might want information that is specific to its geographic area and visitor segment. To get this information the organization may decide to interview a tourism marketer in a neighboring town that has a similar carnival.

Since the purpose of the expert interview is to gain factual information, probing questions are not as frequently used. Instead the interviewer will rely on prepared questions, such as asking about attendance and any reasons for a decline. Using the above example, the interviewer would ask directly how they have alleviated any concern about crime. There may be a temptation to treat an expert interview casually. After all, the person being interviewed may be considered a colleague and, in fact, may be known to the researcher or even be a friend.

However, the researcher should treat the interview seriously, as they are taking valuable time that the expert could put to other uses. Because the researcher wants to minimize the time commitment that is being asked from the expert, the researcher must keep the interview as short as possible. The opening stage would simply be spent thanking the expert for their time. Another way to thank the expert, and to make use of free time, is to conduct the interview over lunch or coffee with the researcher picking up the check. The prepared question stage would be simply asking the expert factual questions. Closing would be a simple 'thanks'.

Expert interview process stages and questions

- Opening
  - researcher thanks participant for time
- Questioning
  - if questioning other organizations ask: Have you had difficulty attracting visitors to a Mardi Gras event?
  - Why, or why not, do you believe this is true?
- Closing
  - thanks! and I'll pick up the check for lunch

Intercept interviews

Intercept or person-on-the street interviews are short, focused interviews consisting of only three to five open-ended questions with a single probing question if there is time. The entire interview should only take two to three minutes. The purpose is not to obtain in-depth information but rather many responses to a specific question than could be obtained through in-depth interviews.

The intercept interviews are held in the location where the participants normally can be found, such as at the Mardi Gras celebration. This interview method is essential when participants are unwilling to participate in a lengthy interview. Because probing questions will be very limited, the researcher does not need to be a skilled interviewer.

To conduct intercept interviews the researcher will first approach visitors who meet the participant profile. The opening stage will consist of researchers introducing themselves on a first name basis and explaining for whom they are working. The researcher will also inform the potential participant of the purpose of the interview and how long the interview will take, and ask permission to start the interview. Once the prepared questions are asked, the researcher will quickly thank the participant for their time and look for another potential participant.

Intercept interview process stages and questions

- Opening
  - researcher introduces purpose of research
- Questioning
  - Did you feel safe at today's event?
  - Why, or why not?
- Closing
  - thanks!

Figure 9.2 Intercept interviews can be conducted where visitors can be found.

Photo Credit: Anton Gvozkikov

Preparing interview questions and logistics

Interviews use open-ended questions that do not provide the participant with any already selected answers from which to choose. When writing interview questions the researcher can choose from among descriptive or causal open-ended questions. Descriptive questions ask the participant to describe their behavior. As long as the question is not perceived as invasive or threatening, these are the easiest questions for participants to answer. Causal questions ask why a behavior takes place. These questions are more challenging for participants to answer as they may not have given much thought to why they engaged in a behavior. To answer the question the participant must think about his or her motivation for taking a particular action.

The process of writing interviews questions should be collaborative (Agee 2009). All departments in the tourism organization conducting the research should be involved in writing interview questions as each may have a different perspective on a problem. If the research study is being funded by a nonprofit or government agency, they should be consulted so that they can add questions of particular interest. Finally, some research studies may even ask potential research subjects what issues the interview questions should address.

Descriptive questions

Descriptive questions ask participants to describe their behavior. They ask questions using the words 'what', 'when', 'where', 'how often' and 'with whom'? What they

Case Study 9.3: The adventure of a lifetime! But for whom?

Many people might have fantasized about visiting Antarctica after reading an adventure story or seeing a documentary, but the closest a tourist could get was a cruise ship. Not anymore! As the demand for unique, authentic and personalized experiences grows, tourism companies have expanded their offerings. A UK company is now providing tourists with a two-week overland trip across the continent of Antarctica. What does the trip offer? Climbing the highest mountain, cross-country skiing over the tundra and locating the point where all 24 time zones meet.

Tourists will have to be physically fit and be ready for some tough travel. While outdoor clothing and heated tents for sleeping are provided, this is not a luxury trip. The cost is $165,000 US and only six travelers go on each trip. There are enough potential travelers that can afford the trip. The issue is screening the travelers to ensure that they understand that they will be traveling overland in trucks in Antarctica, which is very different from taking a cruise. In fact, the company cannot even guarantee the return date as there is always a strong possibility that the travelers will have to stay put during storms until the weather allows travel again (Ekstein 2017).

Question: What interview questions would you ask potential travelers to ensure they will have a trip that will result in good reviews and not complaints?

do not ask is why a behavior takes place. For example, visitors might be asked what hotel services they use, when they visit, at what site they booked the hotel, how often they visit the hotel and what social media they use to share the experience. All of these are factual questions that are simple to answer. Such questions are usually asked early in the interview. They then might be followed up later with probing questions to learn more.

Descriptive questions

- What services do you use at the visitor center?
- How often do you visit the restaurant?
- Who accompanies you on the visits?
- When is the most convenient time for you to take a holiday?
- Where would you prefer the festival to be held?

Causal questions

Interviews should never consist of only descriptive questions. Interviews are an expensive research methodology that limits the number of people who can be involved. These types of descriptive questions could just as easily be answered in a survey form, saving the organization money.

Instead. causal questions designed to uncover the reason for, or causes of a behavior should be asked. They are almost always probing questions because they require the visitor to take the time to consider why they perform behaviors that are usually routine. Using the example of the descriptive questions given above, the causal questions would ask for the motivation behind the behavior. The management of the hotel might assume that someone books a room because they need somewhere to stay. However, a causal question might reveal other motivations, such as need for relaxation, excitement, or romance.

Causal questions can also ask the participant how their feelings or attitudes changed as a result of a behavior. This form of probing question will require visitors to consider aspects of their behavior of which they may be initially unaware. The answers to these questions can provide information as to the benefits that visitors receive from the tourism experience. Even if the participant cannot answer the question as to why they engage in a behavior, a question about how they felt after the behavior may uncover the motivation. For example, a participant may be unable to articulate why they frequently visit a destination. However, when asked how they feel after a visit they may respond that they feel a connection with history. This lets the researchers know that tourists are visiting for the psychological benefits besides the factual history that they learn.

Causal questions

- Besides the obvious reason that you need a place to stay when you visit, what other benefits does a visit to the hotel provide?
- Why do you prefer to attend events with friends?
- Why do you find the walking tours boring?
- Why would a downtown location for the visitor center be more convenient?
- How do you feel when you return home after a visit to our community?

Interview logistics

Once the questions have been written, it is time to consider who will conduct the interviews, when they will be conducted and the best location. First, the organization will need to have a skilled interviewer to conduct the research. The organization must then plan the time for the interviews that is most convenient for the visitors. Finally, the place where the interview will be held will depend on the type of interview being conducted.

Abilities needed by interviewers

Both personal characteristics and learned skills must be possessed by an interviewer to ensure that a successful interview takes place. The personal characteristics include patience and a sincere interest in people. A successful interviewer must have patience as it takes time to gain the trust of the participant. In the early stage of the interview the researcher and visitor may engage in conversation that is only tangentially related to the research topic. While always keeping the interview topic in mind, the researcher must be willing to spend the time to gain the trust of the participant. A researcher will also need a sincere interest in people, not just in the topic under discussion. For at least an hour researchers must focus all of their attention on one person. They then must have the same intense interest in the next research participant.

The interviewer will need excellent communication skills. This includes both verbal and nonverbal communication, as probing questions will challenge the participant to discuss issues of which they may not be aware. Interviewers will need to be skilled in reading the body language of the visitor so that they know when to probe for more information and when they need to back off.

Abilities needed by interviewers

- Patience: to establish rapport
- Interest in people: to ensure each participant feels valued
- Excellent communication skills: to gain the needed information

Location for the interviews

The location chosen for the interviews will depend on the type being conducted. In-depth interviews can be held at the office of the tourism organization, the hotel where the visitor is staying or a neutral third location, such as a restaurant. Expert interviews are usually held at the office of the expert or else at a neutral location. Intercept interviews are held where the visitors can be found.

A common reason for not conducting the interview at the tourism organization's office is that some visitors might find the ambience uninviting or even intimidating. Visitors who are members of groups or communities that feel disenfranchised may feel that they cannot express themselves freely. As a result, they might limit their responses to what they feel should be said, rather than what they truly believe. The best way to eliminate this issue is to conduct the interviews at a location that is comfortable for the visitors. If the interview is held at the hotel where the visitor is staying or at a nearby restaurant, it should be in a private setting so that the participants will not be distracted.

If the visitor is no longer in the area, technology can be used to conduct the interview. While the interview can be conducted over the phone, it would be better to have a video link to help maintain the interest of the research subject.

In-depth interviews are usually conducted at the expert's place of employment so that the time commitment is minimized. There may be situations when the expert may wish to have the interview conducted elsewhere so that they may speak more freely. For example, an event organization working with a festival that is having attendance problems may want to speak to someone who works at another festival. This person may feel uncomfortable speaking about his or her own organization's problems where others may overhear. Therefore the interview should be arranged for a neutral site such as a restaurant.

In addition, expert interviews can be conducted over the phone or via video link. Expert interviews usually do not involve communicating information at an emotional level. For this reason, technology can be used without the worry of missing information communicated through body language. In addition, telephone or online interviewing is necessary when the expert does not live in the local area.

Intercept interviews are always conducted at the location where the participants who match the profile can be located. If the interviews are to be of the destination's current visitors, then they are conducted on site. For example, they may be

Figure 9.3 Intercept interviews may be the best approach with visitors who are not interested in participating in research.

Photo Credit: Lestertair

conducted in the lobby of a hotel, the entrance to a gallery, the visitor center or even a public place such as park or beach. If the organization wants to interview people who are not current visitors they then must decide where these potential users can be found. For example, if a music venue wants to interview young males who do not attend events when visiting during the summer, they may consider conducting the interviews at the local beer garden.

Location choices for types of interviews

- In-depth: researcher's office, neutral location, online
- Expert: expert's office, online, telephone, online
- Intercept: organization's premises, public place where participants congregate

Interview participants

Because so few participants are needed for most interview research, there may be less concern over finding appropriate participants. After all, if a tourism organization only needs to interview five or six visitors, they may believe that it will be easy to wait until the last minute as these few people can be easily found. However, the opposite is true; the fewer the participants involved in a research study the more important it is to find the correct participants as each participant's input into the study is heavily weighted.

Another reason for researchers to spend more time considering the necessary participant profile is the fact that it is harder to recruit participants for interview research. A focus group is a much more stimulating event where the participant has the opportunity to meet and interact with others. An in-depth interview will involve a private discussion with only one person. An additional difficulty when recruiting is that the participant may not find the topic of as much interest as the researcher. Why should they want to give up an hour or more of their day, particularly if they are on holiday? As a result, finding and recruiting the appropriate participants will be challenging.

The organization may wish to consider incentives when recruiting participants for in-depth interviews. The incentive could be a reduction in price to attend an attraction, a voucher for dinner at a restaurant or a free ticket to an event. Cash incentives should be avoided as it should not be the only motivating factor for participation. The incentive is a way of acknowledging and thanking the participant for their assistance.

Developing the profile

Whether the research will be an in-depth, expert or intercept interview study, the first step is to develop a participant profile. This profile will help keep the researchers focused on finding the right visitors when they become discouraged and want to recruit someone who is only marginally qualified. With in-depth or intercept interviews one of the first issues will be based on whether they want to include current visitors or people who are unfamiliar with the attraction or event. The researcher will then need to decide on the demographic characteristics that are important to consider when developing the profile. Such characteristics as age, gender, income, ethnicity, religion, family status and educational level may, or may not, be relevant to the study. For example, the organization may decide that income and ethnicity are important demographic factors to include in the profile. The next question will be if the organization wants to limit the participants to a specific income level or ethnic group or if the organization wants to ensure that the participants are representative of all possibilities.

Psychographic characteristics will also be part of the profile. The organization must decide if the lifestyles, values and attitudes of the participants need to be considered. While age and psychographic characteristics are often related, this is not always true. Young people can have a conservative view of life or be very sedentary in their habits. Meanwhile, older people can have a very liberal view of life and have very active lifestyles.

Sample participant profile for amusement park interviews

- Visitor status
  - participants should be frequent visitors, defined as visiting the amusement park at least once a month in at least two seasons of the year
- Demographic characteristics
  - household with child or children under the age of 16 and income level below $30,000 a year.
- Psychographic characteristics
  - family should value time spent together in a physical activity such as team sports or solitary activities such as walking or gardening

Case Study 9.4: African safaris are going hands-off instead of hands-on

A staple of the safari tourism industry has been allowing people to interact with wild animals. Such attractions as riding an elephant and walking with a young lion were offered. These were considered typical tourism experiences and were popular with tourists. However, stories started to appear about the treatment of the animals used to entertain tourists. For animals to allow humans such close contact required training that was not always a positive experience for the elephant or lion. Governments became concerned about the bad press their countries would receive if the practices continued. The government of Botswana has banned the practices and many safari operators in Zimbabwe and South Africa have voluntarily stopped. Why?

While safari companies are naturally concerned that tourists will be disappointed and no longer book the trips, eco-tourists will not patronize a travel company that books these activities. TripAdvisor will not even allow the bookings on their site. In addition, most people's attitudes toward wild animals have changed. People no longer want to control an animal, they want to see it in its natural habitat, behaving in a natural way. Safari companies have responded by offering educational experiences where people can learn and observe (Holmes 2017).

Question: What interview research should be conducted before developing other types of activities for visitors?

Screening for in-depth interviews

After the profile has been developed the next issue will be where to find the participants. If the participants are to be current visitors to the city, hotel or event, information may be available in the form of visitor sign-in forms or hotel records. If the participants are to be non-visitors the organization may have to rely on snowballing, which uses referrals.

The organization will need the names of more participants than will be required at this stage in the recruitment process, as there will be referrals of people who do not meet the profile or do not wish to participate. It is better to start with too many names than to continually go back and find more.

Once the organization has the names of potential participants they will need to be screened. This screening process can be done online, in person or over the phone. The purpose of the screening is to ensure that the potential participant meets the profile. A short form should be developed to ensure that all relevant questions are asked. The completed form can then be used to explain why certain people who were referred were not selected to be participants.

When conducting the screening process, the researcher should not inform the potential participant of the 'right' answer that will include them in the study. This is to ensure that people answer the questions truthfully and not just so they will be included. If participants are not selected to be included it is not necessary to explain exactly why, but just to say that while the researcher appreciates their interest, their assistance will not be needed.

Sample screening questions for study on amusement park usage:

- Are there children under the age of 16 who are living in your household?
- Is the total income for your household below $30,000 a year?
- Can you name an activity that you do together as a family?

Screening participants for expert interviews

Expert interviews are conducted to obtain factual information about the causes of a problem. Researchers may want to save time by simply talking to anyone who is willing to give advice. However, careful thought in regard to who should be involved in the expert interviews will save time in the long run.

The researchers should consider the need to speak to someone at a tourism organization or service provider who offers a similar tourism product or service. For the example above, the organization conducting a study on amusement park visits by low-income families might contact the marketing department of a similar park in another city for information. However, the organization might also focus on other organizations that serve the same group but with a different product. In this case the organization might contact someone at the local zoo to find if they have been successful in attracting low income families. Finally, the organization may want to speak to someone who is familiar with how to attract families. In this case it might be a very different type of organization that is contacted, such as a youth sports league.

Organization chosen for expert interviews on amusement park visitors

- Product knowledge: marketing department at other amusement park
- Market segment knowledge: zoo that attracts low-income families
- Problem knowledge: youth sports league

The screening process will consist of finding the correct person with whom to speak. This may involve calls to the personnel department of the organization to determine who has the necessary knowledge. More likely, it will be through networking. The expert should then be contacted to explain the purpose of the research and the reason the organization is seeking their expertise. If the person's name was received from a mutual acquaintance this should be mentioned. A written communication should follow to confirm the details of the interview time and place.

Screening for intercept interview

The profile for intercept interviews will focus on visitor status and demographic characteristics. While psychographic characteristics are also considered, they are difficult to assess when only conducting a three- to five-minute interview. Intercept interviews are held where the participants are already congregating as the result of an activity. For example, when wanting to conduct intercept interviews of amusement park visitors, they are conducted in the park. This automatically screens for visitor status. The participant profile for intercept interviews would describe their demographics based on what can be physically observed: for example, whether they are alone or with others, age category and gender.

Participant profile for amusement park user study

- Park visitors
- Family groups with a least one adult
- Children to be young teens or younger

The screening process for intercept interviews has limits. It is difficult in such a short time period to establish enough trust to ask a personal question, such as income level. A substitute question on occupation can be used as occupation and income are usually closely related. Participants would find it easier to discuss their jobs than their financial situation.

The screening can be done visually with no questions needing to be asked. The researcher simply approaches a family group that meets the criteria and asks permission to conduct the interview. At the end of the interview they can ask the question about occupation. Even though some participants may not meet the criteria, the researchers may still find this interview data of interest.

References

Agee, J. 2009. Developing Qualitative Research Questions: A Reflective Process. *International Journal of Qualitative Studies in Education* 22.4: 431–447.

Ekstein, N. 2017. A Road Trip to South Pole Is the Coolest New Adventure [online]. *Bloomberg*, 23 March. Available from www.bloomberg.com/news/articles/2017-03-23/a-road-trip-to-south-pole-is-the-coolest-new-adventure. [Accessed 25 March 2017].

Holmes, R. 2017. Southern Africa's Tour Operators Are Radically Rethinking Wild Animal Attractions [online]. Skift. *Northstar Travel Media*. Retrieved 25 March 2017. Available from skift.com/2017/02/15/southern-africas-tour-operators-are-radically-re thinking-wild-animal-attractions/. [Accessed 15 February 2017].

King, D. 2017. Downhill Digerati: The next Generation of Ski Apps [online]. *Northstar Travel Media*. 21 March. Available from www.travelweekly.com/Travel-News/Travel-Technology/Downhill-digerati-The-next-generation-of-ski-apps. [Accessed 22 March 2017].

Liu, C. 2015. Never Ask What They Want – 3 Better Questions to Ask in User Interviews [online]. *Medium.com*, 9 December. Available from https://medium.com/user-research/never-ask-what-they-want-3-better-questions-to-ask-in-user-interviews-aeddd2a210 1e#.1bgzy3dtg. [Accessed 15 December 2016].

Mohn, T. 2017. The Hostel as Art Gallery, and Pipeline to an Arts Community [online]. *The New York Times*. 13 March 2017. Available from www.nytimes.com/2017/03/13/arts/design/hostels-art-exhibits-budget-travel.html?. [Accessed 29 March 2017].

Steber, C. 2016. The Pros and Cons of Face-to-Face Interviews for Market Research [online]. *Communications for Research*. 7 Feb. 2016. Web. 9 May 2017.Available from www.cfrinc.net/cfrblog/the-pros-and-cons-of-face-to-face-interviews-for-market-research. [Accessed 6 April 2017].

Chapter 10

Using social media to conduct research

Learning objectives

- What types of social media sites can be used to conduct visitor research?
- How can social media analytics be used as a source of data on visitor behavior and the effectiveness of marketing messages?
- Why are social media sites a source of information on visitor trends such as destination preference and service expectations?
- How can online communities be used to conduct netnography?

Chapter summary

- Information online is a source of opinions, ideas, comments, facts and trends but a method is needed for analyzing the data. Social media should be categorized by purpose rather than the names of the individual sites as these will change. The sites used for research must be ones whose information is valid and reliable. There are ethical issues when using online postings on social media that must be considered.
- Social media analytics provide research information on the effectiveness of the organization's social media marketing. The metrics inform the organization on the level of engagement that the visitor has with the site and organization. For more in-depth information these metrics should be used in combination. These insights gained can also be used for SEO optimization.
- Social media research can be used to keep track of fast changing visitor preferences. To do so blogger, aggregator and trend spotting sites should be reviewed. In addition, the effectiveness of content marketing should be analyzed. Online product reviews should be researched for ideas for new segments and product improvements.
- Research of online communities is referred to as netnography. It is used to join existing online communities to listen to conversations about visitor preferences and behavior. Social media can be researched without following the netnography

process but it should not be unstructured. The vast amount of information online means that simply browsing will take up too much time with no guarantee of results.

Social media sites and consumer research

Social media allows the exchange of written information, photos and videos directly between people, which is then shared with a wider community. The information, consisting of opinions, ideas, comments, facts, images and trends, posted on social networking sites can be used for research data. Other research techniques, such as a survey, focus group or interview, first collect data before analysis. The difference with social media marketing research is that the data already exists, but the researcher needs a method for analyzing what is relevant.

The vast amount of information available in social media means that without a process, it will be difficult to use the data to make recommendations. While information can be found by simply browsing, there are research methods that can be used to take a more structured approach. The first step, as with other methods, is to decide upon the research question, such as: What are solo travelers saying online about the service at our hotel? Collecting the data can be automated by using software that will search and find the required information from online postings. If the purchase of such software is not possible, it can be conducted by having a researcher go through postings on specific sites looking for comments and images that are relevant. Even when software is used, the insights of the researcher will still be needed to analyze the findings. The final report will provide more qualitative analysis of insights than charts and graphs. Additional research using traditional methods may be needed to confirm the insights uncovered before enacting recommendations.

Online research participants

In most social media research, the people generating the data are not aware that they are participating in research. For example, past visitors may be online commenting on a new hotel or sharing ideas of activities at a destination. Most of the data they provide will be qualitative including their opinions, complaints and suggestions for improvement. They may also provide quantitative information such as when they stayed, the number of nights that they stayed and who they were with. They will do so freely, either because they feel compelled to vent or they are altruistic and want to help other travelers. The same people that provide the information online may not be willing to participate in a survey, focus group or interview. If the information is posted on a public site, it can be used for research purposes. If the information is accessed by making a friend request, ethical issues arise (Moreno et al. 2013). Such friending implies a personal relationship on some level. The owner of the site may grant a request under the assumption that such a relationship exists. Therefore, such friend requests by a researcher involve deception.

Because the researcher does not need to make personal contact with the participant, social media research can be used to get data from populations that would be difficult to recruit as participants. For example, social media research can be particularly useful for tourism organizations that need to attract visitors from a distance. Another advantage is if the researchers are trying to get information from segments of visitors who may be difficult to recruit for traditional research methods, such as particular ethnic or age groups.

Types of social media sites

Social media sites continue to change as new sites with better features are developed. As a result, there are always new sites that are popular with users. In addition, particular visitor segments may use specific types of sites. While people refer to names of sites, such as Facebook or WeChat, individual sites will grow and fade in popularity due to a competing site offering better features. While the internet is global, some sites are specific to certain countries due to language or cultural differences. Rather than think about the brand name of the sites, it is better to classify social media sites by function.

First, there are the social networking sites that are used for communicating personal information. These sites have privacy features that might limit accessing the information to only friends and family. Some social networking sites are maintained by companies where people exchange information about their product and service and these sites are public. These sites are used to post both critical and helpful information about travel and destinations.

Other sites, such as LinkedIn, are meant to be used to connect professionally. Some are specific to types of professions while others are general. These sites are used to communicate between individuals but are also used by the public to learn more about companies. The types of information that can be researched include posts, likes and recommendations on lodging, destinations and events.

Some sites, such as Reddit, collect social news. People supply links to articles that they find intriguing and then add their own commentary. While any type of subject may be welcomed, the information can be searched by subject or company. These sites can be useful in finding what topics are trending in travel and destinations.

Blogging sites can be traditional, such as Blogger, or micro-blogging sites, such as Twitter. People often use these sites to instantly share favorable and unfavorable views of destinations. Photo and video sharing sites, such as YouTube and Pinterest, show consumers in the act of visiting destinations. Finally, there are many online community groups that focus on travel and hospitality related products.

New sites are constantly being introduced as technology continually develops. This is why thinking of social media as methods of two-way communication rather than brand names is essential. Even before social media research is attempted, the organization must determine what types of sites are used by the segment of visitors they wish to research or which particular sites are used to discuss the topic that is being researched.

Integration with traditional research methods

Sometimes social media research is a first step in developing another research methodology. One way it can be used is to develop survey questions and focus group discussion topics. This can be done by tracking social media conversations and postings to see what types of issues are raised repeatedly. For example, if visitors are frequently discussing the lack of cleanliness at venues, this might mean that a question on the importance of cleanliness should be added to a survey. The survey will then validate whether this is an issue of concern to the particular venue's visitors. It might be found, that while people discuss the issue online it is not of importance to the targeted visitors so will not be the basis for a recommendation. There may be a time when organizations will rely on social media as the main source of marketing research information (Nguyen 2017). Currently, it is more likely that traditional and social marketing research will be used in tandem.

Social media can be helpful in preparing for an expert interview. First social media can be useful in finding the names of influencers in the industry. This might be a blogger who writes on hospitality topics or simply the names of industry leaders. If there are a number of different experts who could be consulted about a marketing issue, then posting on social media will demonstrate which topic is of most concern.

Another way to integrate social media research is to use it for product development. People will often discuss how they wish that travel experiences could be improved. Some of these ideas could be developed by the organization and then could be tried on an experimental basis. Social media can then be used to learn if they are appreciated by visitors before being introduced on a larger scale.

Validity and reliability

One of the concerns with social media research is whether the data gathered is reliable and valid. Reliability refers to whether similar results would be obtained if another researcher undertook the same study. The results of a marketing research study should not be affected by the biases of the researcher. There is always the temptation to find the data that reinforces preconceptions. Because there is so much data available on social media, it would be easy for researchers to simply look for the comments that support their opinions and ignore the rest.

Validity refers to whether the data found actually reflects the truth. While reliability is the result of the integrity of the researcher, validity results from the skill of the researcher. Validity can be affected by the type of social media sites used. Twitter tends to attract and reinforce negative comments. One extreme experience of disappointment with the customer service a visitor experienced can be tweeted and retweeted numerous times. While the comment may be spread widely, the underlying cause may be a single occurrence and not representative of a trend. Another issue with the validity of social media research is whether those making the comments are reflective of the views of the target market segment. The challenge when designing social media research is understanding who is making the statements.

Because of these issues, social media research requires additional skills from the researcher. The person undertaking the research needs to be knowledgeable of the different types of social media sites and the audiences they attract.

Ethical issues in social media research

Most people using social media sites that do not contain privacy settings understand that their comments and contributions can potentially be viewed by anyone who is online. While the person is posting about a travel experience to help other travelers they are not posting to be used by an organization as a research participant.

If someone who comments knows that a site has been created specifically to be used for research purposes this may bias their response either positively or negative. People may post a complaint online as the result of unhappiness that has nothing to do with their tourism experience. Someone who is having a bad day can use social media to vent. Their actual experience may be different from what they have expressed online.

While people who comment on public sites cannot have an expectation of privacy, researchers who use comments must protect the privacy of the user as they have not given their consent to the research study. No identifying information should be used in a research report including either actual names or pseudonyms. In addition, the website name and date posted should not be used. Even direct quotes should be avoided as a search engine can be used to find the source. People posting on a public site have not given permission for their posting to be used for research purposes so their identity must be protected.

While conducting social media marketing research the organization should not at the same time conduct marketing. While researchers are collecting online comments made about their destination or event, they should not at the same time post information.To do so affects the validity of the research as such communication might affect the content of future posts. The researcher might feel that it is simply being helpful to visitors who will find the information useful. Doing so is unethical because it reinforces a narrative that research is just marketing in disguise. This will then make it more difficult to find research participants in the future.

Social media analytics as a source of data

There are tools built into social media that can be used to understand if and how people are interacting with the organization's sites. These tools can be divided into those that measure passive viewing versus engagement. The first passive measure, which shows that someone has come to a site, is reach. This is the total number of people who have found the tourism organization's social media site. If few people are finding the sites, this should be of concern to the marketing department. It also means that the organization's social media cannot be used to conduct consumer research as there aren't enough people on the site to give a range of views. There is another passive measure that can be researched, which is impressions. This can be a misleading measure of the effectiveness of the organization's social media as it includes every time a site is viewed. At first, it might seem that a high number would be proof of effectiveness but the number could include multiple views by the same person. Another passive social media measure is followers, which are the people who regularly view the organization's content or read the blog posts. While these followers are interested in the tourism organization, they have not yet shown the engagement that leads to purchase.

Passive measures

- Reach: number of people who visit a site
- Impressions: number of times a site is visited
- Followers: people who regularly visit a site

Engagement measures are a form of social media analytics that are more meaningful. Engagement happens when individuals provide information to others or back to the tourism organization. The organization should be aware of engagement such as shares and retweets, as they are a form of consumer driven marketing. This

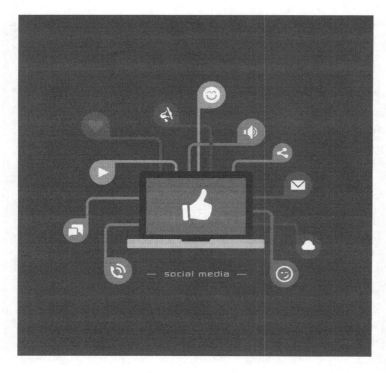

Figure 10.1 Social media research can be used to gauge potential visitors' interaction on sites.

Photo Credit: popcic

happens when potential visitors find the organization's message so compelling that they want their friends to hear it also. Mentions are when the potential visitor uses the organization or brand name in communication with others. Positive mentions are also a form of consumer driven marketing and are proof that the organization's message is compelling. Even negative mentions provide useful marketing research information for improvement. Comments are the most valuable form of social media information. By commenting potential and current visitors provide information without the cost and time of research being conducted. Comments can be used to improve both the product and marketing message.

An additional step in analysis is to track consumer sentiment. This can be done using software that can analyze online conversations for mention of the tourism organization. Using this information calculates the share of voice, which is the percentage of time that the conversation is about them.

Active engagement

- Shares and retweets: marketing message is passed on to others
- Mentions: tourism organization's name is mentioned in communications
- Comments: positive and negative feedback provided
- Share of voice: amount of time that the conversation is about the organization

Social media channels

Channels is a term used to describe how users arrived at a social media site. For example, a tourism organization can determine if someone has arrived directly to

Case Study 10.1: The digital concierge has arrived

Technology is being used to enhance the travel experience by providing advice on what to experience. Travelers want a personalized experience that meets their lifestyle and activity preferences whether they are solo travelers or families. Cruise companies have responded by adding unique activities onboard and on shore excursions that focus on anything from nightlife to environmental issues to volunteer opportunities.

The problem was helping travelers access all the activities. Travelers want to get the most from the cruise experience and don't want to waste time searching, and possibly missing, an event. With today's huge cruise ships and varied opportunities, how do people know where to go and what to do?

The old-fashioned printed daily itinerary was no longer enough to satisfy travelers' demands to get the most out of their experience. Technology presented the answer with a wrist band that is a personal concierge. To use the system cruise ships need to install digital access points and interactive screens. The system then allows the wristband to let travelers know where they are on the ship and help them to navigate to where they want to go. Because friends and family are also on the system, they can be easily located. The system also allows the traveler to easily book reservations for dining, the spa and excursions. As the software learns the travelers' preferences it will even make customized recommendations of where to go and what to see (Stieghorst 2017)!

Question: How could social media research be used to determine what functions such a system should provide for guests?

the social media site or via a search engine. All tourism organizations want their listings to appear as close to top of a search engine site as possible. By researching the channels potential visitors are using, the organization can determine how well their search engine optimization is working. Another way people can arrive at a social media site is by clicking on a social icon on the organization's website. If this link is not being clicked the tourism organization knows that potential visitors are not finding the content on the website compelling enough to want to learn more.

If a website link is included in an email that is sent, analyzing the channels will tell the organization if it has been clicked upon. If someone has come to the organization's social media because of information on another site, this is called a referral and can also be tracked. Finally, an organization will want to know if their paid online ads have resulted in consumers clicking through to their site to view the content.

Consumption metrics

Perhaps most important to marketing research are consumption metrics. While it is not possible to know how many people have viewed a magazine ad or seen a billboard on the side of the road, it is possible to know how many people have consumed content online. Social media analytics does the research, all that is needed is an understanding of what the metrics mean.

Page view, users and sessions are similar but with critical differences. Page views is simply how many times the website page has been viewed by potential visitors. However, a single viewer may come back to see the same page several times. While the organization will want to know if its product is compelling enough for people to return to the page, it is just as important to know how many distinct viewers are coming to the site. The tourism organization will also want to track users, which is the number of individual people who have viewed the page. While page views will be calculated for each page, sessions discounts users who are viewing multiple pages at one time. They will be counted as a single session.

While people might be attracted to an organization's page, the question remains as to whether they stay on the page long enough to read or view the content. Average length on page will provide this information. Another issue that needs to be understood is whether the information on the site engages the reader enough to have them explore more. Bounce rate is the number of viewers who only stay on the single page, while another metric tells how many pages were viewed during a session.

Most important for marketing research are conversion rates, which tally how often the site motivated people to take action. The tourism organization needs to know whether the video it posted was viewed and how often. If PDF files or other forms of information are posted on the site, metrics will show many viewers were motivated to download. Form completions to be sent in for more information can also be tracked. If any of these conversion rate metrics are unsatisfactorily low, the site with the links needs to be modified so that the rate is increased.

Combining social media metrics

While an individual social media metric can tell the tourism organization a great deal, the metrics should also be used in combination. If only one metric is tracked, the organization can congratulate itself on its social media marketing success without the effort resulting in actual visits to the destination. For example, having a large number of followers or likes is not better than having a low number if they do not engage in any other way. Social media does not exist simply to communicate information about a destination but rather to convert the interested into visitors.

One such combination uses bounce rate along with channel information. The tourism organization would like people to stay on the site until they have time to read the content and convert to buyers. The organization should look at bounce rate, which shows if the viewer interacted with more than one page, in combination with the analytic that shows from where the consumer arrived. If viewers that arrive from the organization's other social media sites stay online longer than those that arrive after a Google search, then the organization knows that its social media is effective in delivering the right potential visitors to its site.

Many organizations track the number of followers they have and they also track the numbers of comments per post. However, the two numbers when viewed alone do not provide much information. If the number of comments is looked at as a percentage of followers the number is much more meaningful. What the organization wants is followers who demonstrate a high level of interest in the destination by posting comments or questions. These viewers are most likely to become actual visitors to the destination. Likes is another social media metric that alone is fairly meaningless as it takes so little interest on the part of the viewer to click on like. Comparing the number of likes generated by a post to the number of followers demonstrates a level of intensity that a single metric alone cannot provide.

Search engine optimization research

Any organization involved in tourism, hospitality or events understands that people will be searching online for both activities and experiences. As they may not be aware of the name of a specific organization or destination, they will be conducting generic searches hoping that something or someplace of interest appears on the search engine listings. Search engine optimization, SEO, is a marketing technique that seeks to ensure that the organization's website will appear as the result of a potential visitor's search.

Effective SEO is a process that takes research. To research what terms a potential visitor might use, the organization should list topics that are related to their destination, hotel or event. For example, a marketing department for a hotel might immediately think of the name of the city. It is thought that once the potential visitor is on the city's tourism organization site, they will see the hotel name. However, an effective SEO program will reach beyond the obvious keywords such as the name of the city.

Additional keywords can be found by going online as if the researcher is a potential visitor. By doing so listings may be found for attractions located in the city, such as a children's museum. Potential visitors may start with searching using the museum's name. If the hotel website also includes the name of the museum in its keywords it will show on the list. After all, someone looking to visit the museum will need a place to stay. Appearing on the page when the name of the museum is searched will give the potential visitor the information they will need next.

Other ideas are to think of the activities people pursue when visiting a destination. For example, if a tourism organization for a city located in a mountainous area knows visitors come for hiking, then this 'word' should be part of the tourism organization's sites key words. A local event might list family friendly, educational or live music as part of their keywords. To find additional keywords, after using a keyword to find a page of listings, at the bottom of the page are additional search terms that can be relevant.

Head terms and long tail keywords are two kinds of search strategies that can be used by someone searching online. Head terms are short phrases such as searching for a 'Nashville hotel'. It is difficult to appear at the top of search engine generated list when someone uses a head term because so many listings will appear. An example of a long tail keyword search is the phrase 'what are the best family friendly hotels in Nashville'. Because a long tail keyword search is more specific, if the hotel brands itself as family friendly and uses this term in its keywords it will be easier to rank near the top of the list.

Researching consumer trends online

Every business needs to know what is happening in the external environment including economic, technological and socio-cultural trends. While the tourism researchers do not need a deep understanding of economic theory, they do need to research how the economic environment is affecting consumers' decision as to whether to travel, where they wish to travel and how much money they can, or are willing to, spend on travel. Technology is another aspect of the external environment of which the tourism organization must be aware. There are new travel products using technology that will impact the travel experience. Technology also affects how products are purchased. For example, the tourism industry would be affected by travelers' desire to make payments conveniently. Socio-cultural changes affect visitor preferences for travel experiences. A growing interest in extreme sports or cooking lessons will impact the travel industry as they can use this information to create and sell new experiences. For example, the issue of wellness has given rise to hotels providing yoga mats in rooms.

Bloggers, aggregators and trends

With so much change happening at increasing speed, it is difficult for any organization to keep up. In the past, the organization would need to wait for an editor or writer to research and then report the information on a news site. Social media has now changed this dynamic (Chahal 2017). Since consumers are providing direct evidence of these changes with online postings, tourism organizations can use social media to research current trends.

One of the problems with social media research is that there is such an abundance of interesting information online that it is easy to get sidetracked. To stay on track,

Figure 10.2 Visitor postings are a source of information on trends such as destination preference and service expectations.

Photo Credit: aodaodaodaod

Case Study 10.2: How do you know what people are really seeing online?

Hotels rely on online searches to drive potential visitors to their own websites. So when Google changes how search results appear online, hotel marketing departments are concerned. If online users change their behavior when presented with a list of hotels, the marketing department needs to know so they can adjust the key words for their own site. Such changes might also affect their use of Google AdWords.

When someone goes online to search for a hotel name, such as Bay Shore Inn, a number of results for destinations with the name Bay Shore will be listed. In addition, on the top left of the screen AdWord placements will appear. Below them will be the organic listings for hotels including the name and on the right business listings. But what do people really see when confronted with all this information?

A past eye tracking study, before the page was redesigned, found that people's eyes tracked an 'F' shape. They went across the top from left to right, then down the page until they again tracked right when something caught their attention. Another eye tracking study was commissioned after the research. It found that the page had affected viewers' behavior. Now people spent time viewing the top left portion and then spent an equal amount of time on the top right looking at the business listings. This means the organic listings received less attention as the viewer's eyes stayed at the top of the page.

Viewers' clicks confirmed this change as now 55 per cent of viewers click on a paid ad while only 28 per cent used an organic link listed lower on the page. The study shows that Google AdWords are effective for hotels, which then calls into question the relevance of SEO. After all, why worry about people finding you organically? There is a reason why SEO is still relevant. Even though they click on paid ads, 44 per cent of people say that they place more trust in the information found from organic searches (Heaword 2017).

Question: How else could eye tracking software be used to research viewers' use of the hotel's website?

just as with traditional research methods, a research question must be formulated. For example, a resort that targets families might be concerned by recent news stories about safety at hotel pools. The research question might ask what safety guidelines parents expect for children using public pools. They might research using news articles that have been written about parents' concerns, but these will all predate the more recent postings on social media. The way to go about doing such research is through following professional bloggers, reading aggregator sites and watching what is trending. Bloggers who specialize in a topic take on the role of researcher. There are bloggers on every subject from airline comfort to water safety. Many blog daily on any news item that is part of their interest area. The difference between a blogger and a reporter is that a blogger has a point of view that they express. For this reason, more than one blogger on a subject should be followed.

News aggregator sites take articles from other sites that are attracting interest and post the headline and link. Some sites have a point of view they reinforce with their choice of articles. Others try to show links to articles with a variety of views. To use the water safety example, an aggregator site might have an article that argues that hotels and resorts provide inadequate supervision, while another will argue that parents are no longer teaching their children to behave responsibly.

There are sites devoted to trends that can be used to research the topics currently of interest. Micro-blogging sites such as Twitter are a fast and easy way for people to communicate what is on their minds. Because what is expressed might be based on a fleeting emotion, individual tweets can be misleading. However, such a site is an excellent means of seeing what topics are being talked about. Most of the topics will not pertain to travel, hospitality or events. However, if pool safety for children is a topic that is trending, it will be on the minds of many visitors even if they have not been personally affected.

Social networking sites, such as Facebook, can play the same research role. These networks even provide a feature to show what topic is trending. If people are talking about vacations on a budget, this shows that people are concerned about having enough money to take a trip. If grandparents are talking about taking their grandkids on trips, this lets the researcher know there is an interest in multi-generational travel.

Video and photo sharing sites can also be used to research trends. When researching what is trending on these sites, the research question must be kept in mind as it is easy to become distracted. For example, if the question being researched is what activities families like to do on vacations, then vacation photos should be reviewed.

Finally, there are free and paid services that will follow trends and report on the findings. Google offers a service where they will send an email with a link to the article on any keywords that are specified. If popularity of organic wine is an issue of concern to an organization, Google will watch for content and report. There are also paid services that will allow for more parameters to be specified as to where the content appears and the date.

Content marketing research

Tourism organizations post content onto social media to attract the attention of targeted potential visitors. The messages posted shold not be direct marketing information, but rather should educate or entertain the potential visitor with information that is related to the travel experience. Before posting content, research needs to be conducted on what information is already attracting attention online. This type of research can be done by listening to and producing topics clouds (Smith 2016). It is easy for the researcher to go online and spend hours reading content clicking from one link on to another. However, this is not research but merely browsing. Instead, when reading content online the researcher should be listening for specific terms that relate to the research question. For example, if the tourism organization is interested in learning how much money people spend on holidays, content should be read looking for terms such as, expensive, cheap and budget.

A topic cloud can be used when the research question is about the interests of a specific target market segment. A topic cloud will extract the most common terms used in an online conversation and present them visually. The more times the term is mentioned the larger and bolder the word appears. An example of the use of a topic cloud would be an analysis of young Millennials discussing travel on a website dedicated to discovering new destinations. Even a quick glance at the topic cloud might show that the words 'relaxation' and 'nightlife' appear most frequently.

Another means of conducting marketing research of online content is trend alerts. For example, a destination may be near a site of a significant military battle for which a major anniversary is approaching. The destination may believe that this is a marketing opportunity. Setting up a trend alert that notifies the researcher every time someone is online discussing the battle may find that it is not being mentioned on social media. This means the destination will have to do significant marketing to excite the target market about events they will be having. Or, they may decide that there is not enough public interest to warrant spending money and energy on an event.

Online product review research

Online reviews are a new form of word of mouth marketing. In the past, a consumer had to be able to personally connect with someone who had purchased and used the product. Now they don't need to know someone as they can go online and find people they have never met who will share information. The consumer then decides whether they will trust the reviewer's opinion, which is why they will seek out many reviews from different sites. They will then in turn leave a review online. These reviews will focus on both the positive and negative aspects of the tourism experience. The reviews will answer the types of questions that would have been put to research subjects in a focus group or interview, such as complaints and improvement ideas. Now the answers are available online without the expense of conducting the research. Reviews can be used to spot new trends, get feedback on promotional campaigns or find ways to improve the product.

Social media monitoring or listening is research rather than just browsing when an organization is specifically looking for information about the tourism product or service. The result is that not only will the organization obtain information, it will be able to take immediate action to fix a problem. Such problems would usually become known only when formal research was conducted. Social media online research should not be conducted instead of traditional research but instead as a complement to surveys, focus groups and interviews.

Figure 10.3 Online product reviews should be researched for ideas on new segments and product improvements.

Photo Credit: aradaphotography

Case Study 10.3: Brits love traveling via YouTube

When searching online for travel information, what sites do the British use? A recent research study decided to analyze this question. What they found is not only are the sites used changing, but also how searches are conducted differs. The study found that people are watching more travel videos on YouTube. Video is so popular that it is estimated that by 2020 it will account for 79 per cent of all internet traffic. Obviously, people would rather watch than read.

Another study of British travelers was done in 2016 to determine the popularity of destinations by tracking the number of hits different travel videos received. While all destinations increased, some increases were dramatic. Travel video watching for Iceland increased 118 per cent, while Vietnam increased 75 per cent. What is also interesting is that how people search on YouTube differs from how they use search engines. YouTube searching terminology is much more precise. Almost half, 48 per cent, of searches on YouTube are a single word, such as Iceland. On search engines only 26 per cent of searches are a single word, while over half are three words or longer. This means that people start on search engines with general searches, but when on YouTube, they are looking for a very specific video topic (Hitwise Travel Study 2017).

Question: What type of research would let us know what search words are used when our travel video is found?

There are commercial service providers that will gather information from all relevant tourism review sites that mention the organization or destination. These service providers will then prepare reports providing a percentage of positive versus negative mentions. This allows the organization to prioritize customer issues based on what it believes needs to be addressed immediately.

Research using online communities

One of the uses of social media for conducting research is netnography, a new form of ethnography. In ethnography, the researcher studied cultural differences by traveling to the location where the research was undertaken, often a distant part of the world. With the development of technology, the idea of virtual ethnography, or netnography, developed. Rather than the researcher studying people who share a culture because they live in a specific geographic location, the culture of individuals who come together online is studied. Netnography uses online technology to study relationships that take place only as virtual relationships.

Netnography process

A researcher can use netnography in an effort to understand the reason why travel decisions are made. This is in opposition to social media analytic research which attempts to quantify consumer behavior (DeVault 2017). For example, a researcher might want to know whether the bride or groom makes the destination decision for a honeymoon. They could conduct a survey, but using netnography they can see the process happening. They could do so by visiting a social networking site dedicated to honeymoon planning where they can first observe the online behavior by reading the comments and following conversations where input is received from both brides and grooms. They will then contact specific people who are on the site to ask questions about who has the final say in choosing a destination. Netnography involves the analysis of data, such as the number of interactions, but also the skill of the researcher in developing and handling online relationships with people.

Once the research question has been determined, the netnography research process involves the researcher finding and joining an online community where the research subjects interact. For example, the research question might be on the decision making process of young people planning spring break trips. Once the question is formulated, the appropriate online community where information on spring break destinations is shared must be found. Next, a schedule of interaction must be developed. To learn about the behavior of a group will take repeated interactions on the site. The researcher will follow this schedule by going online to both review current comments and to ask questions of community members. Finally, the results will be analyzed and reported.

The advantage of this type of online research is that rather than just asking for an opinion, the potential traveler's behavior toward a destination can be researched. For example, on a review site someone might post a negative comment about an experience at a concert venue. The negative review may have resulted from a real problem with a venue or from someone who just had a bad day. There is no way for the researcher to learn more unless they are able to communicate directly. However, when the information is shared in an online community other people will post their responses. For example, a complaint might be made that the concert was too noisy. Other community members may then respond that the concert was heavy metal and was expected to be loud.Hearing the response to a complaint in the context of an online community conversation will provide the needed clarification

A decision will need to be made as to whether the researcher will inform the group of the purpose of the research when joining the online group or if they will simply join in the conversation noting interesting research findings as they occur. One of the advantages of publicly declaring the fact that research is being conducted is that researchers can steer the conversation to the research question. For example, an online group of solo travelers may not discuss how their destination decision would have been different if they were traveling with someone else. If the researcher has informed the group of the process they can ask if the decision process would be different. Whether the answer is yes or no, the online comments and conversations will provide insights into the thinking of the group members. Netnography is different from conducting surveys and interviews because it includes listening to ongoing conversations over time with the researcher as an active participant; the research is conducted as conversation rather than question and answer.

Social media online consumer insights

Social media can be used to research insights and ideas without joining an online community. To do so, the researcher simply researches online conversations. However, this should also use a structured approach. The researcher should not

> ## Case Study 10.4: Everyone wants to know if a hotel is green
>
> There are many travelers who will only stay at hotels that follow environmentally friendly practices. How do you know if a hotel is green or just saying so? Now there is a way for hotels to track their environmentally sound practices on a daily level. The Greenview Portal makes it easy by providing one online site where such issues as energy conservation, water usage and waste reduction can be tracked for each property rather than only at corporate headquarters. The site then suggests better ways to implement environmentally sound practices that will save time and reduce costs. There is even an online library of resources so that the hotel staff can learn more. Because the public now expects companies to care about the community, there is also a way for hotels to log in their community based activities.
>
> What does this have to do with guest relations? The hotel can compare how well they are doing on their conservation efforts with other hotels that use the system. Not only does this create friendly competition, it allows the hotel to inform guests on the standing of their environmental standards compared to their competition (4Hoteliers 2017).
>
> *Question: How can a tourism organization use social media to learn more about what environmental issues are of most concern?*

start reading without first determining the questions that need to be answered. When asking a research question on consumer insights, it is useful to research more broadly than only using the organization's name. While an organization will surely want to research what is being said about them online, consumer insight research has a broader focus. The organization should want to learn what consumers are saying about the product category as a whole. So instead of researching a hotel name, the research question might focus on what amenities people are seeking in a hotel. The researcher will need to determine what type of sites, forums or blogs would contain this sort of information. Once this is done, the research can then either use software to analyze the content, or even better, the researcher would be analyzing what is being said.

The reason for having a researcher do the analysis is that software cannot look for what the organization does not know exists. There may be surprising insights that the researcher would not know enough to ask about. For example, reading online comments about hotels and amenities might uncover the fact that people are not going on outdoor adventures when traveling because they do not have room to pack the necessary clothing. As a result, a hotel might decide to start providing backpacks for guest use.

When reviewing the posts, the researcher will develop categories and subcategories. For example, when reading posts about hotels and technology, it would be unsurprising if a number of them mentioned in-room Wi-Fi. This would then be coded as a category. Within this category, subcategories might be found such as cost, strength and ease of connection. In reading more about this issue some outlying comments can be tagged. For example, if there are a few random complaints such as that Wi-Fi is stealing addresses. In this case, the reason for tagging is so that later, the researcher can decide to see if there are other comments on the topic. The fact that the researcher knows this is not true is irrelevant as it is what consumers think is true that is being researched.

When analyzing the data, the researcher is looking for both similarities and differences. There may be similar comments made about technology that apply to all hotels. A comment that room service cannot be ordered via the phone might be an example. However, dissimilar comments can be just as insightful. A comment might be made that someone doesn't want to interrupt phone calls and wishes there was a computer screen in the room that could be used without the hassle of signing in.

The data from this type of research is reported in the form of a story rather than with charts and graphs. To help people wade through all the information the categories, subcategories and tags will be helpful. However, it is the insights that the researcher brings in interpreting the online conversations that are critical. If a more quantifiable approach is then desired, additional research can be conducted on the issues uncovered. If sufficient information is obtained, the organization may be ready to write a survey to confirm the analysis. If not, focus groups or interviews may need to be conducted.

References

Chahal, M. 2017. The Future of Social Insight [online]. *Marketing Week*, 16 May. Available from www.marketingweek.com/2017/02/22/future-social-insight/. [Accessed 19 May 2017].

DeVault, G. 2017. How Market Research Is Like Anthropology [online]. *The Balance*. 28 February. Available www.thebalance.com/investigate-social-media-like-an-anthropolo gist-2297153. [Accessed 19 May 2017].

Heaword, T. 2017. Eye Tracking in 2017 for Google Hotel Searches: Why the Old Rules Don't Apply [online]. *Travel Tripper Inc.*, 20 March. Available from www.traveltripper. com/blog/eye-tracking-in-2017-for-google-hotel-searches-why-the-old-rules-dont-apply/. [Accessed 23 March 2017].

Hitwise Travel Study Shows Growing Power of YouTube. [online] TravelMole, 7 Mar. 2017. Available from http://www.travelmole.com/news_feature.php?news_id=2026229. Web. [Accessed 3 April 2017].

Moreno, M., N. Goniu, P. Moreno, and D. Diekema. 2013. Ethics of Social Media Research: Common Concerns and Practical Considerations. *Cyberpsychology, Behavior and Social Networking* September 16(9): 708–13.

Newly Launched Greenview Portal Simplifies Going 'Green' for Hotels [online]. Hotel, Travel & Hospitality News. *4Hoteliers*, 30 March 2017. Available from www.4hoteliers. com/news/story/17006. [Accessed 30 March 2017].

Nguyen, H. 2017. Should Social Media Analysis Replace Traditional Marketing Research? [online]. NetBase. 22 March. Web. 19 May 2017. Available from www.netbase.com/blog/social-media-analysis-replace-traditional-marketing-research/. [Accessed 19 May 2017].

Smith, K. 2016. 7 Ways to Use Social Media for Content Marketing Research [online]. *Brandwatch*, 12 July. Available from www.brandwatch.com/blog/social-media-con tent-marketing-research/. [Accessed 12 March 2017].

Stieghorst, T. 2017. MSC Cruises Rolling out Personalization Technology [online]. Travel Weekly. *Northstar Travel Media*, 6 March. Available from www.travelweekly.com/Cruise-Travel/MSC-Cruises-rolling-out-personalization-technology? [Accessed 13 March 2017].

Chapter 11

Analyzing research data

Learning objectives

- What differentiates the process of analyzing the data that results from qualitative and quantitative research?
- What are the steps in the process of organizing and transcribing qualitative data so that it can be coded for categories and themes?
- How should the numerical data from quantitative research be analyzed using descriptive and inferential statistics?
- How can a hypothesis be supported using statistical tests using the z-score at different confidence levels?

Chapter summary

- The results of survey questions will be expressed in numbers that can then be analyzed by turning them into percentages or ratios that are easy to understand. In addition, more sophisticated quantitative analysis using correlation can be used. After conducting qualitative research, the researchers will have transcripts of tapes and other written material. This raw data will be coded for concepts to determine which themes are repeatedly present.
- All the written material from qualitative research must be organized and labeled as memories will fade. The tapes from focus groups and interviews can be transcribed using software. It is still recommended that the researcher listen to the tapes to get the emotional meanings of what was said. The researcher can do so while making notes on the written transcript. These notes will then be analyzed to find comments that are frequently repeated and therefore are common themes, and those that are unique. Written and other material from projective techniques should also be analyzed for common themes.
- Quantitative results from surveys need to be calculated. The data can then be analyzed using descriptive statistics to find patterns in the responses. Descriptive

statistics include frequency, central tendency and dispersion. These statistics will not only describe which responses were most frequently given but also the distribution of responses across the different available answers. Inferential statistics can then be used to determine statistical differences.

- To obtain more information on how the individual responses are distributed from the mean, the researchers will need to use statistical measures of dispersion. These include range, variance and standard deviation. Tests of statistical significance can be used to conduct hypothesis testing.

Research analysis process

A tourism organization will have spent a considerable amount of time planning the research process including determining the research question and deciding upon the methodology that will best provide the answer. After these two major decisions, the organization then faced the task of finding participants. Finally, the organization conducted the research.

After conducting the research, it is now time to analyze the research findings. The excitement of conducting the research is over, and the researchers may be ready to move on to a new project. This would be a mistake as just having data does not answer the research question. Without careful analysis of the data, recommendations cannot be made and the entire research process would be wasted.

There may be an assumption that all that is needed is to print out the data and present it in a report. The problem is that people who do not regularly conduct research may not understand the meaning of the data. The research data needs to be interpreted to provide information which can be used to make decisions.

The analysis process varies dramatically depending on whether quantitative or qualitative research has been conducted. A quantitative research method provides information that is in numerical form such as the number of responses to each

Figure 11.1 The data from research can result in recommendations on what services to offer.

Photo Credit: Peter Turner Photography

question. The analysis process uses mathematics and statistics to describe this data. By contrast, qualitative research results in transcribed verbal comments. To analyze this data the researcher will use coding and development of themes and categories to make sense of the findings in a way that will result in recommendations for action.

Differences in analysis

- Quantitative analysis
  - ○ basic analysis requires only counting and math
  - ○ numbers are compared and contrasted for new meanings
  - ○ sophisticated analysis of findings requires knowledge of statistics
  - ○ numbers are used to describe consumers and behavior
  - ○ results are used to disprove or support a hypothesis
- Qualitative analysis
  - ○ coding to develop themes and categories
  - ○ analysis of data occurs while research conducted
  - ○ methodology changed based on findings
  - ○ data repeatedly analyzed by researcher for new insights
  - ○ recommendations based on analysis of data and skill of researcher

Analyzing quantitative data

If the research was a survey that was not done online the organization will be left with a pile of questionnaire forms. The responses on these questionnaires will then need to be counted to find the number of participants who responded to each question by selecting a particular answer. If the survey was conducted online, this counting is done automatically. Either way, the numbers must then be analyzed by turning them into percentages or ratios. Everyone is familiar with research findings that state that 48 per cent of the visitors are male or that 62 per cent of people prefer purchasing their tickets online.

Simple quantitative analysis using only counting and basic math may be all that is needed to describe both visitors and their behavior. For example, a quantitative study can state that 22 per cent of the guests at a family day at the zoo were under the age of 30. Numbers can also state that 37 per cent of the visitors to the zoo recalled seeing an advertisement on a social media site. In addition, math can be used to calculate the variation in the behavior of members of a group. Survey results may find that single visitors spent 38 per cent more in the café or gift shop than families.

Rather than looking at the numbers in isolation, the responses to questions can be compared to provide more information. A tourism attraction may use survey questions to discover what benefits are desired that are missing. Other survey questions may be about the visitor's family status, income or where they live. Correlating the desired benefits with the demographic and geographic data can help to define a new visitor segment. For example, it might be found that a majority of respondents to a survey complain that a small amusement park does not have thrilling rides. Instead of the park spending the money to add attractions, a deeper analysis of the data might reveal another strategy. A correlation of the responses to this question along with family status might find that families from the cities like

Figure 11.2 Before a zoo develops new services such as a zoo train, the visitor desire should be confirmed with a quantitative survey.

Photo Credit: photosunny

the small amusement park just the way it is because it reminds them of simpler times. The park can then use this information to design a promotion campaign aimed at families communicating this message. This may be a more effective strategy than trying to emulate large amusement parks to attract young, thrill-seeking visitors.

More sophisticated quantitative analysis requires an understanding of statistics. While software programs will do the calculations that result in the statistics, the researcher will still need to understand how the statistics should be interpreted. Statistical analysis can be used to disprove or support the hypothesis that was stated when the research began. For example, analyzing the research findings will allow an organization to state that a survey found that a majority of city residents believe that encouraging tourism provides jobs with a 97 per cent confidence that this finding is true.

The analysis of quantitative data only occurs after all the questionnaire forms have been completed. After all there is no reason to analyze findings when only half of the forms that are expected to be returned are in. It would be a waste of effort since the exact same analysis will need to be completed once all the forms are available. However, once the analysis of findings does begin the numbers can be continually compared and contrasted for new meanings. For example, a survey on dining habits of tourists can first examine how much people spend per day on food. The same data can then be examined to determine if age, marital status or income

Case Study 11.1: You start with the Beatles, but then keep going

The 50th anniversary of the release of the Beatles album *Sgt. Pepper's Lonely Hearts Club Band* was in 2017. The album, which sold globally, changed the direction of popular music. As everyone knows, the Beatles are from Liverpool in the UK. It is estimated that Beatles related tourism already brings around US$100 million into the city each year. While the city of Liverpool wants the money to keep coming, the original fans of the Beatles are now well into their senior years. To attract younger visitors the city of Liverpool knew they would have to do something a bit different to celebrate the anniversary other than just have a concert of pop music for the original fans.

Instead, they decided to take a cross-disciplinary approach. The plan was to appeal to fans of other types of music and even art forms so that they would visit, enjoy the events, but also become aware of the continuing influence of the Beatles' music. A different project was chosen for each track of the album. For example, one track was the inspiration for a new mural. Ragafest will showcase the Indian music that inspired one of the songs. Poets will be involved using the song 'When I'm 64' as an inspiration. There will be a parade of traffic wardens in commemoration of the song 'Lovely Rita' and, finally, new compositions will be performed (The Traveller 2017).

Question: If standard demographic data was collected along with performer preference, what type of correlations should be analyzed?

correlate to amount of money spent. The data can then be reexamined for each new question to see if an answer can be found.

Analyzing qualitative data

Analysis of qualitative data is a completely different process. Rather than completed questionnaires whose responses must be counted and turned into percentages, the researchers will have transcripts of tapes and other written material. This raw data will be coded to determine which themes are repeatedly present.

Also unique to qualitative research is the fact that the analysis of findings does not wait until the end of the research process. Unlike quantitative research, qualitative research has started with a research question but not with a hypothesis. This is because qualitative research explores an issue of which little is known. Because of the lack of knowledge the organization is unable to even generate a hypothesis. For example, an organization such as a hotel or tourism attraction may be experiencing low visitor numbers. They could write a survey if their assumption is that the cost of visiting is decreasing attendance. However, since this is simply an assumption, they instead decide to conduct focus groups on why visits are declining. During the first couple of focus groups they may instead learn that the participants are able to afford a visit but are unhappy with the quality of the facilities. The focus group can then change the focus group questions to learn more about visitors' preferences for facility improvements.

Once the research has been completed the researchers will have multiple transcripts of focus groups or interviews. They will also have written material produced during the focus groups such as lists of preferences or concerns and material produced as a result of projective techniques. All of this raw material will be repeatedly analyzed looking for meanings that may not be apparent at first. For example, interviews conducted with parents may contain many references to the parents' concern that a vacation allow for quality time with their children. However, careful listening to the tapes or reading the transcripts will find comments on the fact the parents also wish to spend time away from their children.

Recommendations will then be built from this analysis and the knowledge of the researcher who conducted the interviews. In this case the recommendation may be made that separate activities for both parents and children be included in the itinerary. With quantitative research someone other than the researcher can conduct the statistical analysis. With qualitative research it is the knowledge that the researcher brings to the analysis process along with the findings that result in the recommendations.

Organizing and coding qualitative data

The need to analyze the data should be considered by the researcher as soon as the research is completed. Conducting focus groups and interviews can be an emotionally draining process as it requires intense concentration. It would not be surprising for the researcher to want to take a break as soon as the last participant has left. However, before the researcher leaves it is necessary to organize the data that has been collected during the research.

If the interview or focus group has been recorded on a digital recorder a notation to the tape should be added that identifies the date and topic of the interview or group. After this task has been completed, any written material that has been produced should be labeled. Added to any lists or other material should be the date and topic of the research along with the question that was asked that inspired the list. It frequently happens that by the next day or week, the list or words may no longer make any sense to the researcher. For example, a list may have been have generated on how to attract young adults to cruises. This list of 'reasons' should be labeled with the question so that it can be differentiated from the list that resulted from the question of what can be done, which would be labeled 'solutions'.

In addition to lists the researcher may have asked participants to place ideas on cards. These should have been collected during the research process and set aside. They now can be clipped together by topic and labeled. Handouts such as cartoon completion should be similarly handled. While these may seem mundane tasks, in fact they are just as important as not losing completed questionnaires when conducting survey research. The material is what will be analyzed and if it is not collected and organized, the researcher is left with only memories.

Back in the office the researcher will face the task of transcribing the tapes. In addition, the information on the lists and cards should be typed. Any information on handouts such as cartoon completion, or ad creation should also be typed or scanned. Once the information has been typed, the original material should still be kept, because the written or drawn material will contain information other than just the written words. For example, a participant in a focus group on tourism development for a festival may write in large letters with a red marker the comment 'too crowded'. The fact that the participant wrote the words larger than any other comments and in red communicates the intensity of the feeling in a way that the typed list can never do.

Transcribing taped material

After all the material has been labeled and dated, the next step in the analysis process will be the transcription of taped material resulting from both focus groups and interviews. There is software that will provide a word for word transcription along with an analysis of most commonly used words. With qualitative research the act of transcribing the tapes is not a routine task but part of the analysis process. Therefore, if possible, the researcher even if not doing the transcription should listen because it is not just the words themselves that are important but also how they are spoken. These nuances of tone of voice will have meaning to the researcher who will remember them in the context in which they were made. This information would be lost if only computer software is used for analysis.

During focus groups or interviews, researchers are so focused on the process that they may miss some of the underlying meaning of the words that are being spoken. For example, a researcher may initially miss the anger in someone's statement that they are tired of having to wait at the front desk to check in. While during the focus group the researcher may have thought of this simply as a matter of inconvenience, listening carefully to tape might make the researcher realize that the person making the statement sees having to wait as indicative of an overall uncaring attitude.

In the past tapes of focus groups and interviews would have been professionally transcribed by a typist. While such a transcription was useful, the cost was usually prohibitive. In addition, it would take time for the transcript to be produced. By the time the transcript was ready for analysis the researcher who conducted the focus group or interview might not remember the nonverbal body language that accompanied the comments. Instead, computer software can be used to turn the recorded file into a written transcript. This can be done using a number of programs that can be found online.

When transcribing to the tape, the speakers will not be identified by name and the researcher, who may be conducting more than one focus group or interview, may quickly forget who is speaking. Of course, the actual name of the speaker is not important, but the researcher will want to remember if the comments were made by the older woman who was quiet but intently listening throughout the group session, or the older woman who was quiet because she seemed bored.

Instead of transcription, researchers should read through the computer generated transcript while listening to the tape. They can then make a note of all comments with a form of shorthand. For example, a long statement about the inconvenience of the organization's location and the amount of money it costs to travel to a hotel can be simply noted as 'location inconvenient – parking too expensive'.

The coding of the transcript should not be an onerous task. There are parts of a focus group or interview, particularly at the beginning, when little of importance is being said. These notes can be made at the same speed as the tape is playing. However, other portions of the tape will be rich with material that needs to be typed. At these times the researcher will need to stop the tape in order to type all the necessary comments or even go back and listen again.

Coding transcribed material

At the end of the transcription process the researcher will have the tape transcript, typed lists of information, and perhaps drawings or photographs. While researchers will already have been thinking about the meaning of what has been said, they shouldn't simply go with their first insight, such as deciding price is the problem or the location needs to be changed. Instead the researchers will now start a process called coding, which is a systematic method of analyzing all the typed material, looking for common concepts. While the transcript provides the words, only the researcher can add the emotional meaning behind them (Gläser and Laudel 2013). It is this meaning that provides the emotional information that is difficult to achieve with quantitative methods.

For example, reading through the transcripts and lists that resulted from a focus group on festival attendance, the researchers may notice that the concept of price repeatedly emerges. It may have been stated directly, but there also may have been indirect comments such as 'the economy is not doing well' or 'I am saving money'. Each of these statements would be coded as 'price'. Other price comments might be about the cost of transportation, or the cost of dining out. At this point in time, the researcher does not differentiate but simply codes them all as price issues. Other issues that differ from price that might be coded from such a focus group might be entertainment quality or appropriateness of venue.

Coding Process

The researcher can code the material by simply using a different colored highlighter for each type of issue. The researcher will find that different comments will have the same coding because the participants may state the same issue in different ways.

The researchers will need to review the same transcripts more than once before they are sure that the coding is complete. For some focus groups or interviews the issues will become plain early in the coding process. For example, interviews of parents who bring their children to a historic site may quickly reveal that the parents are motivated by a desire to educate their children on history. This is not a surprising finding and hardly worth the trouble of conducting the interviews. Repeatedly going through the transcripts might also reveal that each of the parents states, although using very different words, that they feel they are better parents for having brought their children. The researcher may then start thinking that besides educating their children another motivation would be to gain status as a 'good' parent.

Developing themes

Once the coding is completed it is now time for the researcher to consider the connections between the codes. At this stage the researchers might realize that

Case Study 11.2: Hotels need housekeepers – but they also need tech workers

Hotel guests now expect technology to be part of their hotel stay, just as it is part of their everyday life at home. Of course, hotels need employees to manage their websites. In addition, employees must maintain data centers for guest information. Every hotel stay consists of many different purchases, and all this financial data must be kept accurate and reported correctly by tech workers. Behind the scenes at the hotel so much technology is being incorporated that 'hospitality tech expert' is now a recognized employment field.

And more hospitality tech experts will be needed in the future. One example is Hilton's change to keyless hotel room entry. Hilton has 4,800 hotels across the world. Currently only 750 offer keyless entry, a number they want to move to 2,500 within a year. This will take a great deal of coding by tech experts, and when the job is done, customers will want technology to do something more (Weed 2017).

Question: What type of information could a hotel find by analyzing their customers' demographic data and correlating it with sales data?

Figure 11.3 Responses from unique tourism segments, such as bachelorette parties, can be analyzed separately to better meet their needs.

Photo Credit: vectorfusionart

codes they thought were separate are common themes and need to be combined. For example, comments on an attraction's inconvenient location, lack of parking, and heavy traffic are all part of the same theme of transportation problems.

The researcher may find they need to separate some coding into different categories. For example, the researcher might separate issues of price into those concerned with the ticket or room price and those related to other issues such as dining and transportation.

At times a new theme will need to be created by the researcher. For example, a focus group on perceptions of visitor centers might have resulted in coded material grouped under separate themes of 'poorly staffed' and 'no one greets'. After some thought the researcher might realize that all this coded material is connected by a single theme of 'unwelcoming'.

This type of insight could then lead directly to a recommendation that the management designate 'greeters' at visitor centers who will make sure that everyone feels welcome when they come in the door. This type of insight is why the analysis of qualitative data requires a skilled researcher and is more of an 'art' than the statistical analysis of quantitative data.

Using statistics to analyze quantitative data

Once quantitative survey research methodology has been completed, the researcher will be left with completed questionnaire forms either in paper or electronic form. To turn these forms into findings from which recommendations can be made, a standard process should be followed. The process includes a pre-analysis stage where the forms will be reviewed, open-ended questions coded and the data entered, if not an online survey. The data can then be analyzed using descriptive statistics. Inferential statistics can then be used to determine statistical differences and also hypothesis testing.

Qualitative analysis process

- Pre-analysis
  - review data for validity, completeness and accuracy
  - code open-ended questions
  - enter data into computer software program, if needed
- Descriptive statistics analysis
  - frequency
  - central tendency
  - dispersion
- Inferential statistics analysis
  - Statistical difference
  - Hypothesis testing

Pre-analysis of survey forms

After the work of preparing and conducting the survey it is understandable if researchers will want to immediately start analyzing the responses. However, they must first take the time to review the questionnaires for validity, completeness and accuracy. This is true whether the questionnaire was on paper or online.

Validity refers to whether the forms were actually completed by the participants. If the researchers conducted the survey themselves, this is not an issue. If someone else conducted the research, the forms need to be checked to ensure that the assistants did not complete all or some of the forms without actually surveying participants. The researchers should check for validity by reviewing the forms while looking for random or nonsensical answers. For example, it would be extremely odd if the researchers found that almost all forms had 'married with children living at home' checked when the participant profile called for a study of university students and their choice of spring break destinations.

While problems with validity should be rare, what is more common is the issue of completeness, especially with self-administered online surveys. It is not uncommon for participants to not complete every page in a survey or every question. This might be because they did not notice a page in the survey or they found some of the questions confusing. The researchers will have to decide how many or which of the questions can be skipped for the survey form still to be useful. For example, if the survey was designed to determine if there is any difference in preference between males and females, and the gender question is unanswered, then this survey form may need to be discarded.

Lastly the survey forms must be checked for accuracy. Before data entry the researchers should review each form to determine if all answers are clearly marked and legible. This must be done before data entry because if the data entry clerks are unable to easily distinguish which answer has been marked, they might just make their best guess.

After the forms have been reviewed, if paper forms are used they are now ready for data entry. As the data will need to be entered as numbers rather than words, the researchers will now need to code the answers to any open-ended questions. For example, if a question was asked about the main motivation for attending a festival, the answers will need to read and then grouped by theme just as is done when analyzing qualitative data. Once the themes are found each will be given a number and the numbers will be placed by the words on the forms. Once the coding of open-ended questions is complete, there is no reason why the data entry cannot be done by someone other than the researchers.

If the survey was conducted using a paper questionnaire the data must be entered into a database or spreadsheet program. After entering the data, the number of the row will be recorded on the questionnaire so that the data entry can be checked for accuracy if needed. The software used should allow the researchers to analyze for frequency, central tendency and dispersion.

If the survey was conducted online, the data is ready to be analyzed by the built-in statistical tools. Most survey forms are now developed using online software that automatically enters the answers in a form that can be analyzed.

Analysis using descriptive statistics

Once the responses from the surveys have been entered in the software program, the researchers are now ready to begin analyzing the findings. The easiest way to do so is using descriptive statistics, which include frequency, central tendency and dispersion. Using descriptive statistics, such as frequency, the researchers should

Case Study 11.3: Want a blanket to keep warm on your flight?

You can have one but the airline will charge you $12! As airlines have lured more passengers with cheap airfares, they have increasingly made up for the lost revenue with added on fees. It wasn't that long ago when food and beverages were provided as a courtesy and of course you could check your baggage with no additional charge. Now airlines are charging for food, drink, baggage, earbuds, newspapers, entertainment and blankets. The amount of money collected from these fees now makes up 10 per cent of airline revenue.

Please don't think of complaining. An 88-year-old man who had to pay $12 for a blanket commented that someone should be 'taken behind the woodshed' for such extortion. As a result of his 'threatening' behavior, the plane made an unscheduled stop and the elderly man was taken off the plane (Sablich 2017)!

Question: What interview questions could be asked to determine travelers' attitudes toward such fees?

be able to find patterns in visitor behavior. Using cross-tabulation of the descriptive results they can then analyze if certain groups of people behavior differently from others.

While the behavior of the individuals who participated in the survey will differ, it will not be completely random. An analysis of central tendency looks at all the survey results to determine what responses are usual or normal for most of the individuals participating in the survey. Besides what is the usual or normal response, the researchers will want to know how much the individuals vary from this norm. Statistical measures of dispersion can provide this information.

Determining frequency

One of the easiest statistical methods to calculate is frequency distribution, which is simply counting how many participants responded with each possible answer to a question. This is the first statistic the researcher should analyze. Examples of frequency include how many participants are male versus female and how many participants noticed versus didn't notice the organization's recent ads for summer holidays.

Besides just counting the number of responses, the researchers should also calculate the percentage of each response group. Instead of just stating 390 respondents were male and 420 were female out of a total of 810, it is much easier to analyze the percentages of 48 per cent male and 52 per cent female. The frequencies will be much more meaningful to the reader when the percentages are included.

Frequency statistics can be used to provide much richer information. For example, the organization may have found that only 43 per cent of participants were aware of the promotional campaign for a summer festival. Of course, this might be a matter of concern for the organization, but this finding provides no information on how to solve the problem of low awareness.

Cross-tabulation splits the responses into two groups, such as male and female, and shows the number of positive and negative responses separately for each group. Using this method, the researchers may learn that a larger percentage of males than females responded that they had not heard the promotional message. The organization might then speculate that the campaign message was not placed on the social media sites used by males. However, the organization might also want to cross-tabulate responses on awareness by other factors. The computer can be asked to calculate the number of positive and negative responses by respondent age. This result may find that specific age groups have a much higher negative response rate than others. Perhaps the issue is not male or female, but the age of the respondent. The computer can then be asked to run a cross-tabulation by males versus females and age at the same time. This will tell the organization which factor, age or gender, is resulting in the negative response rate. Not all free survey software provides this analysis.

Central tendency

Software will calculate the mean, mode, and median of the total responses for each question. Some questions provide only two possible responses, such as male or female, or yes or no. The central tendency that will be calculated for these types of responses is mode. The mode is simply the answer that received the most responses. It would make no sense to average the answers.

The statistical concept of mean is what is usually referred to as the average. Of course, to have an average, the computer must have numbers to calculate. The survey question might have asked for the participant's age or income. The average can be easily calculated from these numbers. This will have more meaning than just the median response which is only the midpoint of the responses but does not take into consideration how far all the individual response are from the midpoint.

The statistical concept of median is used to calculate the mid-range of all answers. It is not the same concept as the 'average' of all responses. It is used when a selection of possible answers is provided but the responses are not quantifiable. Perhaps an organization promoting a festival asked participants a question about the importance of the issue of quality of bedding provided. The answers given might have been 'extremely important', 'very important', 'important', 'neither important or unimportant', 'unimportant', 'very unimportant' and 'extremely important'. The median response might have been 'unimportant'. This means that just as many participants responded with answers above this response as below this response.

Statistical measures of dispersion and hypothesis testing

To obtain more information on how the individual responses are distributed from the mean, the researchers will need to use statistical measures of dispersion. These include range, variance and standard deviation.

The easiest measure to use and understand is the range of the responses. For example, the organization may have asked the survey question of frequent visitors, 'How many nights a year do you stay in a hotel?' Perhaps 232 participants responded to the question and the researcher calculated the mean response as 48. As the mean is the average response, the next question that needs to be answered is what were the highest and the lowest number of nights mentioned. This would be the range of the responses. The researchers might find that the lowest amount given was 7 and the highest was 225.

The reason it is important to calculate the range, is that the researchers need to know if the mean or average has been affected by extreme answers on either side of the range. Perhaps they will find that someone has given the very high number of 225. The researchers might find that the next number listed in descending order was 84. The possibility of having more than one visitor to a town who stays 225 nights in a hotel is low. However, this number is skewing the mean of all responses much higher. Therefore, the researchers may want to drop this response and recalculate the mean.

The variance of the set of responses to the question on how many nights a visitor stays helps the researcher to understand how dispersed each individual response is from the mean. While the researchers may have dropped the one response that was way outside the usual range of responses, they still don't know how dispersed all the responses were from the recalculated mean of 36. One way to calculate this number would be to subtract each individual number from the recalculated mean of 36 and then add the differences. However, this will not work because the negative numbers and the positive numbers will always cancel each other out and the answer will be zero. The total number of nights listed below 36 is exactly the same as the total number of nights listed above, which is why 36 is the mean.

To solve this dilemma, the difference between each individual data number and the mean is first calculated using subtraction. The answer to each subtraction is then squared and these squared answers are then added together. The final step is to divide the sum by the number that is one less than the number of responses. This step allows the researcher to compare the variance between data sets that have different numbers of responses. The final number calculated is the variance. While the computer will calculate this number for the researcher, it is still necessary for the researcher to understand how the statistic was derived so that its meaning is understood.

The researchers might look at this number without a great deal of excitement. After all what does a variance of 2.5 really mean? Actually it will not mean much on its own. Its value is in allowing the researchers to compare the variance between two sets of numbers. For example, the researchers may calculate the nights people stay by gender. They may find that the means are very different, with the mean for males being 48 and the mean for females 22. The question facing the researchers is whether the dispersion of responses is greater or less for males versus females. If the variance for males is 4.05 while the variance for females is 2.72 then the number of nights that men stay in hotels varies more widely than for female visitors.

Standard deviation would be the next calculation made by the researchers. The researchers know that the higher the variance, the more dispersed are the responses in the set of data. They have found that the number of nights that male visitors stay is more dispersed. The problem with the variance number is that being squared, the

Case Study 11.4: When you check into your hotel room – someone may be waiting

Don't worry as it will be a virtual someone named Siri or Alexa. Both Marriott and Wynn hotels are experimenting with placing the technology in their hotel rooms. Every hotel chain wants to win the loyalty of the Millennial traveler. They are heavy users of technology and it is integrated into their everyday activities from checking traffic to ordering groceries. They don't want to check into a hotel room and have to pick up a telephone to get information. Hotels are interested in the devices because they can save staff expenses. If the devices are programmed to act as a personal concierge for such tasks as ordering room service and making spa reservations, the hotel won't have to hire someone to answer the phone to take the information. Technology companies Amazon and Apple are eager to make deals with hotels as they believe that once hotel guests experience the convenience of the devices, they will also want them for their homes.

While hotel companies will need to make a choice between the systems, another question will be what the devices will be able to do. It will be easy to have them check news sites and weather reports. The next level of interaction would allow the guests to access their accounts and make reservations. A higher level of interaction would allow the devices to make recommendations on what to do in the area based on a guest profile that the hotel maintains. If a guest loves sushi, Alexa or Siri will be ready with a list of recommended nearby restaurants (Yu and Soper 2017).

Question: How could the data of all requests made on a hotel's system be analyzed?

number no longer has any meaning on its own. If the square root of the variance is calculated, the answer is the standard deviation, which is in the same units, nights, as the original numbers.

If the standard deviation is added and then subtracted from the variance, this tells the researcher that this range is where the most responses will fall. The standard deviation for females is 2.72 and for males is 4.05. Therefore, the responses provided by males varied more widely. While this is easy to see visually in a small sample of 10 responses, it would not be easy to see when the researcher has a list of 150 responses.

If these standard deviation numbers are then added and subtracted from the mean, they will show where most of the responses lie. For females, this is between 14 and 39. For males, it is 22 and 53. The deviation is much larger with males and so it will be harder to know if they should be targeted as a group.

Descriptive statistics and data analysis

- Frequency: one way, cross-tabulation
- Central tendency: mean, median, mode
- Dispersion: range, variance, standard deviation

Hypothesis testing

The other type of statistical analysis that the researcher can conduct uses inferential statistics. These statistical methods go beyond just describing the data discovered during the research to analyze whether the findings are true. Of course, no marketing research study that uses a sample can 'prove' anything with absolute certainty. What the analysis of quantitative research data can do is indicate whether a hypothesis is likely to be true or false. Using inferential statistics, the researcher can perform statistical tests to determine if the responses from the sample can be used to draw conclusions about the entire population.

Statistical testing process

The first step in using statistical analysis to support the truth of a hypothesis is to state the hypothesis, or guess, about some characteristic of consumers or their behavior. For example, this could be the average fee that people will be willing to pay to attend an event or the percentage of people interested in new menu items. The research will then be designed to measure this characteristic. Once the research study has been completed and the data entered into the computer, the percentage from the sample of participants will be compared with the expected outcome stated in the hypothesis.

It would be rare if the hypotheses and the research results were exactly the same percentage. The issue is if the difference between the hypotheses and the results is so insignificant that it could be the result of random error or if the difference is so significant and the hypothesis is wrong. The z-test, using the z-score, is used to determine if the differences are statistically significant or not.

Stating the hypothesis

A hypothesis is a guess that is made by the tourism organization conducting the research. Perhaps a festival would like to offer afternoon performances. The organization needs to know if there will be sufficient attendance to justify spending the money to offer the performances. The venue's finance department has stated that at least 20 per cent of current attendees would need to express an interest in also attending in the afternoon to make it financially viable.

This first hypothesis is the null hypothesis and will be stated as what the organization does not wish to be true. This null hypothesis is considered true until proven false. For the festival considering holding a festival the null hypothesis is: less than 20 per cent of current attendees will be interested in attending the afternoon performances. The alternative hypothesis would be that 20 per cent or more will be interested. One hypothesis is the opposite of the other and, therefore, both can't be true.

There are no statistical tests that can prove a hypothesis true. This is impossible as the only way to know with 100 per cent accuracy if the hypothesis is true is to survey every current attendee. But statistical tests can be used to state with 90, 95 or 97 per cent accuracy. However, if the null hypothesis is proved false, then the alternative hypothesis, that more than 20 per cent of attendees will be interested, can be accepted as true. Therefore the null hypothesis needs to be expressed so that its rejection leads to the acceptance of the preferred conclusion – offering afternoon performances.

The festival company surveys a sample of 1,000 attenders (which is enough to make the study valid at 95 per cent confidence) and finds that 22 per cent stated they were interested. While this is over the required 20 per cent, the researchers know that a sample is never as accurate as asking everyone. However, the question remains if 22 per cent is so close that it is simply random error that made it over 20 per cent.

The organization needs to determine whether the difference between the results stated in the hypothesis and the survey results is statistically significant. While the word 'significant' usually means important, in statistics it means 'true'. The test to find if the difference is significant or just random error, or z-score, can be automatically calculated by a statistical computer software program. This calculated z-score will be compared with the predetermined z-scores to indicate if the null hypothesis should be rejected. It is standard procedure to have the computer software both calculate the z-score and compare the scores.

The results will vary depending on whether the organization wants to be 90, 95 or 97 per cent confident that the results are accurate. However, the researcher can make a rough calculation by remembering the standard numbers for confidence levels. For a 95 per cent confidence level the number was 1.96. The computer software calculated the z-score for the example of the survey of theatre goers as 1.658, which tells the researchers that they cannot with 95 per cent confidence say the null hypothesis is not true. The percentage of 22 per cent from the sample is just too close to the needed outcome of 20 per cent. After all, not everyone was asked the question. Therefore the null hypothesis remains true and the company does not go ahead with offering afternoon concerts.

Interestingly, if the survey sample returned a result of 23 per cent of festival goers being interested and the computer calculates a new z-score, it would be 2.48 which puts the results well within the range for stating with 95 per cent confidence that the null hypothesis is false. Therefore, the alternative hypothesis must be true and the company starts presenting evening performances. The same type of calculations can be done for comparing a hypothesized average and the average that was found by surveying the sample.

References

Gläser, J. and G. Laudel. 2013. Life With and Without Coding: Two Methods for Early-Stage Data Analysis in Qualitative Research Aiming at Causal Explanations [online]. Forum Qualitative Sozialforschung / Forum: Qualitative Social Research. May. Available from www.qualitative-research.net/index.php/fqs/article/view/1886/3528. [Accessed 26 May 2017].

Sablich, J. 2017. Those Pesky Airline Fees and How to Avoid Them [online]. *The New York Times*. 27 March. Available from www.nytimes.com/2017/03/27/travel/avoiding-pesky-airline-add-on-fees-airfare.html? [Accessed 1 April 2017].

Traveller. 2017. The Beatles' Sgt. Pepper Is Getting Its Own Festival to Mark 50 Years since Its Release [online]. *Sydney Morning Herald*. 26 March. Available from www.traveller.com.au/the-beatles-sgt-pepper-gets-a-50th-birthday-festival-in-liverpool-gv72ws. [Accessed 29 March 2017].

Weed, J. 2017. Hoteliers Comb the Ranks of Tech Workers to Gain an Edge [online]. *The New York Times*. 13 February. Available from www.nytimes.com/2017/02/13/business/hoteliers-comb-the-ranks-of-tech-workers-to-gain-an-edge.htm? [Accessed 1 April 2017].

Yu, H. and S. Soper. 2017. Siri and Alexa Are Fighting to Be Your Hotel Butler [online]. Bloomberg, 22 March. Available from www.bloomberg.com/news/articles/2017-03-22/amazon-s-alexa-takes-its-fight-with-siri-to-marriott-hotel-rooms. [Accessed 24 March 2017].

Chapter 12

Preparing the report and presentation

Learning objectives

- What are the types of written reports that can be produced and for whom?
- Is there a structure to the formal written research report that should be followed?
- How does the way the report is written affect whether it will be read?
- What rules should be followed to ensure an informative and persuasive oral presentation?

Chapter summary

- After the research is completed and the data analyzed there is still one task left to complete, which is to report the recommendations. The report, which should be both written and oral, ensures that everyone understands the purpose and results of the research. It also ensures that there is a record of the findings so efforts will not be duplicated in the future. Several types of reports may be written for different types of readers. There may be a reluctance to produce the reports as the researchers may be ready to move on to a new project, but this would be a mistake.
- Following a structure when writing a report will make the process easier. A title page, table of contents and executive summary are at the beginning of the report. A methodology section explains how the research was conducted. The findings section will focus on the results of the research. Appendices will contain all the supporting information.
- To ensure that the written report will be read, it should be concise and help the reader by using headings and subheadings. It should be written in an appropriate style for the reader and at the correct language level. How a report looks visually will also affect its readability so attention should be paid to how information is presented.

- An oral presentation is recommended. It should never attempt to cover all the information but rather should focus on highlights. Using photos or videos will add interest and keep the audience focused. Persuasive skill is needed to see the recommendations. The visuals used should only reinforce critical information so the attention is on the presenter not slides.

Reporting the findings and recommendations

While the completion of the research methodology may be seen as the end of the research process, all the effort that has gone into conducting the research will be wasted if the organization does not communicate what was learned. The recommendations that have resulted from an analysis of the research findings must be presented in both a written report and an oral presentation. After all, recommendations that are not communicated cannot be implemented. However, a written report must contain more than the recommendations. For the recommendations to be credible, the researchers must also present information on the methodology, the participants and the findings.

The findings and recommendations should also be communicated through either a formal or informal oral report. This report could be to the management of the tourism organization, the employees, stakeholders in the community or members of the public. If appropriate, the oral report may be in a nontraditional format, such as a video. Researchers will choose the formats that work best for communicating with the organization, not the format they would prefer.

Figure 12.1 The recommendations will be useless if no one reads the report.

Photo Credit: isaravut

A useful marketing research report will do more than just report facts. It must tell a story about the reason for the research and end with recommendations for action. The story can be framed around the desires of the visitor and the benefits of the tourism product or service. To communicate this story, the data should be presented using visuals as 80 per cent of the human brain focuses on processing this type of information (Kraus 2013).

Reluctance to produce a written report

Even if it is determined that a video or oral presentation be the primary means of communicating the recommendations to the organization and others, there is still a need for a written report. The researchers may be reluctant to prepare a written report for a number of reasons. First, because writing clearly is a skill that not everyone possesses, preparing a multi-page written report is a daunting task. To write clearly is a very different process from speaking as written language is much more concise than spoken. With spoken language, the speaker is watching the listener. When the speaker notices that the listener looks confused, the message can immediately be clarified using additional and different words. With written language writers must ensure that they are communicating clearly the first time and therefore every word is critical.

Not only is writing clearly difficult, the report must be organized logically. To have this logical order the writer must understand every step of the research process. If the organization of the report is incoherent, the reader will not find the research process credible.

Another reason for reluctance to prepare a written report is when the researcher does not have any recommendations. It is easier to cover a lack of knowledge in an oral report with an engaging and entertaining presentation. With a written report it will clearly become apparent that the researcher does not know what the findings mean to the organization.

Lastly, preparing the written report comes at a time when the researcher's initial enthusiasm is running low. What seemed like a worthwhile research project when it started has now been going on for a long period of time. The researcher is ready to move on to something else at the very same time that a significant amount of energy needs to be put into writing the report.

Purpose of the written report

There are a number of reasons why researchers must make the effort and take the time to produce a formal written research report. First, the report will be read by people both inside and outside the tourism organization who may not have any knowledge of research methodology. The report may be read by organizations that promote tourism, government officials and local cultural groups. The written report needs to provide these readers with background information on how the research was conducted. This would include details on the methodology and participants that researchers would not have time to cover in an oral presentation.

Another purpose for the written report is that it is a means of documenting the required actions to implement the research recommendations. When presented orally the organization may be very enthusiastic to implement the recommendations. However, that enthusiasm may quickly fade because of the routine challenges of running the organization on a day-to-day basis. If this happens the organization

Case Study 12.1: People demand the best personal service even when traveling

People are now accustomed to getting excellent personal services when they are home. When they travel, they may wish they had access to their favorite fitness studio and beauty salon. Because they can't take a personal trainer and stylist with them, there is a second-best option. RoamFitness is a chain of fitness studios located in airports. They offer the same fitness equipment you would find in any gym so that the traveler can keep up their routine. They also offer showers, WiFi, and other amenities. They can even loan workout clothes. A yearly membership gives a traveler access to any of the gyms.

When a woman is traveling, it isn't possible to stop by her local blow out studio or have makeup done at a salon before a big meeting. Nomi Beauty works with local hotels to provide these services in the hotel room for more extended hours than are offered by the hotel salon. Appointments for hairstyling and makeup can be made with the hotel concierge or on the Nomi app. The cost of the service is simply added to the bill. Now not only the rich and famous can afford these services when traveling (Vora 2017).

Question: What would the outline for a report on this new trend in services look like?

can always go back to the written report to find the steps that will need to be taken to implement the recommendations.

In addition, the written report is useful to clarify any misunderstandings. It would not be unusual for two people who listen to the same oral presentation to come away with different recollections of what was said. If this happens, the written report is available for examination. Finally, the written report is there to preserve the research findings for future employees. It may well be that in the future the organization may again decide to conduct research using the same methodology. This is not just a matter of convenience, as the organization may want to use the same survey questions or focus group script to see if the answers have changed over time. If they do conduct similar research, the report will have all the necessary information to both conduct the research and analyze trends.

Purpose of written report

- Explanation of research terminology and methodology
- Action plan for recommendations documented
- Clarification in case of misunderstandings
- Preservation of knowledge for future employees

Types of research report

More than one type of research report may need to be produced to communicate with different types of readers. These reports will differ in the type of information and the amount of detail that are provided to the reader. Reports that are produced for outside stakeholders and the public will include less detail on the methodology and research process. The different types of research reports include preliminary, full, summarized and recommendations.

Even before the research process is completed, the researchers should consider preparing a preliminary report. Those in management who are responsible for commissioning the research, may be concerned with the progress of the research process. To alleviate these concerns a preliminary report can be prepared that will include any issues that have been noted by the researchers during the early stages of the process. For example, the preliminary report to a tourism promotion organization may note that some focus group participants seem hesitant to speak in front of other participants about their visit to the area. As a result, management may decide to also include interviews in the research process.

The preliminary report may also present initial findings, even though they have not been substantiated by all the research methodology. For example, initial findings from interviews may include the fact that visitors have a negative perception of a tourist attraction. Therefore, the organization may decide to conduct additional focus groups to learn why this is so.

After the conclusion of the research the researchers will prepare a full report for the organization's management. This report will include all the details of the methodology, the selection of participants, the research findings and the recommendations based on these findings. This will be the report that will be kept as a reference in the marketing department in case additional research on the subject is needed in the future.

A summarized report should be prepared for those who have an interest in the recommendations but are not interested in all the details of the methodology and selection of participants. These individuals may include the management of local tourist attractions, government officials and other community groups. As they are willing to trust the organization on methodology and participants, all they want to know is what was learned from the research.

A findings and recommendations report may be written for employees of the organization, as these are the people who will be most directly affected by any change in the organization. It will help with implementation if all employees understand that the recommendations were made as the result of the research findings.

Not all of these reports need to be presented as a formal written document. The preliminary report can be in the form of a memo along with an unofficial conversation at a meeting. The summarized report may be posted online but also may be presented orally at a staff or board meeting. The recommendations report may be sent out to employees via email or social media.

Types of research reports

- Preliminary
  - memo and explanation to commissioners of research
  - inform on progress or problems so can adjust methodology if needed
- Full
  - formal document for management and commissioners
  - documents methodology, sampling, findings and recommendations
- Summarized
  - letter or memo to outside stakeholders and public

○ highlights findings and recommendations with short description of methodology
- Findings and recommendations
  ○ email or social media to employees
  ○ informs reader of recommendations

Structure of the written report

The formal full and summary written report should follow a standard format. The reason is that individuals familiar with standard business practices will read the report and this is the type of structure that will be expected. It may be that the researchers will find this highly organized approach confining, or even boring. While they are free to be more creative in their approach to writing reports that are for internal use, reports that will be seen by government officials and management of the organization should follow a standard format.

The structure should start with introductory material including a title page, table of contents and executive summary. The purpose of this section is to set the stage for the information that will follow. The methodology section will include information on the research question, the objectives of the research, how the participants were selected and the details of the methodology. The findings and recommendations section will now tell the reader what was learned during the research and what it means for the organization. Finally, the appendices will contain all the supporting information.

Components of research report

- Introductory material
  ○ title page
  ○ table of contents
  ○ executive summary
- Research methodology
  ○ research question
  ○ research objectives
  ○ sample selection
  ○ methodology
- Findings and recommendations
  ○ quantitative data or qualitative findings
  ○ recommendations
- Appendices
  ○ biographical information on researchers
  ○ further details on sampling procedure
  ○ examples of methodology
  ○ full data

Introductory material

The purpose of this section is to provide legitimacy and context to the report's contents. The title page should include the name of the tourism organization along with

Case Study 12.2: Making Sunday special enough to get them out of the house

Restaurants in New York City have high fixed costs due to being in such an expensive city. And yet, most are closed on Sundays resulting in no revenue. Why? Not enough New Yorkers go out to eat that night to make staying open worthwhile. Now some New York restaurants are trying to change this behavior because missing a day of revenue is making it too difficult to make a profit. The restaurants knew that to attract Sunday guests they had to be different, relaxed and family focused.

To do so they are offering special menus that have a more family feel. Some of the menus feature recipes that are family favorites of the chef's parents or grandparents. There is often only one choice of entrée and the meal is served family style for one fixed price. Restaurants have learned that on Sunday night Millennials want something that is more traditional than the usual newest foodie trend. For example, an Italian restaurant serves traditional spaghetti and meatballs, while a British style restaurant serves a Sunday roast. The new approach has been so successful that it is sometimes difficult to get a table on Sunday night at some restaurants (Passy 2017).

Question: If you were preparing a written report on the success of the new approach, what type of photos could be included to heighten interest?

any logo or appropriate visual. In addition, the name of the head of the organization and the people involved in the research should be included. If the researchers do not work for the organization, the name of the company they work for along with contact information should also be stated. The table of contents is prepared after the report has been completed. Its purpose is to allow readers to quickly find needed information. This is especially important when the report is being discussed in meetings. For example, if questions are raised about the participant profile, everyone will be able to quickly find that section without any need to stop the conversation.

The purpose of the executive summary is to 'sell' the report to the reader. Everyone is busy and only those people involved in the research are going to be willing to read the full report. Other readers might intend to read the report when they have the time – which often will never happen. The executive summary is a very condensed version of the report that will state in a page or less what research was conducted, the findings, and the recommendations. Hopefully, after reading the executive summary, the reader will be interested enough to read the full report. The executive summary also helps as a convenient review of the contents to refresh the memory of the reader.

Research methodology

This section of the report will provide the information that supports the findings and recommendations that are to come. The section will first address the research question, as readers should understand what organizational problem or concern was to be addressed by the research. After a brief explanation, the research question should be directly stated. If the research study was quantitative the research question may be stated in the form of a hypothesis.

The research objectives, which are more action oriented than the research question, concern how the organization will use the research findings. For example, the report may discuss that the city government was concerned about a lack of economic development in the downtown core leading to a loss of tax revenue. The research question was what kinds of tourist attractions are desired by visitors. The objectives might include the organization's plans to use this information to recruit new tourism related businesses.

Of course, the findings and recommendations will not have credibility if the reader is not convinced that the research participants were properly selected. After all, an easy way for the researchers to obtain the research findings they want is to ask people whom they know will answer the question in a certain way. The report should describe how the participants were selected to remove this potential bias.

Finally, the methodology will need to be discussed. First, the researcher should explain why a specific methodology was chosen. It should not be assumed that the reader will automatically understand why a focus group rather than a survey was the proper method to gather information. Then the writer should explain the details of the methodology. For research on the use of hotel lobbies as meeting spaces, this would include the numbers of focus groups, interviews, or observations that were held and the number of surveys conducted. Of course, the dates the research was conducted and the distribution method for surveys should also be included. General information about the questions that were asked or the topics discussed in focus groups or interviews should be explained. There is no need to describe every detail as a copy of the survey form, examples of projective techniques, the focus group script, and the interview guidelines can be included in the appendices.

Findings and recommendations

This section is the heart of the report as it provides the information on what was learned during the research process along with ideas on what actions should be taken as a result of what was learned. It is the information in this section that is the payoff for the time and money that was spent on the research. For example, the research on hotel lobbies might have found that they are being used for business meetings. The resulting recommendation might be that moveable furniture be provided so that all sizes of informal groups can be accommodated.

Because this section of the report cannot contain all the information that was learned during the research process, the researcher must decide what details should be included. This is especially true of quantitative surveys. The numbers that result from surveys can be statistically analyzed in many different ways. Using the example of the types of lodging preferred by visitors, it may be very important to include the results of an analysis of the preferences of older visitors if they make up a significant proportion of the population. However, it is not necessary to focus on every age group, particularly if young visitors are not being targeted.

The next task in this section of the report will be to describe the recommendations or what action should be taken by the organization based on these findings. It is the responsibility of researchers not just to report facts but also to understand the implications of the research by making recommendations. Data are the facts that were found during the research. Analytics is studying the data to understand its meaning. Recommendations are ideas that will lead to the organizations taking action and the reason why time and money is spent on research (Marrs 2016). Even if the organization does not use the recommendations they can spur the organization to think about changes that should be made. If a report does not make recommendations, there is a risk that after it is read, it will end up simply sitting on a shelf, which would be a waste of research time and effort.

The recommendations must be based on the findings and not simply the researcher's own ideas. For example, the tourism researcher who is analyzing the findings from a visitor preference survey might personally feel that a water park is needed to attract tourists. However, if a water park is not supported by the research findings, the recommendation should not be included.

Recommendations may be made by the researchers resulting from surprising findings that were not part of the original research question. For example, the researcher may have decided to analyze the data from the visitor study by ethnic groups. As a result, it was learned that a specific group expressed interest in visiting organic farms. Based on these findings the researchers may recommend that the city encourage local farmers to provide tours.

Appendices

Included in this final section will be relevant information that is too lengthy to include in the body of the report. The researchers will need to decide, based on personal judgment, what should be included to increase the legitimacy and credibility of the findings and recommendations. For example, if the researchers are unknown to the report readers, the appendices could include a short statement on previous research projects along with their educational background. Or, if appropriate a full resumé might be added.

If the researchers believe that the readers might question the sampling procedures, additional detailed information on the process can be included. Examples of the research methodology can be added to the appendix, such as a copy of the complete survey form or a copy of the focus group script. It is much easier to add this information in the appendices than to describe every detail in the body of the report.

Finally, the complete data set of all the findings should be included, such as the answers to all survey questions. In addition, a copy of the transcript of focus groups and interviews should be included. As explained earlier, it is not possible, or recommended, that all the findings be discussed in the report, rather only the most important findings on which recommendations are based.

Writing the report

The final report should be concise, readable and interesting. One of the issues that the researcher must balance is the need to include all relevant information with the need to keep the report as short as possible. People are busy and do not have the time to read an unnecessarily lengthy report. If the report looks too long, some people may be intimidated by the length and it will never even be opened.

To help the reader understand the report, headings and subheadings should be added in the body of the text. Each section listed in the report structure discussed previously, should have its own heading along with any other headings and sub-headings that will help readers move through a long report by informing them of what material is coming next. While the writer must decide where it is appropriate to place these divisions, there should rarely be a page in the report that only has text with no headings.

Factors that make a report readable include the style and level of language used and also the visual layout. The report should be written at the appropriate reading level, which is determined by the length of the sentences and the types of words used. The best way for the researcher to get feedback as to whether the reading level is appropriate is to have a draft read by members of the organization. The report should not contain any jargon that will not be understood by a reader without a marketing research background. If a term needs to be used, such as participant profile, the first time it appears an explanation of its meaning should be given.

Another issue with readability is the visual layout of the report. The font chosen may vary based on whether the report is going to be read on paper or online. The font and size should make the report easy to read with sufficient white space on the page to be visually appealing. These technical details will allow the reader to concentrate on the content without being distracted by any difficulty in reading the report.

Lastly, the report should be interesting. This does not mean that the writer has to write in a creative style. However, there are ways to add interest to the report. Besides just listing facts, the report can also describe incidents that give the reader a flavor of what it was like to conduct the research. For example, the report can discuss the eagerness of potential participants to participate in interviews on improving tourism services. Such descriptions will also remind the reader that the participants are not just statistics but real people whose opinions need to be taken seriously.

Photos of the research process could also be included, such as participants involved in a focus group or of someone completing a survey. If it is not possible to include photos of participants because of privacy issues, the report might include a photo of the researchers and management during a preliminary meeting at the organization. Another idea might be photos of the locations where the observational research took place or even just of the organization's building.

Another way to enliven the report is to include quotes from participants. These of course would be anonymous. Quotes of statements made in interviews or focus groups or comments made in response to an open-ended question in a survey can provide the readers with a feeling of involvement in the process that just reporting findings can never accomplish.

Writing the drafts

The first step in writing a research report is to create an outline that will provide a roadmap to follow during the writing process. The outline will contain the major components of the report but will also include more detail, e.g. under the heading of 'Sample Selection' there might be a subheading of 'Snowballing' if this was the method chosen. If appropriate there might be a section on 'Incentives' if the organization used incentives to increase participation. Writing the report will be much easier once the outline has been completed as the writer will have a starting point rather than just be facing a blank piece of paper.

After the outline has been completed, the first draft will be written. This first draft, which is just the start of the writing process, will be reviewed to ensure

Case Study 12.3: Your bag isn't lost even if you don't have it

Lost baggage is one of the biggest complaints for airline passengers. A passenger might go to the baggage claim area and wait in vain for the bag to appear. Once everyone else had gotten their luggage, the traveler would give up hope and go to the baggage claim area where they would stand in line to file a report and provide instructions as to where the bag should be delivered once it was located.

Then technology started to be used with the airline texting the passenger if their checked baggage did not make the flight. However, the passenger still had to go to the Lost Baggage area to provide instructions as to where to deliver the bag. Now airlines have instituted a new system. When the text is received, the passenger can provide information as to where to deliver the bag. Everyone should be happy except for one factor. The airline no longer considers the bag lost! Therefore, they do not need to report a lost bag, which improves their statistics. Some might say that it's not a big deal. But with US airlines alone getting $4 billion in baggage fees annually, some people say a better solution is not to lose the bag in the first place (McCartney 2017)!

Question: What type of visuals could you use to explain the new system in a written or oral report?

that the organization is correct. Topics that are discussed should fit under the proper heading so the reader does not need to hunt for information. At this point in the process the writer may decide to change the report's organization to one that will make more sense to the reader. In addition, the writer will see if there are redundancies in the report. If topics have been covered at too great a length, they should be edited down. Finally, the writer should check to ensure that all topics have been adequately covered. If not, the writer will need to add more detail to the report.

Once these changes have been made, the structure of the report should be complete. It is now time to edit for wording and produce the second draft. To produce this draft the writer will slowly read through the report noting where wording or sentences should be changed or improved. This can seem to be a tedious process but it is the process that results in a professionally written report.

With these changes made, the report will now be ready for proofreading, which will catch any spelling, grammatical or punctuation errors. While software will catch some errors, careful proofreading is still needed. It would not be surprising if the writer is so tired of the process that it is difficult to look at the report with the attention that is needed to catch these errors. The writer may want to ask someone else to take a fresh look at the report and do the proofreading.

The report is now ready for layout. This means that the writer will check to make sure that all the headings and subheadings are formatted consistently, that page numbers are attached and that the pagination breaks between pages make sense. Again, this can be time consuming and the writer may well want to just print the report and be done. However, it is the layout that provides the first impression of the report and the writer will want this first impression to be professional.

Presenting numerical information

If the research was quantitative and the methodology chosen was a survey, the writer will have many numbers and statistics to be included in the report. However reading numerical information can be tedious. The reader will quickly start skipping over the material if they are faced with sentences such as, 'Of the total of 100 visitors interviewed, 15 were aged 19–30, 34 were aged 30–45, 25 were aged 45–60, and 26 over 65.' The other issue has to do with the relationship between numbers. It is easy for the reader to visualize the relationship between numbers when information such as 40 per cent of participants were male and 60 per cent were female is presented, but when more percentages are added, understanding the relationship becomes difficult.

For these reasons, numerical information is often presented visually. The human brain finds it easier to read numbers that are presented either in rows and columns in a table, or in a chart or graph format. Survey software will create these visuals automatically, but the researcher must decide which form of presentation is best.

If the writer is faced with a series of numbers that all pertain to the same topic, in the past the simplest and most easily understandable way of presenting the information was in a table. Now readers are becoming more familiar with getting data using infographics. For this reason a table must be well designed or else readers may not take the time to understand the contents (DeVault 2016). For example, a presentation on the number of visitors can be quickly understood if presented in columns that show both the total number and the percentage of each age group. As a result in the body of the report the writer no longer needs to mention every number. Instead the writer is now free to highlight the meaning of the most important numbers. For example, the writer might point out that 25 per cent of all visitors are children Therefore the city is successful in attracting families.

Pie charts are a means of visually presenting information to allow the reader to quickly grasp percentages of a whole. A pie chart is best to show this visually. By comparing the pieces of the pie, the reader is actually comparing the percentage of each group of visitors to the entire group. For example, out of all the event tickets sold over a year the types of events for which they were purchased can be shown.

Another way of presenting visual information is using a bar chart that uses length to show the numbers in relationship to each other. The advantage of a bar chart is that it can contain more than one year of data for different groups. For example, older hotel guest totals for last year can be shown next to younger hotel guests. The reader will quickly see the number relationship between the two groups.

Line charts are very useful when comparing numerical data over time. The hotel might conduct research of visitors every year. Comparing two or even three years of data can be done using bar charts, but adding more years makes the bar chart too confusing to be useful. Line charts can compare data over many years. On a line chart the number of older visitors can be tracked over a ten-year period and visually will show with a single glance whether it is increasing, declining or erratic.

Preparing the oral presentation

The researchers should also be prepared to give an oral presentation of their findings and recommendations. There are a number of reasons why it is a valuable use of the researchers' time to prepare and present the information orally. A strong oral presentation may create enough interest to encourage people to read the written report. Secondly, an oral presentation gives the researchers the opportunity to better explain the tie between the research recommendations and the findings on which they are based. While this has been done in the written report, there may still be some individuals who do not understand how the recommendations were derived. The oral presentation can clarify this relationship more fully.

Once the recommendations have been explained, the oral presentation can be used to create excitement for their implementation. This is the researchers' chance to 'sell' to the management of the tourism organization, the employees and other interested stakeholders in the community how the tourism experience can be improved by taking action based on what was learned during the research. Finally, at the end of the presentation, the researchers can ask for questions. This provides the opportunity to clarify any misunderstandings. Some individuals may have read the written report, but may have misunderstood the explanation of the methodology or how the participants were chosen. The oral presentation gives the researchers an opportunity to clarify any misunderstandings that might keep individuals from believing in and implementing the recommendations.

Figure 12.2 Presentations must be interesting to ensure that the audience listens.

Photo Credit: Elizaveta Galitckaia

Case Study 12.4: The dining table was the original Facebook

Before people used technology to keep informed of family and friends, information was shared around the table while eating. With people now wanting authentic experiences while traveling, what better way than having a meal with the locals? Even better would be if you could help prepare the meal. There are now apps that will help you have this experience.

The idea started with local chefs preparing meals in their homes for visitors. It now includes such experiences as cooking classes of local specialties and tours of local food markets. With so many people interested in food when they are home, it is natural that they would want the same experiences when they travel.

More than food is shared, as people converse about everything from their families to politics. People who book the experiences also post photos of themselves and the locals dining together. And, of course, they post pictures of the food (Walters 2017).

Question: How could photos and online reviews be incorporated into a presentation on this topic?

Reasons for oral presentation

- Provide information that will motivate people to read the report
- Explanation of tie between research findings and recommendations
- Create excitement for implementation
- Opportunity to clarify misunderstandings

Presentation structure

The presentation should follow a planned outline. All presentations should start by introducing the presenters along with their titles and their role in the research process. The introduction should provide the audience with an outline of the presentation as people can better focus on what is being said if they know what topics will be covered and when the presentation will be concluded. This introduction should only take two to three minutes, at the most.

The researchers will then state the research question and the objectives that the organization hoped to achieve with the research. A short description of how the participants were chosen will add legitimacy to the findings and recommendations. Finally, the methodology used will be described. The researchers should not go into these topics in depth because of time limitations. Instead the audience can be reminded that for those interested more details are available in the written report.

The next section of the oral presentation will cover the results of the research study. Not all the findings should be discussed, as this would tax the patience of the audience. Instead the findings that must be presented are those that resulted in the recommendations for action. The recommendations should be discussed in as much detail as possible. The recommendations, which are the answer to that problem, are the reason the research was undertaken.

Finally, the presentation will conclude with thanks to the audience for their attention and a call for questions. The presenters must be careful to plan their presentation so that there is adequate time for questions as not doing so may be seen as an attempt to evade answering and lead to suspicion. If there are few questions, the presenters can use this time to remind the audience of any important details that they feel might have been gone over too quickly.

The timing of the presentation will depend on what has been allotted by management. Since people are busy and have short attention spans, the researchers may only have 30 minutes to present. Of these 30 minutes, at least ten should be used for questions at the end. This leaves 20 minutes of which five will be used for the introduction and conclusion leaving only 15 minutes. The methodology should be covered quickly so that the majority of the time can be spent on recommendations.

Presentation outline

- Introduction
  - identify research participants
  - describe contents of presentation
- Methodology
  - state research question and objectives
  - describe methodology
  - explain sample selection procedure
- Recommendations
  - report of findings
  - explain recommendations for action
- Conclusion
  - thank audience and ask for questions

Hints for successful presentations

Everyone knows that a good presentation requires preparation. However, not everyone knows that there are other issues that must be considered if the presentation is to proceed flawlessly. The presenter should review the room where the presentation will take place to check where the audience will sit, where the presenter will stand, whether the layout will allow the presenter to circulate around the room, the availability of any needed computer equipment. In addition, the presenter should investigate the audience including who they are, what they already know about the subject, what they want to learn from the presentation, and what management wants them to learn from the presentation. Before presenting the researcher should practice the presentation using the necessary equipment either alone or in front of others. In fact, if possible a presentation should be practiced in front of a similar audience in the same room that will be used. A practice presentation will mean that when the actual presentation is given, the presenter will be relaxed and able to concentrate on the audience instead of the presentation.

Preparations and structure in a presentation are important to informing the audience. However, selling the audience on the recommendations will also depend on the persuasive power of the presenter (Fine 2016). If the presenter does not believe the recommendations will make a difference in the success of the tourism organ-ization, neither will the listeners. This belief is what needs to be communicated through the presenter's body language and tone of voice.

Presentation guidelines

There are a few guidelines that if followed will result in a more professional pres-entation. First, the report should never be read. At the most the presenter should read a short quotation from the written report. The audience came to hear an oral presentation, they could have stayed in their offices to read the report on their own.

Second, if PowerPoint or some other visual means of communication is used, the slides should be useful and readable. The audience should never be frustrated by being shown any PowerPoint slides that can't be easily read. The presenter should be the focus of the audience, not the slides.

Third, the presenter should interact with the audience. The audience should be warmly greeted and eye contact should be made with audience members when-ever possible. The presenter should never be so rude as to ignore the audience. Nor should the presenter overwhelm the audience with too much detail. After all, humans can only assimilate so much information at a time.

Fourth, the presenter should not bore the audience. A good presentation must be interesting. If the presentation is not interesting, the research recommendations may be ignored because the audience lost attention and they are not heard. The audience should never be bored – life is difficult enough without struggling to stay awake during a presentation.

Finally, the best way to maintain the interest of the audience is for the presenter to demonstrate enthusiasm for the information he or she is conveying. The pre-senter should care about the information that is being presented. After all, if the presenter does not care, neither will the audience.

Using visuals during a presentation

People have become accustomed to receiving information in more than one form at the same time. So it is not surprising that people have a difficult time simply listening to a verbal presentation with no other visual interaction. Even the most interesting oral presentation may leave the audience with minds that are wandering off to what they need to pick up at the grocery store on their way home from work. Therefore, using visual material not only helps to communicate the research infor-mation, it also helps the audience stay focused on the presentation. Visuals used during a presentation may be computer generated. However, low-tech methods can be just as effective.

Probably PowerPoint is the best known method of presenting visual information during oral presentations. But low-tech methods can also be used, including writing on a whiteboard, using flip charts, handouts of relevant information and photo-graphs of products or research participants. Whiteboards and flip charts can be used to draw attention to important facts. If a surprising 78 per cent of the visitors sur-veyed were unaware of the city's new promotional campaign, this number can be written out on the board or paper. The number becomes a written exclamation point for the fact.

Even if the presenter chooses to use PowerPoint during a presentation, it is still useful to use a low-tech method such as handouts of the slides. If PowerPoint is not used handouts are even more important. Audience handouts, which should only list the main findings and recommendations, serve two purposes. They can be used to reinforce what the presenter is explaining and they can also provide a place for the audience to write notes as they are listening. Handouts can also be used that contain other material such as maps of the city or copies of the survey form. Photographs of the venue or destination under discussion can also assist the audience in better understanding the relevance of the data. These photographs can be used as displays around the room where the presentation is taking place.

High-tech presentations aids include projection of an online source, videos and PowerPoint. Using a PC and a projector, presenters can bring up on the screen material that is online. For example, if the research involved perception of the city's image, the home page of the visitor center can be shown. Video clips of participants, such as in focus groups or interviews, can also be used during the presentation. The use of videos is becoming increasingly common when making research presentations. Videos will bring the material to life in way that other material cannot.

PowerPoint slides can be used to help the audience comprehend information. However, when badly used, which they often are, they will only confuse and distract the audience. There are general rules on use of PowerPoint that everyone should follow. First, presenters should remember that PowerPoint is best used for showing summarization of data in charts and graphs. PowerPoint's worst use is for displaying large amounts of text. As PowerPoint is a visual media, the fewer words that are used the better. For example, a PowerPoint slide could be used to show an insightful quote made by a focus group participant. In addition, a few words that came up frequently as answers to an open-ended question on a survey can be shown. These could then be discussed by the presenter.

PowerPoint is used inappropriately if too much information is put on a slide. Not only will the slide be difficult to read, it will also distract the audience from what is being said by the presenter. If the presenter gives the audience time to read the slide before the presentation resumes, it wastes time in the presentation. It will also mean the presenter will have to reestablish the connection with the audience

Figure 12.3
Both high tech and low tech methods can be used to present information.

Photo Credit: Rawpixel. com

when the presentation resumes. In fact, inexperienced presenters sometimes use PowerPoint slides as a shield to hide behind. While providing the audience with factual information is important, it is the persuasive ability of the speaker that 'sells' an idea.

References

DeVault, G. 2016. Guidelines for Designing Tables [online] The Balance. 8 August. Available from understandinggraphics.com/design/data-table-design/. [Accessed 15 May 2017].

Fine, L. 2016. 3 Key Characteristics of Persuasive Presentations [online]. Inc.com. 6 July. Available from www.inc.com/leura-fine/3-key-characteristics-of-persuasive-presentati ons.html. [Accessed 12 February 2017].

Kraus, J. 2013. How to Write High-impact Marketing Research Reports [online]. Quirk's Media, 15 July. Available from www.quirks.com/articles/how-to-write-high-impact-marketing-research-reports. [Accessed 4 February 2017].

Marrs, M. 2016. The Difference Between Data, Analytics, and Insights [online]. Localytics. 10 May. Available from info.localytics.com/blog/difference-between-data-analytics-in sights. [Accessed 13 March 2017].

McCartney, S. 2017. A Faster Answer for Lost Baggage with a Hidden Benefit for Airlines [online]. *The Wall Street Journal*. 29 March. Available from www.wsj.com/articles/a-faster -answer-for-lost-baggage-with-a-hidden-benefit-for-airlines-1490799444. [Accessed 30 March 2017].

Passy, C. 2017. New York Restaurateurs Get Creative for Sunday Supper [online]. *The Wall Street Journal*. 30 March. Available from www.wsj.com/articles/new-york-restaura teurs-get-creative-for-sunday-supper-1490873403. [Accessed 30 March 27].

Vora, S. 2017. New Services for Travelers from Fitness to Food [online]. *New York Times*. 11 February. Available from www.nytimes.com/2017/02/11/travel/new-travel-apps-serv ices-airport-gym-hotel-restaurant-beauty. [Accessed 12 February 2017].

Walters, A. 2017. The Emergence of Social Dining – the Phenomenon Where Strangers Come Together to Enjoy a Meal – Is Allowing Travelers to Immerse Themselves in Their New Surroundings and Get to Know Locals via Unique, Secure Experiences [online]. *Hotel, Travel & Hospitality News*. 13 March. Available from www.4hoteliers. com/itb/newsarticle/566?awsb_c=4hdm&awsb_k=itb. [Accessed 25 March 2017].

Index

Index

Index